Canadian Immunization Guide

Sixth Edition

Sixth Edition — 2002

Published by authority of the
Minister of Health

Population and Public Health Branch
Centre for Infectious Disease Prevention and Control

Également disponible en français sous le titre
Guide canadien d'immunisation

Text prepared by
the National Advisory Committee on Immunization

This Guide was published by the
Canadian Medical Association

Our mission is to help the people of Canada
maintain and improve their health.

Health Canada

Cat. H49-8/2002E
ISBN 0-660-18803-1

— Message from the —
Assistant Deputy Minister Population and Public Health Branch, Health Canada

All recommendations by the National Advisory Committee on Immunization (NACI) on the use of vaccines in Canada are contained in the *Canadian Immunization Guide*. A readership survey revealed that the *Guide* ranked as useful or better than other sources of information on immunization.

The *Guide* will also be available on the Centre for Infectious Disease Prevention and Control (CIDPC) Web site — www.hc-sc.gc.ca/pphb-dgspsp/publicat/cig-gci/. Updates on NACI's new or revised recommendations are published in the *Canada Communicable Disease Report* (CCDR), which is also available on the web site.

If you have suggestions or comments on the *Guide*, we would be pleased to receive them for consideration for the next edition. You can send your comments to: Advisory Committee Secretariat, Division of Immunization and Respiratory Diseases, Centre for Infectious Disease Prevention and Control, P.L. 0603E1, Tunney's Pasture, Ottawa, Ontario K1A 0L2.

Producing such a publication requires considerable dedication and time on the part of those involved. We would like to thank the National Advisory Committee on Immunization; the responsible members of the Biologics and Genetic Therapies Directorate, Health Products and Food Branch, Health Canada; and the Centre for Infectious Disease Prevention and Control, Population and Public Health Branch, Health Canada, for producing this *Guide*.

– Preface –

The sixth edition of the *Canadian Immunization Guide* contains numerous changes from the 1998 version but attempts to remain user friendly. Every chapter has been thoroughly reviewed and updated as needed. New chapters have been added on varicella, Lyme disease and combined hepatitis A and B vaccines. Both the pneumococcal and meningococcal vaccine chapters have been expanded to include the new conjugate vaccines. The section on adverse events has been expanded. A chapter on communications with information about recommended web sites has also been added.

Highlights of some major changes in the *Guide* are as follows:

- varicella vaccine use during an outbreak and in health care workers;
- pneumococcal conjugate vaccine to prevent severe infection in children;
- meningococcal conjugate vaccine to help contain this feared disease;
- Lyme disease vaccine with limited use but helpful for those visiting endemic areas;
- the use of hepatitis A vaccine in outbreak management;
- the use of acellular pertussis vaccines for adolescents;
- internet sites of interest;
- talking with patients about immunization.

Changes in the *Guide* mirror the extraordinary pace of change in the immunization field. This pace has been challenging for members of the National Advisory Committee on Immunization (NACI), who worked for many hours to keep producing new statements while revising the *Guide* itself. I gratefully acknowledge the hard work and expert contributions of members of NACI, the Division of Immunization and Respiratory Diseases and other Centre for Infectious Disease Prevention and Control staff as well as the staff of the Biologics and Genetic Therapies Directorate. Important contributions were made by liaison members from the Canadian Association for Immunization Research and Evaluation, the Canadian Infectious Disease Society, the Canadian Paediatric Society, the College of Family Physicians of Canada, the Committee to Advise on Tropical Medicine and Travel, the Canadian Public Health Association, the Community and Hospital Infection Control Association, the Council of Chief Medical Officers of Health, National Defence and the National Immunization Programs, and the Centers for Disease Control and Prevention, United States Public Health Service. Close liaison with the US Advisory Committee on Immunization Practices has been invaluable.

Thanks go to the Groupe sur l'acte vaccinal (immunization standards group), Montreal, for its review of the French version of the *Guide*, to Dr. Stan Acres for his invaluable help in finalizing the document, and to Scientific Publication and Multimedia Services, Health Canada, for production.

Victor J.H. Marchessault
Chairman (1998 -)
National Advisory Committee on Immunization

National Advisory Committee on Immunization

Chairman

V. Marchessault, MD
Ottawa, Ontario

Members

I. Bowmer, MD
Health Sciences Centre
St. John's, Newfoundland

G. De Serres, MD
Centre de santé publique de Québec
Beauport, Québec

S. Dobson, MD
Vaccine Evaluation Centre
Vancouver, British Columbia

J. Embree, MD
University of Manitoba
Winnipeg, Manitoba

I. Gemmill, MD
Kingston, Frontenac and Lennox &
 Addington Health Unit
Kingston, Ontario

J. Langley, MD
IWK Grace Health Centre
Halifax, Nova Scotia

M. Naus, MD
BC Centre for Disease Control
Vancouver, British Columbia

P. Orr, MD
Health Sciences Centre
Winnipeg, Manitoba

B. Ward, MD
McGill Centre for Tropical Diseases
Montreal, Quebec

A. Zierler
Safe Kids Canada
Toronto, Ontario

Executive Secretary

J. Spika, MD
Bureau of Infectious Diseases*
Health Canada
Ottawa, Ontario
(1993-2001)

A. King, MD
Bureau of Infectious Diseases*
Health Canada
Ottawa, Ontario
(2001-)

Advisory Committee Secretariat Officer

J. Rendall
Bureau of Infectious Diseases*
Health Canada
Ottawa, Ontario

---

*   Now the Centre for Infectious Disease Prevention and Control

Liaison Representatives

Community and Hospital Infection Control Association
S. Callery
Hamilton, Ontario

Canadian Public Health Association
J. Carsley, MD
Montreal, Quebec

Council of Chief Medical Officers of Health
R. Massé, MD
Québec, Québec

Advisory Committee on Epidemiology
M. Douville-Fradet, MD
Québec, Québec

College of Family Physicians of Canada
T. Freeman, MD
London, Ontario

Centers for Disease Control and Prevention
M. Wharton, MD
Atlanta, Georgia,

National Defence Medical Centre
A. McCarthy, Maj
V. Lentini, Lcdr
Ottawa, Ontario

Committee to Advise on Tropical Medicine & Travel
J. Salzman, MD
Vancouver, BC

Canadian Infectious Disease Society
L. Samson, MD
Ottawa, Ontario

Canadian Association for Immunization Research and Evaluation
D. Scheifele, MD
Vancouver, British Columbia

Ex-Officio Representatives

Bureau of Biologics[†]
L. Palkonyay, MD
Ottawa, Ontario

Bureau of Infectious Diseases[‡]
A. King, MD
Ottawa, Ontario
(1999-2001)

Bureau of Infectious Diseases[‡]
T. Tam, MD
Ottawa, Ontario
(2001-)

First Nations and Inuit Health Branch
P. Riben, MD
Vancouver, British Columbia

[†]   Now Biologics and Radiopharmaceutical Evaluation Centre
[‡]   Now the Centre for Infectious Disease Prevention and Control

– Preamble –

The National Advisory Committee on Immunization (NACI) provides Health Canada with ongoing and timely medical, scientific, and public health advice relating to immunization. Health Canada acknowledges that the advice and recommendations set out in this publication are based upon the best current available scientific knowledge, and is disseminating this document for information purposes. Persons administering or using the vaccines should also be aware of the contents of the relevant product monographs. Recommendations for use and other information set out herein may differ from that set out in the product monographs of the Canadian licensed manufacturers of the vaccines. Manufacturers have sought approval of the vaccines and provided evidence as to their safety and efficacy only when used in accordance with the product monographs.

– Table of Contents –

– Part I –
General Considerations

Vaccines are good! There is no reason to suffer from a disease if there is a safe, effective way to prevent it, and vaccines have proven their utility and effectiveness time and time again. Readers are invited to consult the table on the back of this *Guide,* which highlights the incredible victories against disease won by vaccines.

The range of immunizing agents available in Canada continues to expand as new vaccines and immune globulins are licensed, and improvements in or modifications to currently available preparations are made. The use of these agents for both active and passive immunization must, therefore, be evaluated continually as the incidence and significance of the diseases against which they confer protection change spontaneously or as a result of vaccine use. However, when the incidence of a particular communicable disease falls because of the success of a vaccine, the public or health policy makers may question the need to continue the immunization program concerned. This attitude may very well result in lower vaccine coverage and, inevitably, resurgence of the disease, unless it can be totally eradicated. Although the ultimate aim of those concerned with immunization is the elimination of vaccine-preventable diseases, eradication is rarely a practical possibility. Only in infections such as smallpox, poliomyelitis and measles, which are restricted to humans and involve no other host, is eradication possible today. Immunization programs may need continuous evaluation to adjust to new improvements, but policy makers and the public must keep advocating their continuation in order to avoid resurgence.

An ideal vaccine should confer long-lasting, preferably lifelong, protection against the disease with a single or a small number of doses. It should be inexpensive enough for wide-scale use, stable enough to remain potent during shipping and storage, and should have no adverse effect on the recipient. Some vaccines come close to meeting these criteria; others do not. Each vaccine has its own characteristics, and generalizations are difficult to make; consequently, each is considered separately in this *Guide.*

Some vaccines consist of inactivated organisms or purified components. Others, particularly vaccines against viral diseases, contain live microorganisms. These have the advantages that the dose is small (minimizing production costs) because the virus replicates within the recipient, and that the stimulus (or process) more closely resembles that associated with natural infection. However, live vaccines demand particular care in many ways: in storage, when they may inadvertently be inactivated; in the choice of the individual immunized, since live agents are usually not appropriate for immunodeficient people or, in some cases, for pregnant women; and with regard to changes in virulence and possible spread to contacts of vaccinees and to the environment. Also, because live vaccines produce infection, they can on occasion produce some of the symptoms and complications of the disease they are meant to prevent, though at much lower frequency than that associated with the disease.

In this *Guide*, information is presented on the immunizing agents available in Canada and their use in the prevention of communicable diseases. Recommendations on routine immunization of infants and children are discussed in some detail, and an attempt is made to answer most of the day-to-day queries from providers regarding immunization.

Because of variation in manufacturers' products, precise details of the dosage and route of administration of individual products are not usually given. Readers are referred to manufacturers' labelling and package inserts for this information. As well, the manufacturer has sought approval of the vaccine and provided evidence as to its safety and efficacy only when it is used in accordance with the product monograph. Updates of the information in the product monographs are made infrequently. Recommendations for use and other information set out in the *Guide* may differ from those set out in the product monograph(s) of the Canadian licensed manufacturer(s) of the vaccine. The advice and recommendations set out in this *Guide* are based upon the best and most current publicly available scientific knowledge.

Cost Benefit

The World Bank has stated that immunization should be first among the public health initiatives in which governments around the world invest. ***Vaccination programs are considered to be the most cost-beneficial health intervention and one of the few that systematically demonstrate far more benefits than costs.***

Tengs and colleagues reviewed 587 life-saving interventions and their cost-effectiveness, and concluded that routine immunization programs for children were among the most cost-effective and among the very few that save more money than they cost (i.e., it costs more not to undertake these programs in terms of lives or life years saved). The cost of the 587 interventions reviewed ranged from less than zero (i.e., those that save more resources than they cost) to more than $99 billion per year of life saved (Table 1). The median cost was US$42,000 per year of life saved.

Many cost-benefit studies of routine immunization programs have been conducted, and they almost always demonstrate a very positive cost-benefit ratio, commonly ranging from 7:1 to 80:1. Very few studies of immunization programs, however, have been or are being conducted in Canada. Recent cost-benefit studies of the introduction of a routine two-dose measles vaccination schedule and replacement of the pertussis whole-cell vaccine with the new acellular products have indicated that these two strategies were highly cost-beneficial and in the long term would result in savings of several hundred millions of dollars.

The new vaccines being introduced may seem very expensive, at least initially, when compared with vaccines currently in general use. However, in most cases, the cost-

– Table 1 –

Cost per Life Year Saved for Selected Life-saving Interventions (from Tengs et al)

Measles, mumps and rubella immunization for children	≤0
Smoking cessation advice for pregnant women who smoke	≤0
Mandatory seat belt law	$69
Mammography for women aged 50	$810
Chlorination of drinking water	$3,100
Smoking cessation advice for people who smoke more than one pack per day	$9,800
Driver and passenger airbags/manual lap belts (vs. airbag for driver only and belts)	$61,000
Smoke detectors in homes	$210,000
Ban on products containing asbestos (vs. 0.2 fibres/cc standard)	$220,000
Low cholesterol diet for men over age 20 and over 180 mg/dL	$360,000
Crossing control arm for school buses	$410,000
Radiation emission standard for nuclear power plants	$100,000,000
Chloroform private well emission standard at 48 pulp mills	$99,000,000,000

effectiveness (cost to prevent one undesired incident e.g., death, hospitalization, infection and complications) is relatively low and compares very favourably with the other commonly used treatments or preventive measures. These vaccines should be promoted on the basis of the benefits they provide at an acceptable cost. Research should also be encouraged in order to find the best effective delivery schedule at the least cost. As an example, the number of doses needed can be evaluated to determine the most effective combination. Policy makers should promote the inclusion of money in immunization programs for post-marketing studies, which will lead to further improvements to and benefits from those programs.

Selected References

Division of Immunization, Bureau of Infectious Diseases, LCDC. *Canadian national report on immunization, 1996.* CCDR 1997;23S4:40-1.

Tengs TO, Adams ME, Pliskin JS et al. *Five hundred life-saving interventions and their cost-effectiveness.* Risk Anal 1995;15:369-90.

World Bank. *Investing in health.* New York: Oxford University Press, 1993.

General Cautions and Contraindications

A guide to true contraindications to immunization as well as to conditions considered to be precautions rather than contraindications is provided in Table 2. The Table also lists other conditions commonly but inappropriately classified as contraindications, such as mild acute illness with or without fever, mild to moderate local reactions to a previous dose of vaccine, current antimicrobial therapy, and the convalescent phase of an acute illness. For complete information regarding a particular vaccine, the reader is invited to consult the specific vaccine chapter of the *Guide*.

Minor illnesses such as the common cold, with or without fever, frequently occur in young children and are not contraindications to immunization. Such infections do not increase the risk of adverse effects from immunization and do not interfere with immune responses to vaccines. Deferring immunization because of acute mild illnesses often results in incomplete immunization of children who will either need later catch-up vaccinations or develop vaccine-preventable disease. Moderate to severe illness with or without fever is a reason to defer *routine* immunization with most vaccines. This precaution avoids superimposing adverse effects from the vaccine on the underlying illness or mistakenly identifying a manifestation of the underlying illness as a complication of vaccine use. However, if the vaccine is required because of likely exposure to disease or if the child is unlikely to return to continue immunization in a timely fashion, the vaccine may be given despite the intercurrent illness.

Allergic conditions *per se* (e.g., eczema and asthma) are not contraindications to immunization unless there is a specific allergy to a vaccine component. Special precautions may be required for some vaccines prepared in eggs or avian tissue. The section on egg allergy (page 12) and the sections on individual vaccines should be consulted when dealing with an egg allergic individual. Recently, concern has been expressed regarding exposure to thimerosal, a mercurial, contained in vaccines. In Canada, the only thimerosal-containing vaccine included in the regular childhood immunization schedule is hepatitis B vaccine, and thimerosal-free hepatitis B vaccines are now available in Canada. Other routine childhood vaccines such as those for measles, mumps, and rubella (MMR) and Pentacel™ (for diphtheria, tetanus, acellular pertussis, *Haemophilus influenzae* type b, and inactivated polio) do not contain thimerosal as a preservative. Therefore, NACI does not recommend any alteration to the current infant immunization policies. Some vaccines contain trace amounts of antibiotics (e.g., neomycin) or other compounds associated with the vaccine's production or packaging to which patients may be hypersensitive. No currently recommended vaccine contains penicillin or its derivatives. Yeast allergy is not a contraindication to immunization unless there has been documented anaphylactic sensitivity to yeast.

Bovine-derived materials are essential components in the production process of vaccines. The risk of transmitting variant Creutzfeld Jakob Disease (vCJD) from vaccines containing bovine-derived material is theoretical. Studies in the U.K. did not

– Table 2 –

Contraindications to and Precautions for Commonly Used Vaccines*

Vaccine**	True contraindications	Precautions[†]	Not a contraindication
All vaccines	• Anaphylactic reaction to a previous dose of vaccine • Anaphylactic reaction to a constituent of a vaccine	• Moderate to severe illness with or without fever	• Mild to moderate local reactions to previous injection of vaccine • Mild, acute illness with or without fever • Current antimicrobial therapy *with the exception of live bacterial vaccines* • Convalescent phase of an acute illness • Prematurity • Breastfeeding • Recent exposure to infectious disease • Personal or family history of allergy
DPT	• Anaphylactic reaction to a previous dose of vaccine	• Hypotonic-hyporesponsive state within 48 hr after prior dose of DPT	• Fever ≥ 40.5° C after prior dose of DPT • Family history of sudden infant death syndrome • Convulsion within 48 hr of prior dose of DPT • Family history of convulsions • Persistent inconsolable crying lasting ≥ 3 hr within 48 hr after prior dose • Pre-existing neurologic conditions • Prior history of pertussis
IPV	• Anaphylactic reaction to neomycin		
MMR	• Anaphylactic reaction to previous dose or to neomycin • Pregnancy • Severe immunodeficiency (See section on Immunization in Immunocompromised Hosts)	• Recent administration of IG (see Table 7)	• Tuberculosis or positive TB skin test • Simultaneous TB skin testing • Current antimicrobial therapy • Infection with HIV (1994 Pediatric HIV Classification categories E, N1, A1) • Egg allergy
Hib			• History of Hib disease

– Table 2 con't –

Contraindications to and Precautions for Commonly Used Vaccines*

Vaccine**	True contraindications	Precautions†	Not a contraindication
Hepatitis A and B			• Pregnancy
Influenza	• Anaphylactic reaction to a previous dose; known anaphylactic hypersensitivity to eggs manifested as hives, swelling of the mouth and throat, difficulty in breathing, hypotension and shock		• Pregnancy
Meningococcal vaccines	• Hypersensitivity to any component of the vaccine; history of signs of hypersensitivity after previous administration of the vaccine		• Pregnancy
Pneumococcal vaccines	• Hypersensitivity to any component of the vaccine including diphtheria toxoid	• Possible history of latex sensitivity	• Pregnancy
Varicella	• Immunocompromised people (see Varicella chapter) • Pregnancy	• Recent administration of blood, plasma, IG or VZIG (see Table 7)	• History of contact dermatitis to neomycin • Patients with nephrotic syndrome or those undergoing hemodialysis and peritoneal dialysis • Patients taking low doses of inhaled steroids

*   For complete information regarding a particular vaccine, the reader is invited to consult the specific vaccine chapter of the *Guide*.

**   DPT = diphtheria, pertussis and tetanus vaccine, IPV = inactivated poliovirus vaccine, MMR = measles, mumps and rubella vaccine, Hib = *Haemophilus influenzae* type b conjugate vaccine

†   The events or conditions listed as precautions are not contraindications but should be carefully considered in determining the benefits and risks of administering a specific vaccine. If the benefits are believed to outweigh the risks (e.g., during an outbreak or foreign travel) the vaccine should be given.

show a relation between vaccines and any of the 52 vCJD cases. At a Food and Drug Administration meeting in the United States, in July 2000, the theoretical risk of vaccine-related vCJD was estimated at one in 40 billion and may be even less. For more details see http://www.fda.gov/cber/BSE/risk.htm. In Canada, commonly used vaccines included in the routine schedule are made from bovine-derived material coming from countries proven to be free of bovine spongiform encephalopathy (BSE). By the end of this year (2001), all vaccines using bovine-derived material will come from BSE-free countries and, despite the fact that the risk is theoretical, manufacturers are moving towards finding alternative components to these materials.

At the current time, there is no conclusive evidence to support a link between MMR immunization and inflammatory bowel disease (IBD). Neither wild type nor vaccine strain measles virus has been isolated from the tissues of patients with IBD, and immunohistochemical- and nucleic acid-based investigations have yielded conflicting results. An Institute of Medicine review recently concluded that there was no evidence to support a causal association between MMR vaccination and autism.

There is no evidence to support withholding immunization with MMR from anyone for whom it is indicated because of a diagnosis of multiple sclerosis or other conditions considered to involve autoimmunity, muscular dystrophy or other evolving neurologic conditions.

It is prudent to keep vaccinees under observation for immediate reactions or syncope for a period of at least 15 minutes after inoculation or for a longer period if hypersensitivity is a possibility. Epinephrine should be available for immediate use when immunizing agents are injected in order to treat the extremely rare but serious complication of anaphylaxis (see page 14).

Should a significant untoward reaction follow an injection of any vaccine, the provider should postpone further doses, report the reaction to the local public health authority and seek expert advice. **The use of partial doses for continuation of a course of vaccine is not recommended in any circumstances except for desensitization purposes.**

Adverse Events

Safety has always been an important issue in the use of vaccines, both because they are often universally recommended and because they are generally administered to otherwise healthy people to prevent disease. As a result, the level of tolerance for adverse events associated with vaccines is lower than that for therapeutic drugs.

Both local and systemic adverse reactions may follow the use of immunizing agents, most of them occurring shortly after immunization and others appearing only later. Mild vaccine-associated adverse events (e.g., fever and swelling) are relatively common, predictable and self-limited; serious or unexpected adverse reactions can, rarely, develop.

Assessing attributable risk

When an adverse event occurs after immunization, it is possible that it was caused by the vaccine, but it is also possible that it would have happened if no vaccine had been administered, because on any given day there is some illness in the population even in the absence of immunization. It is therefore necessary to take into account this "background" level of health problems when assessing the frequency of adverse events associated with particular vaccines.

The Figure below illustrates that not all health problems noted after immunization are truly caused by it. In a population of immunized children, the number of illnesses or clinical symptoms compatible with an adverse event increased in the week after hepatitis B immunization but returned to pre-vaccination levels thereafter. The vaccine can be implicated only for this "excess" of illness (or attributable risk).

In line with this demonstration, clinical trials have repeatedly shown that placebo recipients occasionally experience adverse events, and these are clearly not attributable to the vaccine. Adverse events with other etiologies are common and simply occur by chance shortly after the administration of a vaccine.

Total Number of Adverse Events in the Weeks Preceding and Following Each of the 3 Doses of Hepatitis B Vaccine and the Proportion of These Events Attributable to the Vaccine (compared with the incidence during the week preceding vaccination)*

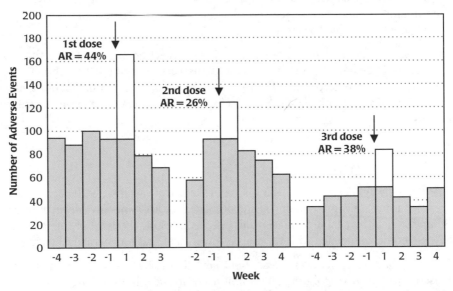

Note. White bars represent relative attributable risk (AR). Arrows indicate vaccination.

* Reproduced with the kind permission of the American Journal of Public Health from De Serres G. et al. *Importance of attributing risk in monitoring adverse events after immunization: hepatitis B vaccination in children.* Am J Public Health 2001;91(2):313-15.

– Table 3 –

Percentage of Children with Fever After MMR Immunization or Placebo Injection in 581 Twin Pairs*

	Days after injection				
	1-6	7-8	9-10	11-12	13-21
MMR	17.2%	20.3%	24.0%	19.9%	16.2%
Placebo	17.0%	18.0%	17.9%	17.5%	16.5%
Difference or attributable risk	0.2%	2.3%	6.1%	2.4%	- 0.3%

* Calculated from data presented in Table II in Peltola H, Heinonen OP. *Frequency of true adverse reactions to measles-mumps-rubella vaccine.* Reprinted with permission from Elsevier Science — Lancet 1986;April 26:939-42.

In a Finnish study of cross-over design, each twin of 581 pairs of twins was given MMR vaccine or placebo in a blinded fashion, and 3 weeks later was administered the other substance. Each child was followed up over 21 days for adverse reactions. As can be seen in Table 3, which illustrates one condition (fever) monitored, some children in the placebo group experienced fever throughout the follow-up period, and the only significant difference (called excess or attributable risk) between placebo and MMR groups occurred between day 7 and day 12.

What happened with fever can happen with other illnesses. Immunized patients suffering from symptoms that became evident after immunization but were not caused by it understandably suspect the vaccine. This chance association illustrates the greatest vulnerability of universal immunization programs, even those involving a vaccine that is 100% safe. It also explains why health care providers are confronted so often with reports of unusual and severe adverse events that are temporally related to but generally not caused by vaccines. Only very large and well-controlled studies are adequate to assess the causality of these fairly rare events. In such studies, the frequency of the adverse events in otherwise comparable vaccinated and unvaccinated individuals is used to estimate the risk that is truly attributable to the vaccine.

Types of reactions

Local reactions after immunization usually consist of swelling or induration, tenderness, and redness or erythema at the injection site. More severe local reactions occasionally occur, such as inflammatory cellulitis without bacterial infection (e.g., after DT or DPT-containing vaccines). Although post-vaccination inflammatory cellulitis can usually be differentiated from bacterial cellulitis by the absence of fever and the general condition of the patient, this distinction can sometimes be difficult to make.

Systemic reactions may include fever, rash, joint or muscle pain, fainting, seizures or other central nervous system symptoms. Fainting immediately after immunization is usually due to apprehension and should not be confused with anaphylaxis.

Allergic reactions, such as urticaria, rhinitis, brochospasm and anaphylaxis, are rare. They may be due to a specific allergy to any component of the vaccine (which may include antibiotics, egg protein, stabilizers such as gelatin, or a preservative). If the specific cause of a serious allergic reaction following immunization can be identified, that particular component must **never** be given again. If the specific cause is not identified, no component of the vaccine should be given again except on the advice and under direct supervision of an experienced physician.

Severe reactions, local or systemic, may indicate that additional doses of the same agent should be avoided. The physician should seek expert advice in such instances, as continuing the immunization series may still be possible (or even necessary, as for post-exposure rabies immunization) under controlled conditions.

Vaccine providers should be aware of the incidence and nature of adverse reactions to immunizing agents. Although signed consent is not required, parents and patients must always be informed about both the benefits and risks of the vaccines. They should be reminded of the risks of the targeted diseases and given the opportunity to ask questions. It should be recorded in patients' charts that such discussion took place. In addition, it may be helpful to provide information brochures written in lay language (see Communication issues in immunization, page 43).

Pregnant women

Immunization of pregnant women with killed or recombinant vaccine is safe; however, the use of live, attenuated vaccines is contraindicated. Should such immunization take place inadvertently, it should be reported. In almost every instance, termination of pregnancy is not warranted (see chapters on the specific vaccines), but in such cases the woman should be followed to term by public health authorities.

Vaccine safety monitoring in Canada

Large-scale trials — however ideal — to detect all possible rare, adverse events cannot usually be carried out before licensure because the number of subjects included in such trials can be quite limited (5,000 to 15,000). Therefore, the reporting of adverse events is vital to monitor the safety of vaccines and generate hypotheses that can be tested by controlled study.

It is important that such reporting include not only well-established adverse events but also any severe or unusual events not previously associated with the vaccine, so as to trigger investigation of possible new associations. This is particularly true for the newer vaccines, of which there is limited use or experience. As a result, truly rare adverse events caused by the vaccine can be detected only with post-marketing surveillance, when large numbers of individuals are immunized. In addition, surveillance of adverse events is important to detect any change in the frequency of known events and to monitor vaccine lots that have been released, should they not perform as expected.

In Canada, there are two main surveillance systems: a passive surveillance system that collects data on any adverse event reported by all health care providers, and an active surveillance system operating through pediatric hospitals, known as IMPACT.

For the passive system, all adverse events should be reported using a standardized form available through public health units. This form permits the reporting of common adverse events but also has a section to describe any severe or unusual occurrences after immunization. Parents and patients should therefore be advised to notify their health care provider about any significant adverse event. To facilitate detailed monitoring and follow-up of adverse reactions, the lot number and manufacturer of the vaccine should be recorded in the vaccine recipient's medical record.

Physicians and other health care personnel should report serious adverse events associated with immunization to their local health unit or medical officer of health. Appendix I provides a list of defined events that should be reported. An example of a reporting form can be found in Appendix II and is available, with instructions, in the *Compendium of Pharmaceuticals and Specialties*. The local public health offices forward completed reports to the provincial health department, which then sends them to the Centre for Infectious Disease Prevention and Control, at Health Canada. This federal office is responsible for post-marketing surveillance of adverse events temporally associated with immunizing agents. Only non-nominal information is sent, and thus confidentiality is maintained. Updated reports on adverse events are published periodically and are available at the Health Canada website (http://www.hc-sc.gc.ca/hpb/lcdc/bid/di/nation_e.html).

To enhance surveillance of rare but severe adverse events, Canada has implemented an active surveillance network: the Immunization Monitoring Program Active (IMPACT), a pediatric, hospital-based network funded by Health Canada. This network collects information on potentially vaccine-related, severe adverse events and serious illness for which new or improved vaccines are being used or may be introduced in the near future. The 13 IMPACT hospitals make up approximately 85% of tertiary care pediatric beds in Canada. This program reports results regularly through the *Canada Communicable Disease Report* (CCDR).

Special review of serious and unusual events is conducted by the Advisory Committee on Causality Assessment (ACCA), which comprises pediatricians, immunologists, epidemiologists and other experts. The mandate of ACCA is to evaluate the degree to which such events are linked to the implicated vaccine in order to detect potential signals of concern (for more information see http://www.hc-sc.gc.ca/hpb/lcdc/bid/di/acca_e.html).

Canadian health authorities are very sensitive to vaccine safety. A national meeting on vaccine safety was convened in November 2000 in order to emphasize the importance of vaccine safety and to issue recommendations to further improve the vaccine safety program in Canada. These recommendations were published in the *CCDR* in October 2001.

Selected References

De Serres G, Duval B, Boulianne N et al. *Importance of attributable risk in monitoring adverse events after immunization: hepatitis B vaccination in children.* Am J Public Health 2001;91(2):313-15.

Health Canada. *Meeting on vaccine safety: a Canadian strategy.* CCDR 2001;27(S4).

Howson CP, Howe CJ, Fineberg HV, eds. Vaccine Safety Committee, Institute of Medicine. *Adverse events following pertussis and rubella vaccines.* Washington, DC: National Academy Press, 1991.

Peltola H, Heinonen OP. *Frequency of true adverse reactions to measles-mumps-rubella vaccine.* Lancet 1986;April 26:939-42.

Scheifele DS. *IMPACT monitoring network: a better mousetrap.* Can J Infect Dis 1993;4:194-95.

Stratton KR, Howe CJ, Johnston RB. eds. Vaccine Safety Committee, Institute of Medicine. *Adverse events associated with childhood vaccines.* Washington, DC: National Academy Press, 1994.

Vaccine adverse events. Bull WHO 2000;78: special issue.

Anaphylactic Hypersensitivity to Egg and Egg-Related Antigens

Vaccines that contain small quantities of egg protein can cause hypersensitivity reactions in some people with allergies to eggs. The likelihood of such reactions occurring varies considerably among vaccines. Adverse reactions are more likely to occur to vaccines against yellow fever and influenza, which are prepared from viruses grown in embryonated eggs. In contrast, the measles and mumps vaccine viruses most widely used in Canada are grown in chick embryo cell culture; after these viruses have undergone extensive purification steps, the final vaccine products *may* contain trace quantities of avian proteins, resembling proteins present in hens' eggs. A measles-rubella combination vaccine, MoRu-Viraten Berna®, contains no avian proteins and can be used without regard to egg allergy.

Anaphylaxis after measles vaccination is rare. It has been reported both in people with anaphylactic hypersensitivity to eggs and in those with no history of egg allergy. In some of these instances **it is hypersensitivity to gelatin that is responsible for the anaphylactic reaction.** As well, allergy to other components of the vaccine, such as neomycin, has been hypothesized but not proven.

Several studies have reported uneventful routine MMR immunization in egg-allergic people and in those with positive MMR skin tests, whereas others have reported occasional adverse reactions despite the use of MMR skin testing and graded challenge vaccination. In the largest summary of the literature, none of the 284 children with egg allergy confirmed by blinded food challenge showed any serious adverse

but patients may remain pale, diaphoretic and mildly hypotensive for several more minutes. The likelihood of fainting is reduced by measures that lower stress in those awaiting immunization, such as short waiting times, comfortable room temperature, preparation of vaccines out of view of recipients and privacy during the procedure. To reduce injuries during fainting spells those at risk are best immunized while seated.

People experiencing an anxiety spell may appear fearful, pale and diaphoretic and complain of lightheadedness, dizziness and numbness, as well as tingling of the face and extremities. Hyperventilation is usually evident. Treatment consists of reassurance and rebreathing using a paper bag until symptoms subside.

Breath-holding spells occur in some young children when they are upset and crying hard. The child is suddenly silent but obviously agitated. Facial flushing and perioral cyanosis deepens as breath-holding continues. Some spells end with resumption of crying, but others end with a brief period of unconsciousness during which breathing resumes. Similar spells may have been evident in other circumstances. No treatment is required beyond reassurance of the child and parents.

In the case of anaphylaxis, changes develop over several minutes and usually involve at least two body systems (affecting the skin, respiration, circulation). Unconsciousness is rarely the sole manifestation of anaphylaxis. It occurs only as a late event in severe cases.

The cardinal features of anaphylaxis are

- itchy, urticarial rash (in over 90% of cases);

- progressive, painless swelling (angioedema) about the face and mouth, which may be preceded by itchiness, tearing, nasal congestion or facial flushing;

- respiratory symptoms, including sneezing, coughing, wheezing, laboured breathing and upper airway swelling (indicated by hoarseness and/or difficulty swallowing) possibly causing airway obstruction;

- hypotension, which generally develops later in the illness and can progress to cause shock and collapse.

An inconstant early feature is swelling and urticarial rash at the injection site. This is more likely to be evident with vaccines injected subcutaneously rather than intramuscularly.

Anaphylaxis is described as mild or early when signs are limited to urticarial rash and injection site swelling. At this stage symptoms may arise from other systems (e.g., sneezing, nasal congestion, tearing, coughing, facial flushing) but are associated with minimal dysfunction. Features of severe disease include obstructive swelling of the upper airway, marked bronchospasm and hypotension.

Management of anaphylaxis

The following steps describe the management of anaphylaxis. Steps 1 to 4 are meant to be done rapidly or simultaneously. **The priority is prompt administration of epinephrine (step 4)**, which should not be delayed if earlier steps cannot quickly be completed.

1. Call for assistance, including an ambulance.

2. Place the patient in a recumbent position (elevating the feet if possible).

3. Establish an oral airway if necessary.

4. **Promptly administer 0.01 mL/kg (maximum 0.5 mL) of aqueous epinephrine 1:1,000 by subcutaneous or intramuscular injection in the opposite limb to that in which the vaccination was given.** Speedy intervention is of paramount importance; failure to use epinephrine promptly is more dangerous than using it improperly.

   The subcutaneous route of epinephrine injection is appropriate for mild or early cases, and a single injection is usually sufficient. Severe cases should receive intramuscular injections because they lead more quickly to generalized distribution of the drug.

   Dosing can be repeated twice at 20-minute intervals if necessary, again avoiding the limb in which the vaccination was given. A different limb is preferred for each dose to maximize drug absorption. Severe reactions could require these repeat doses to be given at shorter intervals (10 to 15 minutes).

   The epinephrine dose should be carefully determined. Calculations based on body weight are preferred when weight is known. Recording the weight of children before routine immunization is recommended when feasible. Excessive doses of epinephrine can add to patients' distress by causing palpitations, tachycardia, flushing and headache. Although unpleasant, such side effects pose little danger. Cardiac dysrhythmias may occur in older adults but are rare in otherwise healthy children.

   When body weight is not known the dose of aqueous epinephrine 1:1,000 can be approximated from the subject's age (Table 4).

   The anaphylactic state in patients receiving beta-adrenergic antagonist therapy (for elevated blood pressure) will be more resistant to epinephrine therapy.

   Since anaphylaxis is rare, epinephrine vials and other emergency supplies should be checked on a regular basis and replaced if outdated.

Adrenaline kit contents:

Copy of the anaphylaxis procedures/doses
2 – 1 cc syringes with attached needles (1 – 25 gauge, 5/8" needle/1 – 25 gauge, 1" needle)
2 vials of adrenaline 1:1,000 (within expiration time frame)
1 vial of diphenhydramine
1 – 25 gauge, 5/8" needle (extra)
1 – 25 gauge, 1" needle (extra)
2 alcohol swabs (optional)

– Table 4 –
Appropriate Dose of Epinephrine According to Age

Age	Dose	
2 to 6 months*	0.07 mL	(0.07 mg)
12 months*	0.10 mL	(0.10mg)
18 months* to 4 years	0.15 mL	(0.15 mg)
5 years	0.20 mL	(0.20 mg)
6-9 years	0.30 mL	(0.30 mg)
10-13 years	0.40 mL†	(0.40 mg)
≥ 14	0.50 mL†	(0.50 mg)

* Dose for children between the ages shown should be approximated, the volume being intermediate between the values shown or increased to the next larger dose, depending on practicability.

† For a mild reaction a dose of 0.3 mL can be considered.

5. If the vaccine was injected subcutaneously, an additional dose of 0.005 mL/kg (maximum 0.3 mL) of aqueous epinephrine 1:1,000 can be injected into the vaccination site to slow absorption. This should be given shortly after the initial dose of epinephrine (Table 4) in moderate to severe cases. It is generally not repeated. Local injection of epinephrine into an intramuscular vaccination site is contraindicated because it dilates vessels and speeds absorption of the vaccine.

6. As an adjunct to epinephrine, a dose of diphenhydramine hydrochloride (Benadryl®) can be given. It should be reserved for patients not responding well to epinephrine or to maintain symptom control in those who have responded to epinephrine (epinephrine being a short-acting agent), especially if transfer to an acute care facility cannot be effected within 30 minutes. Oral treatment (oral dose: 1-2 mg/kg to a maximum single dose of 100 mg) is preferred for conscious patients who are not seriously ill because Benadryl® is painful when given intramuscularly. This drug has a high safety margin, making precise dosing less important. The approximate doses for injection (50 mg/mL solution) are shown in Table 5.

— Table 5 —

Appropriate Dose by Injection of Diphenhydramine Hydrochloride (50 mg/mL Solution)

Age	Dose	
< 2 years	0.25 mL	(12.5 mg)
2-4 years	0.50 mL	(25.0 mg)
5-11 years	1.00 mL	(50.0 mg)
≥12 years	1.00-2.00 mL	(50-100 mg)

7. Monitor vital signs and reassess the situation frequently, to guide medication use.

8. Arrange for rapid transport to an emergency department. Since 20% of anaphylaxis episodes follow a biphasic course with recurrence of the reaction after a 2-9 hour asymptomatic period, hospitalization or a long period of observation is recommended for monitoring. For all but the mildest cases of anaphylaxis, patients should be hospitalized overnight or monitored for at least 12 hours.

Selected References

Ellis AK, Day JH. *Anaphylaxis: diagnosis and treatment*. Allergy Asthma 2000;23-5.

Thibodeau JL. *Office management of childhood vaccine-related anaphylaxis*. Can Fam Phys 1993;40:1602-10.

Immunization During Pregnancy

Immunization during pregnancy may be indicated if the risk of infection is high, the illness would cause significant risk to the mother or fetus, and the risk of adverse effects from the vaccine is acceptably low. When these conditions do not prevail, any vaccination should be deferred until after delivery. There is a theoretical risk to the fetus from live-virus vaccines, but specific fetal damage from administration of currently licensed vaccines during pregnancy has not been reported. Should a congenital defect occur following a pregnancy during which the mother was immunized, blame may be attributed, perhaps wrongly, to the vaccine. When a vaccine is indicated during pregnancy, consider delaying administration until the second or third trimester, if possible, to reduce the risk of inappropriate attribution of cause.

There is no evidence to suggest that pregnant women are at increased risk of allergic reactions after immunization. However, a severe anaphylactic reaction and its treatment can have dramatic adverse consequences for the fetus. As well, fever is a possible reaction to many vaccines; epidemiologic and animal studies indicate that maternal hyperthermia during the first trimester of pregnancy may be teratogenic. The magnitude of this risk is not known precisely.

Inactivated vaccines and toxoids are generally considered safe for the fetus, whereas live vaccines are contraindicated. Tetanus immunization for women who have never received a primary series or who suffer a tetanus-prone wound, and influenza immunization for those at high risk of complications (see chapter on Influenza Vaccine) are particularly important to consider. Live attenuated yellow fever vaccine may be administered to pregnant women only if they will be exposed to an ongoing epidemic. There is no known risk from passive immunization of pregnant women with immune globulins.

Should a pregnant woman receive a contraindicated vaccine inadvertently, the incident should be signaled to the local public health department and the outcome of the pregnancy monitored for possible adverse events. Since there is no or extremely low risk of congenital defects from mumps, measles, and rubella vaccine, pregnancy termination should never be proposed. The effect of varicella vaccine on the fetus is not known, but data collected to date do not suggest that it poses a particular fetal risk.

Immunization with live, attenuated virus for children from families with pregnant women is not contraindicated and should never be postponed for this reason.

Vaccinators are advised to consult with an expert in pregnancy and immunization before deciding on the necessity for immunization during pregnancy.

Selected References

American Academy of Pediatrics. *Active and passive immunization.* In: Pickering LK, ed. *2000 red book: report of the Committee on Infectious Diseases.* 25th Edition. Elk Grove Village, IL: American Academy of Pediatrics, 2000:55.

Centers for Disease Control and Prevention. *Guidelines for vaccinating pregnant women.* www.immunize.org/genr.d/pregguid.htm (June 7, 2001).

Immunization and Breast-Feeding

Breast-feeding does not adversely affect immunization of the infant with either live or killed vaccines and may, in fact, improve the immune response to some vaccines. Infants who are breast-fed should receive all recommended vaccinations at the usual times.

Lactating mothers who have not received the recommended immunizations may safely be given vaccine against rubella, measles, mumps, tetanus, diphtheria, influenza, *Streptococcus pneumoniae*, hepatitis A, hepatitis B, polio and varicella. Inactivated polio vaccine may safely be given to lactating mothers who have not previously been immunized or who are travelling to a highly endemic area.

Selected References

Kanariou M, Petridou E, Liatsis et al. *Age patterns of immunoglobulins G, A and M in healthy children and the influence of breast feeding and vaccination status*. Pediatr Allergy Immunol 1995;6(1):24-9.

Pabst HF, Godel J, Grace M et al. *Effect of breast feeding on immune response to BCG vaccination*. Lancet 1989;1(8633):295-97.

Pabst HF, Spady DW. *Effect of breast feeding on antibody response to conjugate vaccine*. Lancet 1990;336(8710):269-70.

Pickering LK, Granoff DM, Erickson JR et al. *Modulation of the immune system by human milk and infant formula containing nucleotides*. Pediatrics 1998;101(2):242-9.

Immunization of Children with Neurologic Disorders

Children with neurologic disorders can undergo routine vaccinations. For those with seizure disorders that might be exacerbated by fever, prophylactic doses of acetaminophen (15 mg/kg) can be used.

Immunization in Immunocompromised Hosts

The number of immunocompromised people in Canadian society is steadily increasing for a variety of reasons. These include our increasingly sophisticated understanding of "normal" and altered immunity (e.g., IgG subclass deficiencies, mannose binding protein deficiency, cytokine receptor deficiencies); recognition of the subtle immuno-deficiencies associated with chronic illnesses (e.g., diabetes, cirrhosis, alcoholism, renal disease) and the extremes of age; accumulation of individuals with absent or dysfunctional spleens; the expanding range of illnesses treated with immuno-modulatory agents (e.g., autoimmune diseases, inflammatory conditions); the HIV pandemic; accumulation of long-term survivors after organ transplantation; and the increased use of ablative therapy for cancer and other conditions.

The number of immunizations to which immunocompromised people are likely to be exposed is also increasing. There is an ever-enlarging spectrum of vaccines available and an increasing number of vaccines included in universal programs; as well, efforts are under way to fully immunize adolescents, adults and the elderly. Individuals with significant illness can now travel with relative ease (e.g., people infected with HIV, see CATMAT statement on travel and HIV as well as a recent review by Mileno and Bia). Furthermore, both basic and clinical investigations have recently contributed to the discovery of novel strategies (for instance, increased dose, route of delivery, novel adjuvant systems) for eliciting successful immune responses in immuno-compromised individuals.

Therefore, the frequency and complexity of questions dealing with immunization in immunocompromised hosts will only increase with time. Still further complexity is added by the fact that the relative degree of immunodeficiency varies over time in many people. The decision to recommend for or against any particular vaccine will depend upon a careful, case-by-case analysis of the risks and benefits.

There is potential for serious illness and death in both the underimmunization and overimmunization of these people. Immunization of those with significant immuno-deficiency should be performed only in consultation with experts.

General principles

Several general principles apply to the immunization of immunocompromised individuals:

■ maximize benefit while minimizing harm;

■ make no assumptions about susceptibility or protection
  ▪ a history of childhood infection or previous immunization may be irrelevant;

■ immunize at the time when maximum immune response can be anticipated
  ▪ immunize early, when immunologic decline is predictable
  ▪ delay immunization if the immunodeficiency is transient (if this can be done safely)
  ▪ stop or reduce immunosuppression to permit better vaccine response;

■ consider the immunization environment broadly
  ▪ spread of vaccine strain varicella to family members of the vaccinee
  ▪ immunization status of both donor and/or recipient in the setting of bone marrow (BMT) or stem cell transplantation;

■ avoid live vaccines, unless
  ▪ data are available to support their use
  ▪ the risk of natural infection is greater than the risk of immunization;

■ monitor vaccinees carefully and boost aggressively
  ▪ the magnitude and duration of vaccine-induced immunity are often reduced
  ▪ some vaccine strain organisms can persist for years in compromised hosts.

Approach to vaccination of immunodeficient individuals

The approach to immunizing people with immunodeficiency varies with the precise nature of the defect. Additional considerations include the age of the individual (affecting the types of vaccine and the relative urgency of immunization) and factors that influence the risk of exposure to the different pathogens (e.g., endemic, epidemic, professional, travel related). The most common situations are discussed below in broad categories of immunodeficiency. Excellent reviews of this subject are available (Loutan 1997, Pirofski & Casadevall 1998, McFarland 1999, Mileno & Bia 1998, Burroughs & Moscona 2000, Molrine & Hibberd 2001).

Otherwise "normal" individuals with chronic illness or advanced age

These individuals are not necessarily more susceptible to vaccine-preventable diseases but are more likely to suffer significant illness and death from these infections. With the possible exception of yellow fever immunization in those > 65 years of age (see Yellow Fever Vaccine), there are no absolute contraindications to the use of any vaccine in these people.

Particular attention should be paid to annual influenza immunization and at least one dose of pneumococcal vaccine and Td every 10 years (see appropriate vaccine specific chapters). Hepatitis A and/or B immunization may be appropriate in people with chronic liver disease, since they are at risk of fulminant hepatitis. Consider early immunization for individuals who are likely to need solid organ transplantation (e.g., immunization against hepatitis B in those with deteriorating renal disease).

The immune response to vaccines will be suboptimal in many of these people, but there is now good evidence that such limited responses may be improved in some cases with readily accessible strategies, such as increasing the antigen dose (e.g., 40 µg hepatitis B surface antigen dose for patients undergoing hemodialysis). Active verification of immune status (e.g., annual verification of hepatitis B serostatus in hemodialysis patients) and immunization or re-immunization (e.g., against *Haemophilus influenzae* in children < 10 years of age) may be important for some individuals who are at continued high risk.

Splenic disorders

Asplenia or hyposplenism may be congenital, surgical or functional. A number of conditions not typically thought of as immunocompromising can lead to functional hyposplenism. These include sickle cell anemia, thalassemia major, essential thrombocytopenia, celiac disease and inflammatory bowel disease. There are no contraindications to the use of any vaccine in these patients. Particular attention should be paid to ensuring optimal protection against ubiquitous encapsulated bacteria (*Streptococcus pneumoniae*, *Haemophilus influenzae*), to which these individuals are highly susceptible. They should also receive annual influenza immunization. Meningococcal immunization (quadrivalent) is essential for hyposplenic and asplenic individuals who reside in or travel to areas where meningococcal disease is endemic.

There are no data dealing specifically with the periodicity of booster doses in hyposplenic and asplenic patients, although antibody titres are known to decrease with time. Certainly, the 23-valent pneumococcal vaccine should be recommended for everyone who received the original 14-valent product. The current vaccine can be used to safely boost antibody titres at least once after 5 years. Meningococcal immunization can be boosted every 2 to 3 years. (In young patients < 10 years it may be prudent to verify the presence of antibodies directed against *H. influenzae* and re-immunize as needed.)

Careful attention should be paid to immunization status when "elective" surgical splenectomy is planned so that all of the necessary vaccines can be delivered at least 2 weeks before removal of the spleen. It is likely that the protein-conjugated meningococcal and pneumococcal vaccines will significantly improve responses in these individuals. At the current time, however, the number of meningococcal and pneumococcal serotypes for which conjugated formulations are available is quite limited (e.g., 7 or 9 pneumococcal capsular polysaccharides versus 23 in the unconjugated formulation). As a result, conjugated polysaccharide vaccines should be added to immunization schedules as they become available rather than replacing the currently available polysaccharide products. (Note: when available, the conjugated products should be given first.)

Congenital immunodeficiency states

This is a varied group of conditions that includes defects in antibody production (e.g., agammaglobulinemia, isotype and IgG subclass deficiencies and hyper-IgM syndromes), complement deficiencies, defects in one or more aspects of cell-mediated immunity (CMI) and mixed deficits. Individuals with defects in antibody and complement have unusual susceptibility to the encapsulated bacteria and members of the enteroviridae family (e.g., polio, coxsackie and echoviruses), and individuals with mixed and T cell defects are particularly susceptible to intracellular pathogens (virtually all viruses and some bacteria, fungi and parasites). Although the defects and susceptibility patterns are very different, the approach to immunization is quite similar for these individuals. Component and inactivated vaccines can and should be administered in all of these conditions, despite the fact that many vaccinees will respond poorly, if at all. Live vaccines are generally not recommended for these patients, although limited clinical data suggest that MMR can be administered without undue risk in many of those with pure antibody defects.

Antibody defects: Particular attention should be given to ensuring that individuals with this condition are immunized against pneumococcal and meningococcal disease and *Haemophilus influenzae*. Although oral poliovirus vaccine (OPV) is no longer routinely used in Canada, it remains a licensed product and is used in many other countries. OPV should not be used in the affected individual or any of his or her family members. Other live vaccines may be considered on a case-by-case basis after a thorough review of the risks and benefits.

As a general rule, people with antibody defects can be protected from many of the vaccine-preventable infections with the use of intravenous immunoglobulin (IVIG) or pathogen-specific IG preparations. Inactivated vaccines should be given when IVIG-supported immunoglobulin levels are as low as possible. Again, improved responses with the conjugated polysaccharide products can be anticipated in many individuals, but careful attention will need to be given to coverage of pneumococcal and meningococcal serotypes and appropriate boosting.

T cell, natural killer and mixed CMI-antibody defects: Live vaccines are contraindicated. Inadvertent live vaccine administration and exposure to natural infections must be dealt with by rapid administration of serum IG or pathogen-specific IG with or without appropriate antiviral or antibacterial treatment.

Granulocyte defects: There are no contraindications to the use of any vaccine.

Long-term steroids/azathioprine/cyclosporine/cyclophosphamide/Remicade

Long-term immunosuppressive therapy is used for organ transplantation and an increasing range of chronic infectious and inflammatory conditions (e.g., inflammatory bowel disease, psoriasis, systemic lupus erythematosis). These therapies have their greatest impact on cell-mediated immunity, although T cell-dependent antibody production can also be adversely affected. Ideally, all appropriate vaccines or boosters should be administered to these individuals at least 10-14 days before the initiation of therapy. If this cannot be done safely, immunization should be delayed until at least 3 months after immunosuppressive drugs have been stopped or until such therapy is at the lowest possible level.

There is no contraindication to the use of any inactivated vaccine in these people, and particular attention should be paid to the completion of childhood immunizations, annual influenza immunization and pneumococcal immunization (with a booster after 5 years). Active verification of immune status and immunization or re-immunization may be important for some individuals (e.g., against *H. influenzae* in children < 10 years of age or hepatitis B for renal transplant recipients). Live vaccines are generally contraindicated, although the risk to benefit ratio for several of these vaccines can favour immunization if only low doses of immunosuppressive drugs are required and there is significant risk of wild-type infection (e.g., varicella vaccine in seronegative individuals). On the theoretical grounds that vaccine-induced immunostimulation might trigger an anti-transplant response, some centres choose to rely on IG preparations (e.g., in a measles outbreak) with or without appropriate antimicrobial drugs, to avoid vaccines.

High dose steroids: Only high dose, systemic steroids (e.g., 2mg/kg of prednisone or a maximum daily dose of 20 mg for more than 2 weeks) interfere with vaccine-induced immune responses. Of course, reasonable clinical judgement must be exercised in the risk to benefit review of each case. Topical and inhaled steroids have no known impact on oral or injected vaccines. A period of at least 3 months should elapse between high dose steroid use and administration of both inactivated or component vaccines (to ensure immunogenicity) and live vaccines (to reduce the risk of dissemination). Children with adrenogenital syndrome and those receiving physiologic replacement doses of glucocorticoids can follow the routine immunization schedule without restriction.

Immunoablative therapy (e.g., cancer therapy, total body irradiation, marrow/stem cell transplantation)

If time permits, careful consideration must be given to the pre-ablation immunization status of the patient and, in the case of allogenic BMT, the donor. It is well established that disease and immunization histories in both the host and the donor (i.e., in adoptive transfer) can influence immunity after ablation or transplantation. Although the logic underlying programmatic immunization of these patients is compelling, there are relatively few data that address important immunization-related questions after ablative therapies (e.g., optimal timing, requirement for boosters, overall efficacy, cost-benefit). A recent U.S. national survey demonstrated striking inconsistencies in pre- and post-ablative immunization policies and what the authors felt to be "under-utilization" of vaccines in this setting.

General principles in this setting include the following:

- Live vaccines are contraindicated before ablation when significant marrow infiltration is present (varicella immunization in patients with leukemia may be an exception to this rule when given under protocol).

- Administer all appropriate vaccines or boosters at least 10-14 days before ablative therapy if this can be accomplished without delaying the initiation of chemotherapy.

- In allogenic BMT, consider the administration of all appropriate vaccines or boosters to the donor at least 10-14 days before the marrow harvest.

- Wait at least 12 months after ablative therapy before administering live vaccines and then only if there is no ongoing immune suppressive treatment or graft-versus-host disease.

- Inactivated or component vaccines can be given as soon as the total lymphocyte count exceeds 500, but responses are likely to be very poor soon after transplantation. A primary immunization schedule should be re-initiated at 12 months after transplantation in children whose original schedule was disrupted. Immunization or re-immunization should also be offered to adults with either a full primary series or verification of response after at least two booster doses of each vaccine.

- Consider documentation of responses to the most important pathogens (e.g., *H influenzae*, measles, varicella).

Illnesses that progressively weaken the immune system (e.g., HIV, myelodysplasias)

With the exception of BCG (Bacille Calmette-Guérin), there are no contraindications to the use of any vaccine (including MMR) early in the course of these illnesses. As these conditions progress, the use of live vaccines becomes increasingly dangerous, and the risks and benefits of a particular vaccine (and the alternative therapies available) need to be carefully considered.

Early immunization is not only safer but is also more effective in these conditions. There is no contraindication to the use of inactivated or component vaccines at any time. Particular attention should be paid to the completion of childhood immunizations, pneumococcal immunization (boosted once after 5 years), annual influenza immunization and possibly booster doses against *H. influenzae*. Exposure to wild-type infections must be addressed promptly with general serum or specific IG preparations with or without antimicrobial therapy, since the rates of death in people with these illnesses can be very high (e.g., 50% to 70% mortality from measles in patients with AIDS).

In the case of HIV, consensus "cut-offs" have been determined for the use of some vaccines (Table 6). Although concerns have been raised about increases in HIV viral load, which can occur after a number of routine immunizations, these changes are transient and should not prevent the administration of any appropriate vaccine. The only situation in which deferral of an otherwise appropriate immunization might be recommended would be that of an HIV-positive woman who has decided (against medical advice) to breast-feed.

Immunocompromised travellers

Although the degree and range of infectious disease risks can increase dramatically when an immunocompromised individual boards an airplane or boat, the basic principles already outlined still apply. Evidence is accumulating to suggest that several live vaccines (including yellow fever vaccine) can be considered for people with asymptomatic HIV infection whose CD4$^+$ T cell count is > 200. However, the risks and benefits of each live vaccine must be carefully evaluated for every traveller. When a certificate of yellow fever vaccination is required but this vaccine is contraindicated, a letter of deferral should be supplied to the patient.

– Table 6 –

Vaccination of Individuals with Immunodeficiency

Vaccine	HIV/AIDS	Severe immuno-deficiency	Solid organ transplantation	BMT	Chronic disease age/alcoholism	Hypo- or
Inactivated/Component Vaccines						
DPT (Td)	Routine use*	Routine use	Recommended†	Recommended	Routine use	Routine use
IPV	Routine use	Routine use	Recommended	Recommended	Routine use	Routine use
Hib	Routine use	Routine use	Recommended	Recommended	Routine use	Recommended (confirm in children <10)
Influenza	Recommended	Recommended	Recommended	Recommended	Recommended	Recommended
Pneumococcal	Recommended	Recommended	Recommended	Recommended	Recommended	Recommended
Meningococcal	Use if indicated	Use if indicated	Use if indicated	Use if indicated	Use if indicated	Use if indicated
Hepatitis A	Recommended (gay men, IVDU)	Use if indicated	Use if indicated	Use if indicated	Recommended (chronic liver disease)	Use if indicated
Hepatitis B	Recommended (gay men, IVDU)	Routine use	Routine use	Routine use	Recommended (chronic liver or renal disease)	Routine use

27

– Table 6 cont –

Vaccination of Individuals with Immunodeficiency

Vaccine	HIV/AIDS	Severe immuno-deficiency	Solid organ transplantation	BMT	Chronic disease age/alcoholism	Hypo- or
Live Vaccines						
MMR	Routine use[‡] (if no significant compromise)	Contraindicated	Consider at 24 mo (min. suppressive Rx)	Consider at 24 mo (no suppressive Rx, no GVHD)	Use if indicated	Use if indicated
OPV	Contraindicated (use IPV instead)	Contraindicated (use IPV instead)	Contraindicated (use IPV instead)	Contraindicated (use IPV instead)	If indicated use IPV	If indicated use IPV
Varicella	Use if indicated (asymptomatic disease)	Contraindicated	Consider at 24 mo (min. suppressive Rx)	Consider at 24 mo (no suppressive Rx, no GVHD)	Use if indicated	Use if indicated
Oral typhoid	Contraindicated (use IM vaccine instead)	Contraindicated (use IM vaccine instead)	Contraindicated (use IM vaccine instead)	Contraindicated (use IM vaccine instead)	If indicated use IM	If indicated use
BCG	Contraindicated	Contraindicated	Contraindicated	Contraindicated	Use if indicated	Use if indicated
Yellow fever	Contraindicated	Contraindicated	Consider at 24 mo (no suppressive Rx, no GVHD)	Consider at 24 mo (no suppressive Rx, no GVHD)	Use if indicated	Use if indicated
Oral cholera	Contraindicated	Contraindicated	Contraindicated	Contraindicated	Use if indicated	Use if indicated

* Routine vaccination schedules should be followed with age-appropriate booster doses.

† Vaccination and/or re-vaccination recommended with or without verification of serologic response.

‡ Most HIV positive children can receive the first MMR vaccine without significant risk. Administration of the second MMR dose (particularly in adults) must be ated on a case-by-case basis.

Selected References

Al Arishi HM, Frayha HH, Qari HY et al. *Clinical features and outcome of eleven patients with disseminated bacille Calmette-Guerin (BCG) infection.* Ann Saudi Med 1996;16:512-16.

Ambrosina DM, Molrine DC. *Critical appraisal of immunization strategies for prevention of infection in the compromised host.* Hematol Oncol Clin North Am 1993;7:1027-50.

Avery RK. *Vaccination of the immunosuppressed adult patient with rheumatologic disease.* Rheum Dis Clin North Am 1999;25:567-84.

Burroughs M, Moscona A. *Immunization of pediatric solid organ transplant candidates and recipients.* Clin Infect Dis 2000;30:857-69.

Carlone G, Holder P, Lexhava T et al. *Safety of revaccination with pneumococcal polysaccharide vaccine.* JAMA 1999;281:243-8.

CATMAT. *Statement on travellers and HIV/AIDS.* CCDR 1994;20:147-49.

CDC. *Recommendations of the Advisory Committee on Immunization Practices (ACIP): use of vaccines and immune globulins in persons with altered immunocompetence.* MMWR 1993;42:1-18.

Chan CY, Molrine DC, Antin JH et al. *Antibody response to tetanus toxoid and **Haemophilus influenzae** type B conjugate vaccines following autologous peripheral blood stem cell transplantation (PBX).* Bone Marrow Transplant 1997;20:33-8.

Geiger R, Fink FM, Solder B et al. *Persistent rubella infection after erroneous vaccination in an immunocompromised patient with acute lymphoblastic leukemia in remission.* J Med Virol 1995;47:442-4.

Gershorn AA, Steinberg SP. *Persistence of immunity to varicella in children with leukemia immunized with live attenuated varicella vaccine.* N Engl J Med 1989;320:892-7.

Glesby MJ, Hoover DR, Farzadegan H et al. *The effect of influenza vaccination on human immunodeficiency virus type 1 load: a randomized, double-blind, placebo controlled study.* J Infect Dis 1996;174:1332-6.

Grimfors G, Bjorkholm M, Hammarstrom L et al. *Type-specific anti-pneumococcal antibody subclass response to vaccination after splenectomy with special reference to lymphoma patients.* Eur J Haematol 1989;43:404-10.

Henning KJ, White MH, Sepkowitz KA et al. *A national survey of immunization practices following allogenic bone marrow transplantation.* JAMA 1997; 277:1148-51.

Hibberd PL, Rubin RH. *Approach to immunization in the immunosuppressed host.* Infect Dis Clin North Am 1990;4:123-42.

Hughes I, Jenney ME, Newton RW et al. *Measles encephalitis during immunosuppressive treatment for acute lymphoblastic leukemia.* Arch Dis Child 1993;68:775-8.

Ilan Y, Nagler A, Shouval D et al. *Adoptive transfer of immunity to hepatitis B virus after T cell-depleted allogenic bone marrow transplantation.* Hepatology 1993;18:246-52.

Jackson LA, Benson P, Sneller VP et al. *Immunizations for immunocompromised adults.* In: *Guide for adult immunization.* 3rd edition. Philadelphia: ACP Task Force on Adult Immunization, American College of Physicians, 1994:49-59.

Larussa P, Steinberg S, Gershorn AA. *Varicella vaccine for immunocompromised children: results of collaborative studies in the United States and Canada.* J Infect Dis 1996;174(suppl 3):S320-23.

Ljungman P. *Immunization in the immunocompromised host.* Curr Opin Infect Dis 1995;8:254-57.

Loutan L. *Vaccination of the immunocompromised patient.* Biologicals 1997;25:231-6.

McFarland E. *Immunizations for the immunocompromised child.* Pediatr Ann 1999;28:487-96.

Mileno MD, Bia FJ. *The compromised traveler.* Infect Dis Clin North Am 1998;2:369-412.

Molrine DC, Hibberd PL. *Vaccines for transplant recipients.* Infect Dis Clin North Am 2001;15:273-305.

Parkkali T, Olander RM, Ruutu T et al. *A randomized comparison between early and late vaccination with tetanus toxoid vaccine after allegenic BMT.* Bone Marrow Transplant 1997;19:933-38.

Pirofski LA, Casadevall A. *Use of licensed vaccines for active immunization of the immunocompromised host.* Clin Microbiol Rev 1998;11:1-26.

Polychronopoulou-Androulakaki S, Panagiotou JP, Kostaridou S et al. *Immune response of immunocompromised children with malignancies to a recombinant hepatitis B vaccine.* Petriatr Hematol Oncol 1996;13:425-31.

Ridgeway D, Wolff LJ. *Active immunization of children with leukemia and other malignancies.* Leuk Lymphoma 1993;9:177-92.

Rosen HR, Stierer M, Wolf HM et al. *Impaired primary antibody responses after vaccination against hepatitis B in patients with breast cancer.* Breast Cancer Res Treat 1992;23:233-40.

Roy V, Ochs L, Weisdorf D. *Late infections following allogenic bone marrow transplantation – suggested strategies for prophylaxis.* Leuk Lymphoma 1997; 26:1-15.

Shenep JL, Feldman S, Gigliotti F et al. *Response of immunocompromised children with solid tumors to a conjugate vaccine for **Haemophilus influenzae** type b.* J Pediatrics 1994;125:581-4.

Somani J, Larsn RA. *Reimmunization after allogenic bone marrow transplantation.* Am J Med 1995;98:389-98.

Stanley SK, Ostrowski MA, Justement JS et al. *Effect of immunization with a common recall antigen on viral expression in patients infected with human immunodefciency virus type 1.* N Engl J Med 1996;334:1222-30.

Volti SL, Digregorio F, Romeo MA et al. *Immune status and the immune response to hepatitis B virus vaccine in thalassemic patients after allogeneic bone marrow transplantation.* Bone Marrow Transplant 1997;19:157-60.

Working Party of the British Committee for Standards in Haematology – Clinical Haematology Task Force. *Guidelines for the prevention and treatment of infection in patients with an absent or dysfunctional spleen.* BMJ 1996;312: 430-34.

Yeung CY, Liang DC. *Varicella vaccine in children with acute lymphoblastic leukemia and non-Hodgkins lymphoma.* Ped Hematol Oncol 1992;9:29-34.

Immunization of People with Hemophilia and Other Bleeding Disorders

For individuals with bleeding disorders, immunization should be carried out using a fine gauge needle of appropriate length. After the injection, firm pressure should be applied, without rubbing, to the injection site for at least 5 minutes. Administration can be subcutaneous or intramuscular depending on the product. If there is concern that an injection may stimulate bleeding, it can be scheduled shortly after administration of anti-hemophilia therapy.

Any patient with a bleeding disorder who needs plasma-derived products is at higher risk of contracting hepatitis A or B and should be offered the vaccine. Please refer to the appropriate chapter in the Guide for information on dosage.

Immunization of Infants Born Prematurely

Premature infants whose clinical condition is satisfactory should be immunized with full doses of vaccine at the same chronological age and according to the same schedule as full-term infants, regardless of birth weight. In premature infants, maternally derived antibody is present at lower titres and for a shorter duration than in mature infants. As well, the severity of vaccine-preventable illnesses may be greater in this population. Therefore, immunization of premature infants should not be delayed.

Antibody response to immunization is generally a function of post-natal age and not of maturity. Although studies demonstrate conflicting results, premature infants may have weaker antibody responses to several vaccinations than full-term controls. Despite this, vaccine efficacy remains high.

Healthy premature infants generally tolerate immunizations well, as compared with full-term infants. However, premature infants who are sick and have been hospitalized and those who have had significant apnea as a result of prematurity or chronic lung disease may experience a transient increase or recurrence of apnea after immunization.

The response to hepatitis B vaccine may be diminished in infants with birth weights below 2000 g. Routine immunization of infants of mothers negative for hepatitis B surface antigen (HBsAg) should be delayed until the infant reaches 2000 g or 2 months of age. Infants born to women who are HBsAg positive should receive hepatitis B immune globulin (HBIG) within 12 hours of birth and the appropriate dose of vaccine (see chapter on Hepatitis B Vaccine).

If the mother's status is unknown, the vaccine should be given in accordance with the recommendations for the infant of an HBsAg positive mother. The maternal status should be determined within 12 hours, and if the mother is HBsAg positive the infant should receive HBIG.

Pre-term infants with chronic respiratory disease should be immunized against influenza annually, beginning in the fall when they have reached 6 months of age. Delay of immunization has resulted in unnecessary deaths. Certain premature infants should also receive respiratory syncytial virus (RSV) immune globulin to decrease the likelihood of serious RSV infection requiring hospitalization and supplemental oxygen therapy (see chapter on Passive Immunizing Agents).

Timing of Vaccine Administration

For most products that require more than one dose or booster doses for full immunization, intervals longer than those recommended between doses do not lead to a reduction in final antibody concentrations. Therefore, as a general rule, *interruption of a series of vaccinations for any reason does not require starting the series over again, regardless of the interval elapsed.* However, there are exceptions, such as immunization against rabies. By contrast, doses given at less than the recommended interval may result in less than optimal antibody response and should not be counted as part of a primary series.

There are obvious practical advantages to giving more than one vaccine at the same time, especially in preparation for foreign travel or when there is doubt that the patient will return for further doses of vaccine. Most of the commonly used antigens can safely be given simultaneously. No increase in the frequency or severity of clinically significant side effects has been observed. The immune response to each antigen is generally adequate and comparable to that found in patients receiving these vaccines at separate times. Commercially prepared combinations of vaccines are convenient to use.

Unless specified by the manufacturer, inactivated vaccines should never be mixed in the same syringe. They can be given simultaneously, but at separate anatomic sites, consideration being given to the precautions that apply to each individual vaccine. No inactivated vaccine has been shown to interfere with the immune response to another inactivated vaccine; thus, no particular interval between inactivated vaccines need be respected, except when it is the second dose of the same vaccine, e.g., inactivated polio virus vaccine.

Live parenteral vaccines should never be mixed in the same syringe, but may be administered simultaneously at different sites. One live parenteral vaccine may interfere with the effectiveness of another, and to minimize this possibility two or more live vaccines should preferably be administered either on the same day or be separated by an interval of at least 4 weeks. The administration of oral typhoid vaccine (Ty21a) and oral cholera vaccine should be separated by at least 8 hours.

Recent Administration of Human Immune Globulin Products

Passive immunization with products of human origin can interfere with the immune response to live viral vaccines. For measles vaccine, the recommended interval between immune globulin (IG) administration and subsequent immunization varies from 3 to 10 months, depending on the specific product given, as shown in Table 7.

For an optimum response to rubella or mumps vaccine given as individual components, there should be an interval of at least 3 months between administration of IG or blood products and immunization. If given as combined MMR, then the longer intervals, as recommended in Table 7, should be followed to ensure that there is an adequate response to the measles component. For women susceptible to rubella who are given Rh immune globulins in the peripartum period, consult the chapter on Rubella Vaccine for specific recommendations regarding the timing of rubella immunization.

If administration of an IG preparation becomes necessary **after** MMR vaccine or its individual component vaccines have been given, interference can also occur. If the interval between administration of any of these vaccines and subsequent administration of an IG preparation is < 14 days, immunization should be repeated at the interval indicated in the Table, unless serologic test results indicate that antibodies were produced. If the IG product is given more than 14 days after the vaccine, immunization does not have to be repeated.

Because there is little interaction between IG preparations and inactivated vaccines, the latter can be given concurrently or after an IG preparation has been used. The vaccine and IG preparation should be given at different sites. There are no data to indicate that IG administration interferes with the response to inactivated vaccines, toxoids or the live vaccines for yellow fever, typhoid, cholera and polio.

Storage and Handling of Immunizing Agents

Immunizing agents are biological materials that are subject to gradual loss of potency from deterioration and denaturation. Loss of potency can be accelerated under certain conditions of transport, storage and handling, and may result in failure to stimulate an adequate immunologic response, leading to lower levels of protection against disease. Conditions that result in loss of potency vary among products. Manufacturer and NACI recommendations generally specify that most products should be stored at temperatures from +2° to +8° C. Exceptions exist (e.g., yellow fever and varicella vaccines) for which the recommended storage conditions are outlined in the manufacturer's product leaflets.

The term "cold chain" as used in this statement refers to all equipment and procedures used to ensure that vaccines are protected from inappropriate temperatures and light, from the time of transport from the manufacturer to the time of administration.

– Table 7 –

Guidelines for the Interval Between Administration of Immune Globulin Preparation or Blood, and Vaccines Containing Live Measles Virus

Product	Indication	Dose	Interval (Months)
Immune globulin (IG)	Hepatitis A		
	• Contact prophylaxis	0.02 mL/kg	3
	• International travel	0.06 mL/kg	3
	Measles prophylaxis		
	• Normal contact	0.25 mL/kg	5
	• Immunocompromised host	0.5 mL/kg	6
Intravenous immune globulin (IVIG)	Treatment of antibody deficiency	160 mg/kg 320 mg/kg 640 mg/kg	7 8 9
	Treatment of idiopathic thrombocytopenic purpura or Kawasaki disease	> 1280 mg/kg to ≤ 2000 mg/kg	11
Hepatitis B immune globulin (HBIG)	Hepatitis B prophylaxis	0.06 mL/kg	3
Rabies immune globulin (RIG)	Rabies prophylaxis	20 IU/kg	4
Tetanus Immune globulin (TIG)	Tetanus prophylaxis	250 units	3
Varicella immune globulin (VIG)	Varicella prophylaxis	125 units/ 10 kg	5
Washed red blood cells		10 mL/kg IV	0
Reconstituted red blood cells		10 mL/kg IV	3
Whole blood (Hct 36%)		10 mL/kg IV	6
Packed red blood cells		10 mL/kg IV	6
Plasma/platelet products		10 mL/kg IV	7
Intramuscular respiratory syncytial virus immune globulin		15 mg/kg	0
Intravenous respiratory syncytial virus immune globulin		750 mg/kg/ month	9

The effects of exposure to adverse environmental conditions, such as freezing, heat, and light, are cumulative. Data are available to indicate that certain products remain stable at temperatures outside of +2° to +8°C for specified periods of time, but mechanisms rarely exist for monitoring cumulative exposures. Additionally, different products are often transported and stored in the same container. Therefore, it is recommended that all biologicals for immunization be maintained at +2° +8°C at all times, unless otherwise specified in the product leaflet. Management of products that have been exposed to adverse conditions should be guided by specific instructions pertaining to the event from the vaccine supplier.

Monitoring of the vaccine cold chain is required to ensure that biologicals are being stored and transported at recommended temperatures. Testing of product potency or seroconversion rates as indicators of cold chain integrity are rarely feasible.

Refer to the product leaflet of each immunizing agent for specific instructions related to storage and handling. The following general principles apply.

Multi-dose vials: Multi-dose vials should be removed from the refrigerator only to draw up the dose required and should be replaced immediately.

Lyophilized (freeze dried) vaccines: For optimal potency, freeze dried vaccines (e.g., MMR, varicella, BCG, conjugate *Haemophilus* b) should be reconstituted immediately before use with the diluent provided for that purpose. Reconstituted vaccines, including yellow fever vaccine, should be used within 1 hour of reconstitution; if unused, they should be discarded. There are slight variations in the time intervals recommended by specific manufacturers, and users should refer to the product leaflet to guide timing of reconstitution.

Light exposure: Measles, mumps, rubella, varicella and BCG vaccines should be protected from light at all times by storage of the vials in the cartons provided. After reconstitution, if vaccines are not used immediately, they **must** be kept at +2° to +8° C and protected from light.

Freezing: The liquid inactivated and adsorbed vaccines should not be used if they have been frozen. These include DTaP, DT, DTaP-Polio, DT-Polio, Td, Td-Polio, hepatitis A and B vaccines, influenza and pneumococcal vaccines. Prior to use, liquid vaccines should be inspected and should not be used if visible indications of freezing are apparent or if a temperature recording device shows that the vaccine was exposed to temperatures below -2° C.

A positive "shake test" is the finding that liquid vaccine that was frozen and then thawed contains granular particles that can be seen immediately upon shaking. One half-hour after shaking, the supernatant is almost clear but granular particles form on the bottom of the vial. The "shake test" may be positive after freezing of adsorbed vaccines (e.g., DPT Polio, DPT, DT, Td and Td Polio); however, a positive shake test result does not consistently occur after freezing. Therefore, when other signs indicate that the vaccine may have been frozen, the vaccine should not be used, even if the "shake test" is negative.

Unreconstituted live virus vaccines, such as MMR and rubella vaccines, may be used after they have been frozen, but repeated freezing and thawing should be avoided.

Expiry: Vaccines should not be used beyond their expiry date. For expiry dates specified as month/year, products are deemed to expire on the last day of the specified month.

All vaccines that cannot be used because of expiry or adverse environmental exposure should be returned to the source for appropriate recording of returns and disposal, or should be appropriately disposed of locally and the quantities involved reported to the officials in charge of vaccine management in the jurisdiction. The vaccine supplier will be able to provide specific instructions.

Refrigerators: The temperature in frost-free refrigerators may cycle widely and should be monitored to ensure that cycling is within the acceptable range. Special "maximum-minimum" thermometers are commercially available for purchase and are useful for most office storage. More expensive, constant chart-recording thermometers with alarms are appropriate for larger vaccine storage depots. Non-frost-free refrigerators should be defrosted regularly and immunizing agents stored in a functioning fridge during the defrosting process. Fridges older than 10 years are more likely to malfunction and to have breaks in the seal around the door, leading to temperature instability. Half-size "under the counter" fridges are less reliable than full size "kitchen" fridges. Placement of full plastic water bottles in the lower compartment and door shelves of the fridge and ice packs in the freezer compartment will help stabilize temperatures, especially in the event of a power failure.

Recommended office procedures

The following office procedures should be implemented to ensure that storage of vaccines is optimized:

- Designate and train a specific staff person to be responsible for managing vaccines.

- Post storage and handling guidelines on the refrigerator.

- Use insulated storage containers with ice packs for transport of vaccines; to avoid freezing, do not place vaccine packages in direct contact with ice packs.

- Place newly delivered vaccines into the refrigerator immediately upon delivery to the office.

- Store vaccines in the middle of the refrigerator to avoid the coldest and warmest parts of the refrigerator; do not store vaccines on the door shelves.

- Place a maximum-minimum thermometer on the middle shelf of the fridge.

- Read, record and re-set the thermometer at least once daily.

- Secure the electrical cord from the fridge to the wall outlet to prevent accidental power interruptions.

- Ensure that the fridge door does not swing open by installing a fail-safe (e.g., Velcro™) closing mechanism.

- Do not store food or biological specimens in the same fridge as vaccines.

- Rotate stock so that vaccines with the earliest expiry date are at the front of the shelf.

- Only remove vaccine from fridge immediately before administration.

- If refrigerator malfunction is suspected on the basis of temperature readings, obtain servicing immediately and store the vaccine in an alternative fridge in the meantime.

- In the event of an identified cold chain break, seek advice from your local public health authority about whether the vaccine(s) may continue to be used; while awaiting advice, keep the vaccines stored in appropriate conditions.

- When a cold chain break is identified after vaccine has been administered, consult with your local health department about management of the situation. Information required to assess the circumstances will include the name of the vaccine(s), and the duration and temperatures of exposure. People immunized with vaccines whose potency is likely to have been jeopardized may need to be tested for serologic evidence of immunity or be re vaccinated.

Periodic cold chain surveys are worthwhile to evaluate awareness, equipment and practices as well as the frequency of breaks in the cold chain during transport from depots and storage in peripheral offices. These should be undertaken by provincial/territorial and local immunization programs.

Selected References

Brazeau M, Delisle G. *Cold chain study: danger of freezing vaccines*. CCDR 1993;19(5):33-8.

Carrasco P, Herrera C, Rancruel D et al. *Protecting vaccines from freezing in extremely cold environments*. CCDR 1995;21(11):97-101.

Cheyne J. *Vaccine delivery management*. Rev Infect Dis 1989;2(S3):S617-S622.

Deasy T, Deshpande R, Naus M. *Evaluating the cold chain in Ontario: results of a province-wide study*. Public Health Epidemiol Rep Ont 1997;8:44-54.

Dimayuga RC, Scheifele DW, Bell AA. *Survey of vaccine storage practices: Is your office refrigerator satisfactory?* BC Med J 1996;38(2):74-7.

Expanded programme on immunization: stability of vaccines. WHO Bull 1990;68:118-20.

Gold MS, Martin L, Nayda CL et al. *Electronic temperature monitoring and feedback to correct adverse vaccine storage in general practice*. Med J Aust 1999;171(2):83-4.

Guthridge SL, Miller NC. *Cold chain in a hot climate*. Aust N Z J Public Health 1996;20(6):657-60.

Jeremijenko A, Kelly H, Sibthorpe B et al. *Improving vaccine storage in general practice refrigerators*. BMJ 1996;312(7047):1651-52.

Kendal AP, Snyder R, Garrison PJ. *Validation of cold chain procedures suitable for distribution of vaccines by public health programs in the USA*. Vaccine 1997;15(12-13):1459-65.

Krugman RD, Meyer BC, Enterline JC et al. *Impotency of live-virus vaccines as a result of improper handling in clinical practice*. J Pediatr 1974;85:512-14.

LCDC. *National guidelines for vaccine storage and transportation*. CCDR 1995;21(11):93-7.

Lerman SJ, Gold E. *Measles in children previously vaccinated against measles*. JAMA 1971;216:1311-14.

Milhomme P. *Cold chain study: danger of freezing vaccines*. CCDR 1993;19-5:33-8.

Steinmetz N, Furesz J, Reinhold C et al. *Storage conditions of live measles, mumps and rubella virus vaccines in Montreal*. Can Med Assoc J 1983;128:162-63.

Woodyard E, Woodyard L, Alto WA. *Vaccine storage in the physician's office: a community study*. J Am Board Family Practitioners 1995;8:91-4.

World Health Organization. *Report of the Technical Review Group Meeting, 7-8 June 1998: Achievements and plan of activities, July 1998-June 1999*. Geneva: World Health Organization, 1998 (Technical Report Series, No. 98.02).

Yuan L, Daniels S, Naus M et al. *Vaccine storage and handling: knowledge and practice in primary care physicians' offices*. Can Fam Physician 1995;41:1169-76.

Immunization Technique

Injection site

The injection site should be carefully chosen to avoid major nerves and blood vessels. The best sites for subcutaneous or intramuscular immunizations are the deltoid area or the anterolateral surface of the thigh. The latter is the site of choice for infants < 1 year of age because it provides the largest muscle. In children > 1 year of age, the deltoid is the preferred site since use of the anterolateral thigh results in frequent complaints of limping due to muscle pain. Children should be well restrained before injection.

The chosen site should be cleansed with a suitable antiseptic, such as isopropyl alcohol, which is allowed to dry on the skin before the injection is given. A separate, sterile needle and syringe should be used for each injection, and after use should be carefully disposed of in a container designed for this purpose.

Because of decreased immunogenicity reported with several vaccines, the buttock is not recommended as an immunization site, except when large volumes must be given, e.g., of immunoglobulin. If the buttock is used, care must be exercised to avoid injury to the sciatic nerve by selecting a site in the upper, outer quadrant of the gluteus maximus and avoiding the central area.

Route of administration

Immunization should be given by the route of administration recommended by the manufacturer of each vaccine (see Table 8). An appropriate size and length of needle

– Table 8 –

Routes of Administration

Vaccine	Preferred route of administration
BCG	Intradermal
Cholera	Oral
Diphtheria toxoid (fluid)	Subcutaneous (SC)*
Diphtheria toxoid (adsorbed)†	Intramuscular (IM)
Hepatitis A	IM
Hepatitis B	IM
Haemophilus influenzae type b conjugate vaccine	IM
Influenza	IM
Japanese encephalitis	SC
Meningococcal polysaccharide	SC
Meningococcal conjugate	IM
Measles	SC
MMR (measles, mumps and rubella)	SC
MR (measles and rubella)	SC
Penta and Pentacel†	IM
Pertussis (monovalent acellular)	IM
Pneumococcal polysaccharide	SC
Pneumococcal conjugate	IM
Polio (IPV)	SC
Polio (OPV)	Oral
Rabies	IM
Rubella	SC
Tetanus toxoid (adsorbed)†	IM
Typhoid – oral	Oral
– Vi capsular	IM
Varicella	SC
Yellow fever	SC

*   The vaccines that are listed as SC only should not be given intramuscularly because of the lack of efficacy data for this route.

†   Any vaccine combination containing adsorbed antigen must be administered intramuscularly because of the risk of subcutaneous nodule or sterile abscess if it is administered subcutaneously. Examples are Td (tetanus and diphtheria), DTaP.

should be chosen to ensure that the vaccine is deposited within the proper tissue layer.

For subcutaneous injections, a 25 gauge, 1.6 cm (5/8 inch) needle is normally recommended. Insert it at a 45° angle into the tissues below the dermal layer of the skin.

For intramuscular injections, a longer needle is needed:

- at least 2.2 cm (7/8 inch) for those with little muscle mass, such as infants
- at least 2.5 cm (1 inch) for others

Needles of these lengths are recommended to avoid sterile abscess in subcutaneous tissue. There is no risk if the injection is too deep.

After inserting the needle into the site, pull back on the plunger to determine whether the needle has entered a blood vessel. If so, withdraw the needle, select a new site, and use new materials.

For intradermal injections, choose a fine gauge needle (e.g., 26 or 27 gauge). With the bevel facing upwards, insert the needle under the outer layer of skin at an angle almost parallel to the skin. Insert the needle so that the bevel penetrates the skin. Inject the solution slowly for greater patient comfort and to avoid spraying and leaking. If this is done correctly, a bleb should appear in the skin at the injection site.

Immunization Records

Each person who is immunized should be given a permanent personal immunization record. Individuals should be instructed to retain the record, produce it for updating whenever they receive a vaccination and keep it in a safe place. Parents should maintain these records on behalf of their children. In the future, improvements in information technology may allow retrieval of the immunization record from the personal health card or from health data registries. However, these changes will not replace the need for personal, written records.

Record-keeping procedures should facilitate the retrieval of immunization records. It is essential that the health care provider maintain a separate, permanent record of the immunization history of each individual on the medical chart, in a readily accessible section that is not to be archived. Headings on this record should include the following:

- trade name of the product
- disease(s) against which it protects
- date given
- dose
- site and route of administration

- manufacturer
- lot number.

Manufacturers should be encouraged to produce peel-off labels for use on the chart when the product is administered, to assist with completeness of the record. The record should also include relevant serologic data (e.g., rubella serologic results) and documented episodes of adverse vaccine events.

Refer to the *National Guidelines for Childhood and Adult Immunization Practices* (page 58) for additional information about the use and maintenance of immunization records.

Immunization of Children and Adults with Inadequate Immunization Records

Many people present to health care providers and public health officials with inadequate immunization records. In the absence of a standardized approach to their management, they may be under- or over-immunized. The greatest concern with over-immunization relates to vaccine against diphtheria, pertussis or tetanus because of the potential for a higher incidence of local adverse reactions.

In every instance, an attempt should be made to obtain the person's immunization records from his or her previous health care provider. Written documentation of immunization is preferred; in some instances, information obtained by telephone from the health care provider with the exact dates of immunization may be accepted. For children, parental reports of prior immunization correlate poorly with actual immunity and should not be accepted as evidence of immunization.

Although the potency of vaccines administered in other countries can be generally assumed to be adequate, immunization schedules vary, and the age at immunization (e.g., against measles), the number of doses and the intervals between doses should be reviewed in determining the need for additional doses of vaccines. In many countries outside of Canada, mumps and rubella vaccines are in limited use, and measles vaccine alone is generally given. *Haemophilus influenzae* type b conjugate, hepatitis B and varicella vaccines are also in limited use.

Routine serologic testing of children and adults without records to determine immunity is not practical. Instead, the following approach is recommended:

- All children and adults lacking written documentation of immunization should be started on a primary immunization schedule as appropriate for their age (see pages 61 and 62).

- MMR, polio, *Haemophilus influenzae* type b conjugate, pneumococcal conjugate, meningococcal conjugate, hepatitis B, varicella and influenza vaccines can be given without concern about prior receipt of these vaccines because adverse effects of repeated immunization have not been demonstrated.

- Children who develop a serious adverse local reaction after administration of DPT, DTaP, DT or Td should be individually assessed before they receive additional doses of these vaccines. Serologic testing for specific IgG antibodies against diphtheria and tetanus may demonstrate immune status and guide the need for continued immunization. There are no established serologic correlates for protection against pertussis.

- Pneumococcal polysaccharide or conjugate vaccine should be given if the individual is in a high-risk group (see Pneumococcal Vaccine) and a record cannot be found, since in most studies local reaction rates after revaccination have been similar to rates following initial vaccination.

Selected Reference

Canadian Consensus Conference on a National Immunization Record System. CCDR 1998;24(17):137-140.

Talking with Patients About Immunization

This section is a departure from the usual style of the Guide. While the chapters on specific vaccines and general recommendations provide scientific guidance, the following two sections contain material to assist in counselling individuals and parents about questions they may have regarding the safety and effectiveness of immunizations. Suggestions for communicating with news media are also included.

There is a real concern in Canada's public health community that misconceptions about vaccine safety threaten to reduce immunization coverage to levels that would open the door to epidemics of disease rarely seen in developed countries today. Indeed, this has already happened in several countries in recent decades.

As well, the success of vaccines in preventing disease means that many health care providers practising today, and certainly most parents of young children, may never have seen a life-threatening case of diphtheria, polio or even measles. Because immunization requires informed consent and the number of approved vaccines is growing, the continued success of immunization programs will depend on a very high level of public confidence. Widely trusted as a source of information among parents and adult patients, health care providers have a vital role to play in keeping the success of vaccine programs strong.

Appropriately, more and more questions are being asked about the vaccines being offered. Unfortunately, however, a small minority of people actively oppose immunization, and their messages are often dramatic, misleading and widely disseminated. On television and radio, on the Internet, in public libraries and print media, parents and adult patients are often confronted with conflicting information about immunization. In their genuine concern for the safety of their children, parents especially may give undue weight to reports of vaccine-related concerns. The "good news" —

about the safety and effectiveness of vaccines in controlling diseases that once disabled or killed in large numbers — can be much harder to find.

I. Communication issues in immunization

Communication skills play a vital role in the proper implementation of immunization programs at several levels. The advice of a trusted health care provider is recognized as an important factor in determining whether a person is immunized or not. Physicians and other health care workers are viewed as reliable sources of information about immunization issues. Public health officials are called upon to address the public during outbreaks of infectious diseases.

Dialogue with patients and guardians

Provider behaviour may be the most important determinant of parents' acceptance of immunization for their children, but a minority of parents will require more detailed explanations. Adherence to recommendations made by medical personnel has been found to be directly related to the degree to which their discussions are patient-centred. When preventive measures and health promotion are being dealt with, the patient-centred approach means listening to concerns with respect, answering any questions forthrightly and arriving at a common understanding as to the goals and roles of both patient and care provider. It is important to have relevant information readily at hand in a number of formats and languages. The reading level of this information must be appropriate for various levels of education. There are a variety of sources for accurate information about vaccines in printed format and on the World Wide Web (see Selected References).

Good risk communication requires that we understand how risks are perceived and that we recognize the inherent biases of both the public and health care providers. It has been demonstrated that perceptions of risk are not based strictly on a numerical evaluation of risks and benefits. Risk perception reflects an individual's previous experience as well as religious and cultural contexts. Risks perceived as uncontrollable or those involving children are, generally, more feared than other types of risks; man-made risks are considered in a more negative light than those that are perceived as natural. Parents are unlikely, then, to undertake immunization for their children unless they perceive a serious threat as well as some control over the risk. It is important to recognize that people use heuristics or shortcuts to arrive at decisions and rarely resort to simple cost-benefit determinations. This means that the framing of the risk is very important i.e., framing a vaccine in terms of its benefits and not only its risks. The goals of communication include advocacy, education and the development of a decision-making partnership. The method and the content of the communication should reflect these goals.

There are four components to effective risk communication:

1. Communicating existing knowledge, taking into account what an individual already knows. Examples of sources of immunization information are the information sheets provided by provincial/territorial ministries of health or the book

Your Child's Best Shot, published by the Canadian Paediatric Society. It is useful to have varied information formats (visual, audio, printed) tailored to a range of educational levels and languages appropriate to the wide variety of cultures in our society.

2. Respecting differences of opinion about immunization and taking time to understand them. Some parents will express reluctance or refusal to have their children immunized, and it is necessary that the health care worker come to an understanding of the personal (sources of information, prior experiences), cultural and religious background to this. Parents need to be educated about the risks of the diseases and be participants in the immunization decision so that they are given the necessary sense of control.

3. Physicians and other health care workers should be on guard against their own personal opinions and should represent the risks and benefits of vaccines fairly. Such workers are a trusted source of information and are ideally suited to discuss these issues.

4. Effective decision making is best done in a partnership between the vaccinator and the parent or patient. Central to this is the understanding that parents have some input into the decision to immunize and retain responsibility for their child's health.

Communicating with the media

Public health officials, practitioners and other health care professionals are called upon to communicate with the public in a number of instances, such as dealing with media reports of those opposed to immunization or informing people of outbreaks of vaccine-preventable diseases.

It is important to identify a single spokesperson regarding any particular issue. This should be someone who is informed, empathetic and sincere, and can be available to the media. There should be a back-up person identified as well. In larger organizations it is very helpful to have a media coordinator to organize and identify important information, and help the media meet any deadlines. In the case of breaking news, such as the occurrence of an outbreak, it is important to involve the media proactively and early, as part of the total response.

In preparing to deal with the media there are 10 important items to keep in mind:

1. Prepare key messages in advance. There should be a limited number (three is ideal, five the maximum) of clear, concise messages. These should be backed up by facts, statistics and examples.

2. Identify your audience.

3. Understand any controversial issues, for example, the views of those who object to immunization, and deal with these concerns in an honest and forthright manner.

4. Never guess. If you do not know the answer, say so, but offer to find it.

5. Be polite; never lose your temper.

6. Stick to your areas of responsibility.

7. Keep in mind that the goal is to be message-driven, not question-driven.

8. Prepare and rehearse with your media advisor or someone experienced in working with media.

9. Keep your personal opinions out of your communications.

10. When speaking to the media, nothing is off the record.

II. Questions and answers about immunization

The questions and answers that follow, adapted from a number of sources (see Selected References and the list of helpful Web sites on the inside back cover), are intended to assist in counselling about immunization; the wording and style are targeted at a general audience. The answers expand on the key messages about vaccine safety listed in Box 1 while addressing the common misconceptions listed in Box 2.

Box 1: Key messages on vaccine safety in Canada

• The vaccines used in Canada are extremely effective and extremely safe.

• Serious adverse reactions are rare. The dangers of vaccine-preventable diseases are many times greater than the risks of a serious adverse reaction to the vaccine.

• Health authorities worldwide take vaccine safety very seriously. Expert committees in Canada investigate reports of serious adverse events.

• There is no evidence that vaccines cause chronic diseases, autism or sudden infant death syndrome. Alleged links – for example between hepatitis B vaccine and multiple sclerosis – have been disproved by rigorous scientific study.

Box 2: Common misconceptions about vaccines

• Vaccines are not safe.

• Vaccines cause serious side effects. Vaccines are linked to chronic diseases.

• Vaccines are not necessary. The diseases are gone.

• Vaccines contain poisonous substances.

• Vaccines weaken the immune system.

• Natural medicines provide safer protection.

• There are greater risks from the vaccines than from the illnesses they can prevent.

Do vaccines work?

Yes. Vaccines work very well in preventing specific diseases. They are so effective that most of the diseases they prevent are now rare in Canada.

Some people do not develop full immunity after being vaccinated. This is why some immunization programs include a second or third dose of a vaccine. For some diseases, we need "booster" doses because the protection of the vaccine wears off over time. However, no vaccine will work for 100% of the people who receive it. How often a vaccine might fail to work varies with each type of vaccine and each vaccine product. For more details, please see the chapters on specific vaccines in this *Guide*.

Some vaccines also work by creating "herd immunity". When most people in a community have received a vaccine for a particular disease, the chance of an outbreak of that disease is greatly reduced. This "herd immunity" protects the small number of people who cannot be immunized for medical reasons or for whom the vaccine did not work. For herd immunity to be effective, however, as many people as possible must be vaccinated.

Are vaccines safe?

Yes. Vaccines are among the safest tools of modern medicine. Serious side effects are rare. For example, severe allergic reactions can occur, but they very rarely do. In Canada, this kind of reaction has occurred less than once in every 1 million doses of vaccine, and there are effective treatments for this condition. The dangers of vaccine-preventable diseases are many times greater than the risks of a serious adverse reaction to the vaccine.

For information on who should not receive specific vaccines, please see the Contra-indications and Precautions section of each vaccine chapter in this *Guide*.

Minor side effects from vaccines, on the other hand, are common. Many patients get a mild fever after immunizaton or soreness where they receive the injection. These reactions are a nuisance but do not usually last long. They can be part of the body's normal response to the vaccine.

No one in the field of public health takes the safety of vaccines for granted. Vaccine safety is an international concern. Information on possible safety concerns is communicated very rapidly among different countries. This careful monitoring ensures that public health authorities can act quickly to address concerns. In addition, research continues to improve vaccines. Some examples follow:

■ In 1999, some babies in the U.S. developed a rare form of bowel obstruction after receiving a new vaccine to prevent rotavirus infection (a cause of diarrhea, sometimes severe, in infants). Pre-licence studies had suggested that there might be an increased risk of this condition, and monitoring effectively picked up the problem. (In the first 1.5 million doses of rotavirus vaccine, 15 cases of bowel obstruction were reported.) Use of this vaccine was stopped in the U.S., and the manufacturer withdrew its request to license the vaccine in Canada.

- The oral polio vaccine (OPV), introduced in the 1950s, prevented hundreds of thousands of polio cases. It was also found to cause a form of paralysis once in every 3 million doses. A vaccine that uses inactivated virus (IPV) is now used almost exclusively throughout the world and cannot cause even this rare adverse event.

- The original whole-cell pertussis (whooping cough) vaccine sometimes caused high fever, seizures or collapse. A vaccine was developed that uses only part of the cell of the pertussis bacterium. This vaccine has fewer side effects and is now used instead.

In considering the safety of vaccines, it is important to look at both risks and benefits. If there were no benefit from a vaccine, even one serious side effect in a million doses could not be justified. If there were no vaccines, however, there would be many more cases of disease, more serious side effects from disease, and more deaths. The examples from countries that have stopped or decreased their immunization programs have illustrated this fact many times in recent years. The diseases we can prevent with vaccines can lead to pneumonia, deafness, brain damage, heart problems, blindness and paralysis in children who are not protected. We are fortunate in Canada to have vaccines for diseases that still kill and disable children throughout the world every day. The risks of *not* getting immunized are a lot greater than any risk of immunization itself.

How are vaccines made and licensed in Canada?

Vaccines for humans are regulated in Canada by the Biologics and Genetic Therapeutics Directorate of Health Canada. Like all medicines, vaccines must undergo several stages of rigorous testing before they are approved for use. The Directorate also supervises all aspects of vaccine production by the manufacturers. Before any vaccine is licensed and approved for use in Canada, the factory where it is manufactured must be inspected to ensure that all stages of production meet the requirements for safety, sterility and quality control. Before release by the manufacturer, each batch of vaccine is tested for safety and quality under guidelines specified by the Biologics and Radiopharmaceuticals Evaluation Centre. Most safety tests are carried out by both the manufacturer and, independently, by the laboratory of the Directorate.

Once vaccines are in use, Canada has several systems in place to ensure that they are carefully monitored and that any problems are dealt with quickly. These systems are described in the section "Adverse Events" in this *Guide*.

What would happen if we stopped immunizing?

Experience from other countries shows that diseases quickly return when fewer people are immunized:

- Ireland saw measles soar to more than 1,200 cases in the year 2000, as compared with just 148 the previous year, because immunization rates fell to around 76%. Several children died in this outbreak.

- A large outbreak of rubella (German measles) occurred in Nebraska in 1999. All 83 cases in this outbreak involved adults who had not been immunized. Most of them came from countries where rubella immunization is not routine. The outbreak spread from a meat-packing plant to the general community, including several pregnant women and two day care centres. The greatest danger from rubella is to infants, who may be born with congenital rubella syndrome if their mothers are infected during pregnancy.

- In 1994, there were 5,000 deaths due to diphtheria in Russia after the organized immunization system was suspended. Previously, Russia (like Canada) had had only a few cases of diphtheria each year and no deaths. Diphtheria toxoid came into routine use in the 1930s, but even today diphtheria remains a severe disease. About one person in 10 with diphtheria still dies in spite of medical treatment.

- In the U.K., a major drop in rates of immunization against pertussis (whooping cough) in 1974 was followed by an epidemic of more than 100,000 cases and 36 deaths in 1978.

- Japan had 13,000 cases and 41 deaths from whooping cough in 1979, after only 30% of children received pertussis immunization. In earlier years, when most children received vaccine, Japan had only a few hundred cases of whooping cough and no deaths.

- Sweden had a similar experience with pertussis. When vaccination programs restarted, the number of cases fell once again.

Why do we still need vaccines if the diseases they prevent have disappeared from our part of the world?

It is important to continue vaccine programs for four basic reasons:

- First, unless a disease has completely disappeared, there is a real risk that small outbreaks can turn into large epidemics if most of the community is not protected. The only disease that has been entirely eliminated in the world so far is smallpox. Some diseases, such as tetanus, are caused by bacteria that live naturally in the soil. The risk of diseases like tetanus will never disappear, so continued immunization is important.

- Second, no vaccine is 100% effective. There will always be some people who are not immune, even though they have had their shots. This small minority will be protected as long as people around them are immunized.

- Third, there are a small number of people who cannot receive vaccines. These may be people who have previously had a severe allergic reaction to a component of the vaccine, or they have a medical condition that makes receiving vaccines too risky for them. These people are not protected from disease, and for some diseases it is very important that people around them are immune and cannot pass disease along to them. By protecting themselves, immunized people can also protect those around them who are vulnerable to disease.

- And fourth, most vaccine-preventable diseases are still common in other parts of the world. Travellers can carry them from country to country. If we are not protected by immunization, these diseases will quickly spread. For example, most cases of measles in Canada today can be traced to someone who travelled here from a country where measles is more common.

Why can't I take a chance that my child won't get sick, as long as most other people are vaccinated?

Unvaccinated children have a much greater chance of getting disease than children who have received the vaccine.

Two recent studies of disease outbreaks in the U.S. illustrate this concern. Children whose parents chose not to have them immunized against measles were 22 to 35 times more likely to get measles than were immunized children. Children who did not receive the vaccine for pertussis (whooping cough) were almost 6 times more likely to get whooping cough than immunized children; the risks were even higher for the younger children (children < 11 years old), who were 62 times more likely to get measles if they were not immunized and 16 times more likely to get pertussis in these outbreaks.

Unimmunized children also add to the risk for children who cannot receive vaccinations or for whom the vaccine did not provide full protection from disease. People who are not immunized can be carriers of disease and pose a risk to those around them, even if they do not get sick themselves.

Do vaccines weaken the immune system?

No. Vaccines strengthen the immune system to protect children and adults from specific diseases. This is true even for newborn infants. Infants and children are exposed to many kinds of germs every day, through normal eating, drinking and playing. Scientists estimate the immune system can recognize and respond to hundreds of thousands, if not millions, of different organisms. The vaccines recommended for children and adults use only a small portion of the immune system's "memory".

Infants need to be protected with vaccines because they are more likely to get very sick from the diseases that vaccines can prevent, such as diphtheria, whooping cough and meningitis due to *Haemophilus influenzae* type b (Hib). The recommended immunization schedule for infants in Canada is carefully timed to ensure that newborns and older babies get safe and effective protection from the diseases that are most likely to seriously harm them.

Can giving a child several vaccines at the same time overload the immune system?

No. Only vaccines that have been shown to be safe and effective when given together are administered at the same time. When new vaccines go through the extensive testing process, they are given along with all of the recommended childhood vaccines. Scientific studies assess the effect of giving these vaccines at the same time.

Children may receive several vaccines during the same clinic visit, but only after studies have shown that this is a safe practice. In order to receive a licence to combine vaccines, the manufacturer must also prove that the combined product does not make any of the vaccine components less effective or raise new safety concerns.

Giving several vaccines at one time keeps children safe by protecting them against more diseases sooner. As an added benefit, it also reduces children's discomfort by reducing the number of injections they receive, and it saves parents the time and expense of additional office visits.

Can natural infection or a healthy lifestyle be effective alternatives to vaccines?

Vaccines create immunity to specific diseases without causing the suffering of the disease itself. Children do develop immunity to many different germs through their everyday exposure to these infections. However, the diseases we can prevent with vaccines kill and disable children. For some diseases (e.g. tetanus and meningitis) the vaccine creates stronger immunity than natural infection does.

Boosting the immune system in general through herbs or vitamins does not offer specific protection from the viruses and bacteria that cause vaccine-preventable diseases. For infants, breast-feeding offers protection against some infections, such as colds, ear infections and diarrhea, because the infant receives immune-boosting proteins in the mother's milk. Despite its many benefits, however, breast-feeding does not protect infants from the specific diseases we can prevent with vaccines.

Vaccines also use a natural mechanism to keep us healthy by taking advantage of our natural immune response. A vaccine stimulates antibodies so that if we are exposed to that specific virus or bacterium in the future, our immune system can mount an effective attack.

Why do we need vaccines if we have better hygiene and sanitation to help prevent disease in Canada?

Better living conditions have been important in controlling some kinds of infectious diseases, such as diseases spread by dirty water. For the specific diseases that vaccines can prevent, however, disease rates only began to drop dramatically after the vaccines for those diseases were licensed and came into widespread use:

- Measles vaccine was first approved in Canada in 1963. Sanitation and living conditions in Canada have not changed greatly since that time. Before immunization, almost everyone got measles. For many children, the disease was serious: about 5,000 were hospitalized every year, and 50 to 75 children died. Today, because the vaccine is in wide use, there are few cases of measles in all of North and South America, including communities where living conditions are much poorer than in Canada.

- Meningitis (infection around the brain) and other severe infections due to Hib were common until just a few years ago. About one in every 300 Canadian children developed Hib disease by age 5. About 100 infants died each year from Hib meningitis, and many more suffered brain damage or deafness. Immunization against Hib became routine in the early 1990s. Since then, Hib disease has almost disappeared in Canada, from about 2,000 cases a year to less than four cases in the year 2000. Sanitation is no better now than it was in 1990, so it is hard to credit anything but the widespread use of Hib vaccine for this dramatic improvement.

■ Many children in Canada still get very sick from pertussis (whooping cough) each year, and every year one child dies from this disease. Nearly all of the children affected got the disease because they were not immunized against pertussis.

What about reports that vaccines are linked to chronic diseases or problems such as sudden infant death syndrome (SIDS)?

Vaccines are sometimes blamed for conditions that are poorly understood. A child's first year of life is a time of tremendous growth and development, and it is a time when serious problems may start to appear. It is also the time when most vaccines are given, but this does not mean that vaccines cause these problems. Many of our vaccines have been in use for decades with no evidence of long-term adverse effects. Still, research to ensure the safety of vaccines continues.

Anti-vaccine books and web sites claim that vaccines cause autism, seizure disorders, multiple sclerosis (MS) or Crohn's disease, among other health problems. These connections have never held up to scientific scrutiny. Recent research using the best scientific methods and reviews of studies from around the world provide very strong evidence that

■ MMR vaccine does not cause autism or inflammatory bowel disease.

■ Hepatitis B vaccine does not cause multiple sclerosis or relapses of pre-existing MS.

■ Pertussis vaccine does not cause brain damage.

■ Childhood vaccines do not increase the risk of asthma.

■ Vaccines do not cause SIDS. (Fortunately, we have learned that other factors, such as sleeping position and second-hand smoke, *are* linked with SIDS, and successful public education campaigns about these factors have helped to reduce the rate of SIDS in Canada.)

More extensive discussion of specific vaccine concerns is available in the resources for patients and parents listed at the end of this chapter (see Selected References).

Do vaccines contain toxic ingredients?

The main ingredient in most vaccines is the killed or weakened germ (virus or bacterium), which stimulates our immune system to recognize and prevent future disease. Some newer vaccines are made from only part of the germ's cell (for example, a purified sugar or a purified protein).

- In addition, vaccines usually contain sterile water or salt solution.

- Some vaccines are prepared with a preservative or antibiotic to prevent bacterial growth.

- Some vaccines also contain substances known as stabilizers, to help maintain quality during storage.

- Some vaccines contain an "adjuvant." These substances work to boost our immune response to the vaccine and make it more effective.

The amount of any of these ingredients in a vaccine is extremely small, and every batch of vaccine is tested for safety and quality in Canada before it is released for public use.

A preservative called thimerosal received attention in the U.S. in 1999 because it contains mercury and it is used in some vaccines for children. As a precaution, U.S. authorities recommended that the use of vaccines containing thimerosal be reduced or eliminated. In 2001, an independent panel of the U.S. Institute of Medicine conducted an extensive review of this concern. The panel found no evidence that the amount of mercury in childhood vaccines causes damage to a child's nervous system.

In Canada, the only routine vaccine for children that contained thimerosal was the hepatitis B vaccine. Canadian infants were never subject to the same level of mercury exposure from vaccines as U.S. infants. A new formula for hepatitis B vaccine, with no thimerosal, is now available. Meanwhile, research into whether thimerosal in vaccines is truly a risk to infants is continuing.

The ingredients for each vaccine in use in Canada is described in the specific vaccine chapters in this Guide.

Can vaccines transmit animal disease to people?

Because vaccines are a natural product, they sometimes require the use of animal cells during production. This process is strictly controlled so that it does not pose a risk to people. No brain cells are used in manufacturing vaccines in Canada. During the manufacturing process, the vaccines are purified, and all animal cells are removed. However, each batch of vaccine is tested to ensure that it is free from infectious agents.

For some vaccines in Canada, material derived from cows (for example, gelatin and lactose) have been used in the manufacturing process, and this has raised the question of whether vaccines can transmit "mad cow disease" to humans. Scientists in several countries have studied this risk and estimated that, in theory, there could be a risk of one person in 40 billion being exposed to the disease through a vaccine. Even though the risk is extremely small, vaccine manufacturers are working to find alternatives to these components. Meanwhile, Canada is making sure that any vaccine ingredients derived from cows come only from countries that are free from mad cow disease.

Is immunization compulsory in Canada? Does my child have to be immunized?

Immunization is not compulsory or "forced" in Canada, but we do have regulations that help ensure that as many people as possible are protected by vaccines from the diseases they prevent. Some provinces require certain vaccines to be given before a child can enter school, but these are not mandatory in the usual sense of the term. Rather, parents (or children, if they are old enough to give consent) are required to declare a choice of whether to have their child (or themselves) immunized or not. If they choose not to, the child may be told that he or she must stay home from school if there is an outbreak of disease. This rule is designed to keep unimmunized children from getting sick and to keep the outbreak from spreading. School entry regulations also give parents an opportunity to bring their child's immunizations up to date.

Health care workers may also be required to have certain vaccinations, such as hepatitis B vaccine and an annual 'flu shot. If they refuse, they may be required to stay away from work during an outbreak. This practice protects their patients, who could be in grave danger if they became ill with a communicable disease.

Conclusion

Because the diseases that vaccines can prevent are so rarely seen by the general public today, it is understandable that vaccine safety concerns have such a high profile. Careful and timely counselling can help patients weigh the benefits of vaccines and the risks of disease, as well as the small risk of the vaccine itself. By providing vaccines in a climate of appropriate informed consent, including discussion of the common misconceptions that are circulating, immunization will maintain its status as one of the most effective preventive measures in the history of medicine.

Selected References

Ascherio A, Zhang S, Hernan M et al. *Hepatitis B vaccination and the risk of multiple sclerosis*. N Engl J Med 2001;344:327-32.

Ball LK, Evans G, Bostrom A. *Risky business: challenges in vaccine risk communication*. Pediatrics 1998;101(3pt1):453-58.

Confavreau C, Suissa S, Saddier P et al. *Vaccinations and risk of relapse of multiple sclerosis*. N Engl J Med 2001;344:319-26.

Davis R, Kramarz P, Bohlke K et al. *Measles-mumps-rubella and other measles-containing vaccines do not increase the risk for inflammatory bowel disease*. Arch Pediatr Adolesc Med 2001;155:354-59.

Feikin D, Lezotte D, Hamman R et al. *Individual and community risks of measles and pertussis associated with personal exemptions to immunization*. JAMA 2000;284:3145-50.

Fleming P, Blair P, Platt M et al. *The UK accelerated immunization programme and sudden unexpected death in infancy: case-control study*. BMJ 2001;322:1-5.

Gangarosa E, Galazka A, Wolfe C et al. *Impact of anti-vaccine movements on pertussis control: the untold story*. Lancet 1998;351:356-61.

Gellin B. *The risk of vaccination – the importance of "negative" studies* [editorial]. N Engl J Med 2001;344(5):372-73.

Halsey N, Hyman S and the Conference Writing Panel. *Measles-mumps-rubella vaccine and autistic spectrum disorder: report from the New Challenges in Childhood Immunization Conference convened in Oak Brook, Illinois, June 12-13, 2000*. Pediatrics 2001;107(5): e84-e106. www.pediatrics.org/cgi/content/full/107/5/e84.

Salmon D, Haber M, Gangarosa E et al. *Health consequences of religious and philosophical exemptions from immunization laws: individual and societal risk of measles*. JAMA 1999;282:47-53.

Strauss B, Bigham M. *Does measles-mumps-rubella (MMR) vaccination cause inflammatory bowel disease and autism?* CCDR 2001;27(8):65-72.

Stoto MA, Evans G, Bostrom A. *Vaccine risk communication*. Am J Prev Med 1998;14(3):237-39.

Stratton K, Gable A, McCormick, eds. *Immunization safety review: thimerosal-containing vaccines and neurodevelopmental disorders*. Institute of Medicine. Washington, DC: National Academy Press, 2001.

Resources for parents and patients

Canadian Health Network web site. *Immunization/frequently asked questions.* <www.Canadian-health-network.ca/html/faq/chntopiccategory_13.html>

Canadian Immunization Awareness Program web site <www.immunize.cpha.ca> (CIAP is supported by a coalition of Canadian organizations including the Canadian Institute of Child Health, Canadian Medical Association, Canadian Nurses Association, Canadian Nursing Coalition for Immunization, Canadian Paediatric Society, Canadian Pharmacists Association, Canadian Public Health Association, College of Family Physicians of Canada, Conférence des Régies régionales de la santé et des services sociaux du Québec, Council of Chief Medical Officers of Health, and Health Canada.)

Canadian Paediatric Society. *Your child's best shot: a parent's guide to vaccination*. Ottawa: Canadian Paediatric Society, 1997. (CPS web site <www.cps.ca> contains ordering information and the Questions and Answers about Immunization section of this book: www.cps.ca/english/carekids/immunization/ImmunizationFacts.htm)

Health Canada web site <www.hc-sc.gc.ca>

Mitchell, D (ed.). *Getting our point across: immunization information resources for staff in Ontario health units*. Communicable Disease Control Services, Halton Region (Ontario) Health Department, 2000.

National Network for Immunization Information. *Communicating with patients about immunization: a resource kit*. 2000. (NNII is a U.S.-based initiative of the Infectious Diseases Society of America, the Pediatric Infectious Diseases Society, the American Academy of Pediatrics, and the American Nurses Association. The Resource Kit is available on the NNII web site www.immunizationinfo.org)

– Part 2 –
Recommended Immunization for Infants, Children and Adults

A. Immunization Schedules for Infants and Children

Few measures in preventive medicine are of such proven value and as easy to implement as routine immunization against infectious diseases. Immunization carried out as recommended in the following schedules will provide good basic protection for most children against the diseases shown.

Following a standard schedule ensures maximal achievable protection. However, modifications of the recommended schedule may be necessary because of missed appointments or intercurrent illness. Interruption of a recommended series does not require starting the series over again, regardless of the interval elapsed.

Similar vaccines are now available from different manufacturers, but they may not be identical. It is therefore essential for the user to read the appropriate chapter in this *Guide* as well as the manufacturer's package insert.

– Table 1 –

Routine Immunization Schedule for Infants and Children

Age at Vaccination	DTaP[1]	IPV	Hib[2]	MMR	Td[3] or dTap[10]	Hep B[4] (3 doses)	V	PC	MC
Birth									
2 months	X	X	X					X[8]	X[9]
4 months	X	X	X			Infancy		X	X
6 months	X	(X)[5]	X			or		X	X
12 months				X		preadolescence	X[7]	X	
18 months	X	X	X	(X)[6] or		(9-13 years)			or
4-6 years	X	X		(X)[6]					
14-16 years					X[10]				X[9]

DTaP	Diphtheria, tetanus, pertussis (acellular) vaccine
IPV	Inactivated poliovirus vaccine
Hib	*Haemophilus influenzae* type b conjugate vaccine
MMR	Measles, mumps and rubella vaccine
Td	Tetanus and diphtheria toxoid, adult type with reduced diphtheria toxoid
dTap	Tetanus and diphtheria toxoid, acellular pertussis, adolescent/adult type with reduced diphtheria and pertussis components
Hep B	Hepatitis B vaccine
V	Varicella
PC	Pneumococcal conjugate vaccine
MC	Meningococcal C conjugate vaccine

– Table 2 –

Routine Immunization Schedule for Children < 7 Years of Age Not Immunized in Early Infancy

Timing	DTaP[1]	IPV	Hib	MMR	Td[3] or dTap[10]	Hep B[4] (3 doses)	V	P	M
First visit	X	X	X[11]	X[12]		X	X[7]	X[8]	X[9]
2 months later	X	X	X	(X)[6]		X		(X)	(X)
2 months later	X	(X)[5]						(X)	
6-12 months later	X	X	(X)[11]			X			
4-6 years of age[13]	X	X							
14-16 years of age					X				

P	Pneumococcal vaccine
M	Meningococcal vaccine

– Table 3 –

Routine Immunization Schedule for Children
≥ 7 Years of Age Not Immunized in Early Infancy

Timing	dTaP[10]	IPV	MMR	Hep B[4] (3 doses)	V	M
First visit	X	X	X	X	X	X[9]
2 months later	X	X	X[6]	X	(X)[7]	
6-12 months later	X	X		X		
10 years later	X					
M Meningococcal vaccine						

Notes:

1. DTaP (diphtheria, tetanus, acellular or component pertussis) vaccine is the preferred vaccine for all doses in the vaccination series, including completion of the series in children who have received ≥ 1 dose of DPT (whole cell) vaccine.

2. Hib schedule shown is for PRP-T or HbOC vaccine. If PRP-OMP is used, give at 2, 4 and 12 months of age.

3. Td (tetanus and diphtheria toxoid), a combined adsorbed "adult type" preparation for use in people ≥ 7 years of age, contains less diphtheria toxoid than preparations given to younger children and is less likely to cause reactions in older people.

4. Hepatitis B vaccine can be routinely given to infants or preadolescents, depending on the provincial/territorial policy; three doses at 0, 1 and 6 month intervals are preferred. The second dose should be administered at least 1 month after the first dose, and the third at least 2 months after the second dose. A two-dose schedule for adolescents is also possible (see chapter on Hepatitis B Vaccine).

5. This dose is not needed routinely, but can be included for convenience.

6. A second dose of MMR is recommended, at least 1 month after the first dose for the purpose of better measles protection. For convenience, options include giving it with the next scheduled vaccination at 18 months of age or with school entry (4-6 years) vaccinations (depending on the provincial/territorial policy), or at any intervening age that is practicable. The need for a second dose of mumps and rubella vaccine is not established but may benefit (given for convenience as MMR). The second dose of MMR should be given at the same visit as DTaP IPV (± Hib) to ensure high uptake rates.

7. Children aged 12 months to 12 years should receive one dose of varicella vaccine. Individuals ≥ 13 years of age should receive two doses at least 28 days apart.

8. Recommended schedule, number of doses and subsequent use of 23 valent polysaccharide pneumococcal vaccine depend on the age of the child when vaccination is begun (see page 177 for specific recommendations).

9. Recommended schedule and number of doses of meningococcal vaccine depends on the age of the child (see page 151 for specific recommendations).

10. dTap adult formulation with reduced diphtheria toxoid and pertussis component.

11. Recommended schedule and number of doses depend on the product used and age of the child when vaccination is begun (see page 87 for specific recommendations). Not required past age 5.

12. Delay until subsequent visit if child is < 12 months of age.

13. Omit these doses if the previous doses of DTaP and polio were given after the fourth birthday.

National Guidelines for Childhood Immunization Practices

Preamble

The current edition of the Guide contains many examples of the effectiveness of provincial/territorial childhood immunization programs in Canada as carried out by both private and public providers. These include elimination of wild-type poliovirus and a decrease of over 95% in the incidence of *Haemophilus influenzae* type b and measles infections. To ensure continued success it is essential that policy makers, program administrators and providers work together, proactively, to plan, conduct and regularly review childhood immunization programs. Furthermore, several challenges remain, such as continued documented occurrences of "missed opportunities for immunization"; subgroups of Canadian children with lower than optimal vaccine coverage; evidence of incorrect handling and storage of vaccine by providers; wide variations in the reporting of vaccine-associated adverse events; and evidence that there is insufficient communication regarding the risks and benefits of vaccines.

Accordingly, in 1995 the National Advisory Committee on Immunization initiated a process to develop guidelines for childhood immunization practices applicable to both public and private systems of vaccine delivery. The guidelines that follow resulted from extensive consultation, over a 2-year period, with provincial/territorial health authorities; medical, nursing, public health and hospital organizations; and individual providers and child advocacy groups. The guidelines have been officially endorsed by the Canadian Paediatric Society, Advisory Committee on Epidemiology, College of Family Physicians of Canada, Canadian Medical Association, Canadian Nurses Association, Aboriginal Nurses Association of Canada, Society of Obstetricians and Gynaecologists of Canada and the Canadian Public Health Association.

The guidelines are deliberately broad, far-reaching and rigorous. They define the most desirable immunization practices that health care providers can use to assess their own current practices, and identify areas of excellence as well as deficiency. It is recognized that some of the guidelines require involvement of the provinces and territories (e.g., regarding the need to track immunizations and audit coverage levels). Furthermore, some providers/programs may not have the funds necessary to fully implement the guidelines immediately. In such cases the guidelines can act as a tool to clarify immunization needs and to facilitate obtaining additional resources in order to achieve national goals and targets.

The following terms have been used throughout:

- *Provider*: any individual, nurse or physician qualified to give a vaccine

- *Regular provider*: individual usually responsible for a given child's vaccinations

- *Child/children*: the individuals (infancy to adolescence) being considered for immunization

- *Parent*: the individual(s) legally responsible for the child

These guidelines are recommended for use by all health professionals in the public and private sector who administer vaccines to or manage immunization services for infants and children. Although some guidelines will be more directly applicable to one or other setting, all providers and local health officials should collaborate in their efforts to ensure high coverage rates throughout the community and thus achieve and maintain the highest possible degree of community protection against vaccine-preventable diseases.

Guideline 1

Immunization services should be readily available.
Immunization services should be responsive to the needs of parents and children. When feasible, providers should schedule immunization appointments in conjunction with appointments for other health services for children. Immunization services, whether public-health clinics or physicians' offices, should be available during the week and at hours that are convenient for working parents. Services should be available on working days, as well as during some other hours (e.g., weekends, evenings, early mornings, or lunch hours).

Guideline 2

There should be no barriers or unnecessary prerequisites to the receipt of vaccines.
While appointment systems facilitate clinic planning and avoid unnecessarily long waits for children, appointment only systems may act as barriers to the receipt of vaccines. Children who appear on an unscheduled basis for vaccination should be accommodated when possible. Such children should be rapidly and efficiently screened without requiring other comprehensive health services.

A reliable decision to vaccinate can be based exclusively on the information elicited from a parent, and on the provider's observations and judgment about the child's wellness at the time. At a minimum, this includes

- asking the parent if the child is well
- questioning the parent about potential contraindications
- questioning the parent about reactions to previous vaccinations
- observing the child's general state of health.

Policies and protocols should be developed and implemented so that the administration of vaccine does not depend on individual written orders or on a referral from a primary-care provider.

Guideline 3

Providers should use all clinical encounters to screen for needed vaccines and, when indicated, vaccinate children.
Each encounter with a health-care provider, including those that occur during hospitalization, is an opportunity to review the immunization status, and if indicated, administer needed vaccines. Physicians who offer care to infants and children should consider the immunization status at every visit and offer immunization service as a routine part of that care or encourage attendance at the appropriate public health or physician clinic. At each hospital admission the vaccination record should be reviewed, and before discharge from the hospital, children should receive the vaccines for which they are eligible by age or health status. The child's current immunization provider should be informed about the vaccines administered in hospital. However, successful implementation requires significant improvements in keeping records of immunization histories (see Guideline 8).

Guideline 4

Providers should educate parents in general terms about immunization.
Providers should educate parents in a culturally sensitive way, preferably in their own language, about the importance of vaccination, the diseases vaccines prevent, the recommended immunization schedules, the need to receive vaccines at recommended ages, and the importance of bringing their child's vaccination record to every health-care visit. Parents should be encouraged to take responsibility for ensuring that their child completes the full series. Providers should answer all questions parents may have and provide appropriate education materials at suitable reading levels, preferably in the parents' preferred language. Providers should familiarize themselves with information on immunization provided by the appropriate health departments as well as other sources.

Guideline 5

Providers should inform parents in specific terms about the risks and benefits of vaccines their child is to receive.

Information pamphlets about routine childhood vaccines are available from ministries of health in many provinces and the territories, and also from the Canadian Paediatric Society. Such pamphlets are helpful in answering many questions that parents may have about immunization. Providers should document in the medical record that they have asked the parents if they have any questions and should ensure that satisfactory answers to any questions were given.

Guideline 6

Providers should recommend deferral or withholding of vaccines for true contraindications only.

There are very few true contraindications to vaccination according to current Canadian guidelines and providers must be aware of them. Accepting conditions that are not true contraindications often results in the needless deferral of indicated vaccines. Minimal acceptable screening procedures for precautions and contraindications include asking questions to elicit a history of possible adverse events following prior vaccinations, and determining any existing precautions or contraindications.

Guideline 7

Providers should administer all vaccine doses for which a child is eligible at the time of each visit.

Available evidence indicates that most routine childhood vaccines can be administered at the same visit, safely and effectively. Some vaccines are provided in a combination format whereby more than one is given in a single injection and others require separate injection.

Guideline 8

Providers should ensure that all vaccinations are accurately and completely recorded.

8.1 Data to be recorded in the child's record at the time of vaccination

For each vaccine administered the minimum data to be recorded in the child's record should include the name of the vaccine, the date (day, month, and year) and route of administration, the name of the vaccine manufacturer, the lot number, and the name and title of the person administering the vaccine.

8.2 Updating and maintaining the personal vaccination record

All providers should encourage the parents to maintain a copy of their child's personal vaccination record card and present it at each health-care visit so that it can be updated. If a parent fails to bring a child's card, the provider should ensure that adequate information is given so the parent can update the card with the name(s) of the vaccine(s), the date, the provider and the facility.

8.3 Documentation for vaccines given by other providers

Providers should facilitate the transfer of information in the vaccination record to other providers and to appropriate agencies in accordance with legislation. When a provider who does not routinely vaccinate or care for a child administers a vaccine to that child, the regular provider should be informed.

Guideline 9

Providers should maintain easily retrievable summaries of the vaccination records to facilitate age-appropriate vaccination.

Providers should maintain separate or easily retrievable summaries of vaccination records to facilitate assessment of coverage as well as the identification and recall of children who miss appointments. In addition, immunization files should be sorted periodically, with inactive records placed into a separate file. Providers should indicate in their records, or in an appropriately identified place, all primary-care services that each child receives in order to facilitate scheduling with other services.

Guideline 10

Providers should report clinically significant adverse events following vaccination – promptly, accurately, and completely.

Prompt reporting of adverse events following vaccination is essential to ensure vaccine safety, allowing for timely corrective action when needed, and to continually update information regarding vaccine risk-benefit and contraindications.

Providers should instruct parents to inform them of adverse events following vaccination. Providers should report all clinically significant events to the local public-health authority, regardless of whether they believe the events are caused by the vaccine or not. Providers should fully document the adverse event in the medical record at the time of the event or as soon as possible thereafter. At each immunization visit, information should be sought regarding serious adverse events that may have occurred following previous vaccinations.

Guideline 11

Providers should report all cases of vaccine-preventable diseases as required under provincial and territorial legislation.

Providers should know the local requirements for disease reporting. Reporting of vaccine-preventable diseases is essential for the ongoing evaluation of the effectiveness of immunization programs, to facilitate public-health investigation of vaccine failure, and to facilitate appropriate medical investigation of a child's failure to respond to a vaccine appropriately given.

Guideline 12

Providers should adhere to appropriate procedures for vaccine management.
Vaccines must be handled and stored as recommended in manufacturers' package inserts. The temperatures at which vaccines are transported and stored should be monitored daily. Vaccines must not be administered after their expiry date.

Providers should report usage, wastage, loss, and inventory as required by provincial, territorial or local public-health authorities.

Providers should be familiar with published national and local guidelines for vaccine storage and handling. Providers must ensure that any office staff designated to handle vaccines are also familiar with the guidelines.

Guideline 13

Providers should maintain up-to-date, easily retrievable protocols at all locations where vaccines are administered.
Providers administering vaccines should maintain a protocol that, at a minimum, discusses the appropriate vaccine dosage, vaccine contraindications, the recommended sites and techniques of vaccine administration, as well as possible adverse events and their emergency management. The Canadian Immunization Guide and updates, along with package inserts, can serve as references for the development of protocols. Such protocols should specify the necessary emergency equipment, drugs (including dosage), and personnel to manage safely and competently any medical emergency arising after administration of a vaccine. All providers should be familiar with the content of these protocols, their location, and how to follow them.

Guideline 14

Providers should be properly trained and maintain ongoing education regarding current immunization recommendations.
Vaccines must be administered only by properly trained persons who are recognized as qualified in their specific jurisdiction. Training and ongoing education should be based on current guidelines and recommendations of NACI and provincial and territorial ministries of health, the Guidelines for Childhood Immunization Practices, and other sources of information on immunization.

Guideline 15

Providers should operate a tracking system.
A tracking system should generate reminders of upcoming vaccinations as well as recalls for children who are overdue for their vaccinations. A system may be manual or automated, and may include mailed or telephone messages. All providers should identify, for additional intensive tracking efforts, children considered at high risk for failing to complete the immunization series on schedule (e.g., children who start their series late or children who fall behind schedule).

As an added measure, providers should encourage the development of, and cooperation with, a comprehensive provincial and territorial immunization tracking system.

Guideline 16

Audits should be conducted in all immunization clinics to assess the quality of immunization records and assess immunization coverage levels.
In both public and private sectors, an audit of immunization services should include assessment of all or a random sample of immunization records to assess the quality of documentation, and to determine the immunization coverage level (e.g., the percentage of 2-year-old children who are up-to-date). The results of the audit should be discussed by providers as part of their ongoing quality assurance reviews, and used to develop solutions to the problems identified.

B. Immunization for Adults

Childhood immunization programs have proven to be an effective and safe method of preventing many infectious diseases. The delivery and implementation of adult immunization programs have not matched the successes achieved in the pediatric population. However, given increased emphasis on disease prevention and health promotion, physicians and the general public must be made aware of the need to improve immunization programs for adults. Immunization status should be considered an integral part of the health assessment of any adult. Opportunities to provide vaccines to adults are being missed.

Prevention of infection by immunization is a lifelong process that should be tailored to meet individual variations in risk resulting from occupation, foreign travel, underlying illness, lifestyle and age. All adults should receive adequate doses of all routinely recommended vaccines, and other vaccinations should be given for selected circumstances when appropriate. Particular emphasis should be placed on improving appropriate utilization of influenza, pneumococcal and hepatitis B vaccines in Canadian adults. For elderly people, influenza and pneumococcal vaccines are reported as more cost-effective than all other preventive, screening and treatment interventions that have been studied.

Recommended Antigens

All Canadian adults require maintenance of immunity to tetanus and diphtheria, preferably with combined (Td) toxoid.

The first priority is to ensure that children receive the recommended series of doses, including the school leaving dose at 14 to 16 years of age, and that adults have completed primary immunization with Td.

The acceptable options for adult booster doses are

1) to continue to offer boosters of Td at 10-yearly intervals at mid decade years, i.e., at age 15, 25, 35, etc. or

2) as a minimum, to review immunization status at least once during adult life, e.g., at 50 years of age, and offer a single dose of Td to everyone who has not had one within the previous 10 years.

In addition, people who are travelling to areas where they are likely to be exposed to diphtheria may be offered a booster dose of Td if more than 10 years have elapsed since their most recent booster.

People ≥ 65 years of age should receive influenza vaccine every year and, on a one-time basis, a dose of pneumococcal vaccine. Special recall strategies may be necessary to ensure high coverage, particularly for those who are at greatest risk of influenza-related complications, e.g., people with chronic cardiopulmonary disease.

Adults < 65 with high-risk medical conditions for complications of influenza and pneumococcal infection should also receive influenza vaccine every year and a single dose of pneumococcal vaccine (see page 177 for high-risk conditions).

Adults born before 1970 may be considered immune to measles. Adults born in 1970 or later who do not have documentation of adequate measles immunization or who are known to be seronegative should receive measles vaccine (given as MMR). For adults who have already received one dose of measles vaccine, a second dose of vaccine would provide optimal protection. Priority for a second dose should be given to health care workers, college students and travellers to areas where measles is epidemic.

Most individuals born before 1970 may also be considered immune to mumps. Mumps vaccine (given as MMR) is recommended for young adults with no history of mumps.

Rubella vaccine should be given to all female adolescents and women of childbearing age unless they have documented evidence of detectable antibody or documented evidence of vaccination. Combined measles, mumps and rubella (MMR) vaccine is preferred. In addition, MMR vaccine should be given to rubella-susceptible health care workers of either sex who may, through frequent face-to-face contact, expose pregnant women to rubella.

Universal immunization for hepatitis B is recommended in Canada. Opportunities should be provided for adults to receive hepatitis B vaccine. In addition, adults who are at increased risk of exposure to hepatitis B by virtue of their occupation, lifestyle or environment should receive hepatitis B vaccine at the earliest possible clinical encounter (see page 102).

In the future, booster doses of adult formulation of acellular pertussis vaccine may be recommended to prevent occurrence and spread of the disease. Further studies are needed in this area.

Table 4 lists antigens that are indicated for routine use in adults. Detailed information on immunization for health care workers and travellers can be found in Part 5 and 6 (pages 251 and 255) of the *Guide*.

– Table 4 –

Routine Immunization of Adults

Vaccine or toxoid (reference page)	Indication	Further doses
Diphtheria (adult preparation) (page 82)	All adults	Every 10 years, preferably given with tetanus toxoid (Td)
Tetanus (page 208)	All adults	Every 10 years, preferably given as Td
Influenza (page 120)	Adults ≥ 65 years; adults < 65 years at high risk of influenza-related complications and other select groups (see chapter)	Every year using current vaccine formulation
Pneumococcal (page 177)	Adults ≥ 65 years; conditions with increased risk of pneumococcal diseases	See page 181
Measles (page 143)	All adults born in 1970 or later who are susceptible to measles	May be given as MMR
Rubella (page 200)	Susceptible women of child-bearing age and health care workers	May be given as MMR
Mumps (page 166)	Adults born in 1970 or later with no history of mumps	May be given as MMR

Strategies to Improve Vaccine Delivery to Adults

Despite favourable attitudes among Canadian physicians towards the use of vaccines in adults, such vaccines are underused. It is estimated that only 45% of high-risk individuals receive influenza vaccine annually. An organized systematic approach to vaccine delivery is required. Physicians play a major role in the identification of adults in need of immunization. Methods of identification include reminder notices in patient records, pre-employment medical examinations, school and college entry questionnaires, employee health nurse visits and letter reminders. Emergency rooms, public health clinics, hospitals and other health care institutions may also play an important role in vaccine delivery. Health visits of recent immigrants can identify this particular population at risk. When people are offered vaccines, high rates of compliance are usually noted. Adult immunization can be successful if well-organized provincial/territorial/institutional programs are established and maintained.

See Table 5 for a summary of immunization in selected cases.

– Table 5 –
Summary of Selected Immunization for Adults

Vaccine (reference page)	Indication
BCG (Seldom used, see page 71)	High-risk exposure
Hepatitis A (page 93)	Occupational, life-style or environmental exposure
Hepatitis B (page 102)	Universally recommended in Canada, especially for occupational, life-style or environmental exposure
Japanese encephalitis (page 128)	Travel to endemic area or other exposure risk
Lyme disease (page 135)	Travel to endemic areas. Risk determination should determine high, moderate, low or no risk
Meningococcal (page 151)	High-risk exposure or travel
Pertussis (page 169)	See pertussis chapter, page 171
Poliomyelitis (page 185)	Travel to endemic area or other exposure risk
Rabies pre-exposure use (page 191)	Occupational or other risk
Typhoid (page 214)	High-risk exposure
Varicella (page 223)	Occupational, household contacts of susceptible individuals and those susceptible because of underlying disease
Yellow fever (page 233)	Travel to endemic area or if required for foreign travel

Teenagers, young adults and recent immigrants require special attention. Some may not have received recommended vaccines while others may have received vaccines of lower potency than those currently available. Given the infrequency with which these groups seek medical care, practitioners and health officials should use every opportunity to review and update their protection.

C. Opportunity for Immunization in Acute Care Institutions

Taking an immunization history from those admitted to hospital provides an important opportunity to maintain up-to-date immunization for all patients. For patients without regular sources of care or those followed in specialized clinics, the only opportunities for immunization may be during hospital outpatient visits or hospitalization. For children, particularly, emergency room visits should be exploited to check immunization status and immunize if necessary.

The admission of elderly patients and others at high risk of influenza complications should be regarded as an opportunity to ensure that these people are immunized against influenza. Programs to immunize such patients before discharge will ensure that these very high-risk patients will not miss immunization in the community because of hospitalization during influenza season. The routine presence of standing orders or delegated acts for immunization in these institutions, along with clear departmental protocols, can help to reduce administrative barriers to incorporating these preventive acts in an institution traditionally preoccupied with treatment.

Pneumococcal vaccine should be administered before discharge to unvaccinated patients ≥ 65 years of age and those with chronic health problems for which immunization is recommended.

All pregnant women should be screened for hepatitis B surface antigen (HBsAg), and the newborn of an HBsAg positive woman should be given hepatitis B immune globulin (HBIG) and started on a course of vaccine. In jurisdictions where routine hepatitis B immunization is not offered to all children at birth, newborns at high risk of exposure to hepatitis B should receive the first dose of a course of vaccine before discharge. These children might have an infected family member other than their mother, have family circumstances leading to high risk of acute infection, or belong to an immigrant community from an area where hepatitis B is endemic.

Women susceptible to rubella should receive vaccine post-partum, before discharge from hospital.

D. Immunization of Residents of Long-Term Care Institutions

Children living in residential or long-term care institutions should receive all routine immunizations appropriate for their age. Adults should be immunized against tetanus and diphtheria. If required, a primary series should be administered, although in most cases only a booster dose(s), repeated every 10 years, will be needed.

Annual immunization against influenza is strongly recommended for individuals in residential and long-term care institutions, and a program to ensure that this occurs should be in place. Patients or their surrogate decision makers should be informed of the immunization policy on admission, and every effort made to obtain and document informed consent before the influenza season.

Pneumococcal vaccine is recommended for the elderly and the chronically ill, particularly in closed populations. A single dose of the vaccine should be administered to all previously unvaccinated individuals admitted to such facilities and to current unvaccinated residents.

Residents of institutions for people with developmental disabilities should also receive hepatitis A and B vaccines.

Selected References

ACP Task Force on Adult Immunization and Infectious Diseases Society of America. *Guide for adult immunization*. 2nd ed. Philadelphia, PA: American College of Physicians, 1990.

American Academy of Pediatrics, Committee on Infectious Diseases. *Immunization of adolescents: recommendations of the Advisory Committee on Immigration Practices, the American Academy of Pediatrics, the American Academy of Family Physicians, and the American Medical Association*. Pediatrics 1997;99:479-88.

CDC. National Immunization Program. *Adult immunization: a report by the National Vaccine Advisory Committee, National Vaccine Program*. Atlanta, GA: US. Department of Health & Human Services, 1994.

CDC. *Update on adult immunization: recommendations of the Advisory Committee on Immunization Practices (ACIP)*. MMWR 1991;40(RR-12):1-94.

Gardner P, Schaffner W. *Immunization of adults*. N Engl J Med 1993;328;1252-58.

Williams WW, Hickson MA, Kane MA et al. *Immunization policies and vaccine coverage among adults: risk for missed opportunities*. Ann Intern Med 1988;108:616-25.

– Part 3 –
Active Immunizing Agents

BCG Vaccine

Mortality and morbidity from tuberculosis (TB) have declined significantly in Canada since the Second World War (see Figure). There was a 35% decrease in the number of reported cases of TB from 1980 (2,762 cases) to 1998 (1,798 cases). Between 1994 and 1998 an average of 1,929 cases were reported annually. Among children < 5 years the reported incidence of cases was 4.2 per 100,000 in 1998.

Of the infectious diseases, TB is a leading cause of morbidity and mortality worldwide. There is growing global concern about the emergence of drug-resistant strains, which are threatening to make TB incurable again; moreover, the resurgence of the disease is being accelerated by the spread of HIV. In 1993, the WHO declared tuberculosis to be a "global emergency".

In Canada, the incidence of TB varies from one geographic region to another. Rates increase with age among both sexes, particularly males. Groups at highest risk include Aboriginal populations and immigrants from areas with a high prevalence of the disease. Other people at high risk include those infected with both HIV and tubercle bacilli, close contacts of people with untreated TB, the elderly and the homeless.

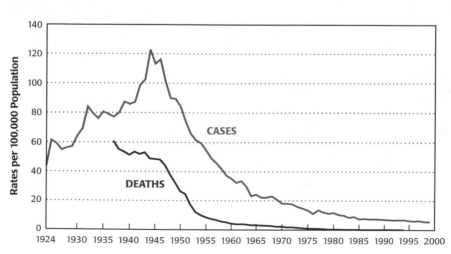

Tuberculosis – Reported Cases, 1924-1999, and Deaths, 1937-1998, Canada

TB control measures include (1) early identification of people with active (infectious) disease and treatment of each case until cured; (2) appropriate chemotherapy for those infected with *Mycobacterium tuberculosis* but without active disease; (3) measures in health care facilities and other institutions to prevent nosocomial/institutional spread; and (4) BCG immunization of selected population groups.

Preparations Licensed for Immunization

Bacille Calmette-Guérin (BCG) vaccine contains live, attenuated bacteria of a strain of *M. bovis*. It is available as a lyophilized preparation for intradermal/intracutaneous use. Instructions in the manufacturer's product leaflet for suspending and administering vaccine should always be followed, especially when BCG vaccine is used in children < 2 years old, since the dose is reduced.

Efficacy and Immunogenicity

There are many BCG vaccines available in the world today. All are derived from the original strain, but they vary in immunogenicity, efficacy and reactogenicity. In particular, the field efficacy of BCG immunization has varied in several studies. A recent meta-analysis of 13 prospective studies showed an overall protective effect of 51% (95% confidence interval [CI] 30%-66%) in preventing TB and a 71% (95% CI 47%-84%) protective effect against death due to tuberculosis. An analysis of 10 case-control studies showed similar results, with a protective effect of 50% (95% CI 36%-61%) against TB. The protective effect was greater in infants and children than adults in the meta-analyses. An enhanced protective effect was also noted in studies in which BCG was given to newborns or infants. These studies are consistent with two case-control studies involving Canadian Aboriginal populations. Five studies reporting on tuberculous meningitis showed a protective effect of 64% (95% CI 30%-82%).

The protective effect of immunization increases with increased distance from the equator. The significance of this finding is unclear at present. Many factors have been considered to explain variations among studies, including BCG strain, infection with non-tuberculous mycobacteria, climate, storage of vaccine, vitamin D and sunlight, and population genetics. BCG strain differences were not an independent risk factor in the meta-analysis. At the present time there is no clear explanation for the variation among studies or in the duration of immunity when efficacy has been shown.

The BCG vaccines available in Canada are licensed for their ability to produce a positive tuberculin reaction. In individuals receiving BCG immunization to prevent TB, a positive tuberculin skin test usually results. However, there is no clear relation between the development of cutaneous, delayed-type hypersensitivity and protection from tuberculous disease.

BCG vaccine does not provide permanent or absolute protection against TB. This disease should be considered as a possible diagnosis in any vaccinee who presents with a suggestive history, or signs or symptoms of TB.

Preparations Used for Immunotherapy

Lyophilized preparations of BCG for intravesical use in the treatment of primary and relapsed carcinoma *in situ* of the urinary bladder are formulated at a much higher strength and must **not** be used for TB immunization purposes.

Recommended Usage

Because BCG immunization usually results in a positive tuberculin skin test, the benefits gained by immunization must be carefully weighed against the potential loss of the tuberculin test as a primary tool to identify infection with *M. tuberculosis*. In Canada, TB rates are relatively low, and the tuberculin test has become increasingly useful as an epidemiologic, case finding and diagnostic tool. In the United States, the increase in rates of multidrug-resistant TB has led to a re-evaluation of the use of BCG in selected settings as a primary intervention, but no broadening of criteria for more widespread use has been suggested.

BCG should be given only to people with a negative tuberculin skin test (Mantoux 5 TU PPD-S). Infants < 6 weeks of age do not need to be tuberculin tested before receiving BCG vaccine since reactivity does not develop before this age.

BCG immunization will not prevent the development of active TB in individuals who are already infected with *M. tuberculosis*.

BCG vaccine is recommended for the following people:

- Infants and children belonging to groups with high rates of new infections, i.e., in excess of 1% per year, when other control measures have proved ineffective.

- Infants and children with negative tuberculin skin tests who are at high risk of intimate and prolonged exposure to persistently untreated or ineffectively treated patients (e.g., because of multidrug resistance) with infectious pulmonary TB, unless they can be removed from the source of exposure or given long-term preventive therapy.

- Individuals repeatedly exposed to people with untreated or inadequately treated active TB in conditions under which normal preventive measures are not possible or have been unsuccessful, e.g., when multidrug-resistant TB is involved.

- BCG immunization may be considered for health care workers (including medical laboratory workers) at considerable risk of exposure to tubercle bacilli, especially drug-resistant bacilli, when protective measures against infection are known to be ineffective or not feasible. Consultation with a regional TB and/or infectious disease expert is recommended before BCG vaccine is administered.

- BCG immunization may be considered for travellers planning extended stays in areas of high tuberculosis prevalence, particularly where a program of serial skin testing and appropriate chemotherapy may not be feasible or where primary isoniazid resistance of *M. tuberculosis* is high. Travellers are advised to consult a specialist in travel medicine or infectious disease when considering a decision for or against BCG immunization.

Usual Response to Immunization

The development of erythema, papule formation or superficial ulceration 3 to 6 weeks after intradermal BCG injection usually indicates successful immunization. Some enlargement of the regional lymph nodes usually accompanies the lesions at the immunization site. Most authorities believe that development of a typical pustule and scar at the site indicates that protection has been conferred.

The relation between development of a positive tuberculin skin test and the protective efficacy of BCG has not been well studied. However, present methods of immunization usually induce positive tuberculin tests for approximately 5 years in the majority of vaccinees. The size of response to a tuberculin skin test decreases with time. Tuberculin reactivity may be diminished or transiently abolished during the course of certain viral infections, particularly measles.

Booster Doses and Re-immunization

Re-immunization with BCG is not recommended and should be addressed in consultation with regional TB or infectious disease experts. Tuberculin skin testing used as a basis for decisions on BCG re-immunization should be discontinued.

Storage Requirements

The vaccine should be protected from heat and direct sunlight and stored according to the manufacturer's instructions, usually at a temperature $\leq 5°\,C$. Reconstituted freeze-dried vaccine should be kept refrigerated when not in use and discarded if not used within 8 hours.

Simultaneous Administration with Other Vaccines

BCG should not be given within 4 weeks after administration of any live vaccine, since these vaccines are known to suppress the tuberculin reaction.

Adverse Reactions

Adverse reactions are more common in young vaccinees (infants versus older children) and are frequently related to improper technique in administration (mainly improper dilution). Most reactions are generally mild and do not require treatment. A change to the current infant dose of vaccine has decreased the incidence of these reactions among infants to < 2%.

Reactions may include persistent or spreading skin ulceration at the immunization site, inflammatory adenitis and keloid formation. Moderately severe and, very rarely, severe reactions can occur. Rates of such incidents appear to vary with the strain of vaccine, dose and method of immunization, and the age of the recipient. Moderately severe reactions, such as marked lymphadenitis or suppurative adenitis, occur in 0.2 to 4.0 per 1,000 vaccinees.

Disseminated BCG infection, which may be fatal, occurs very rarely (about 1 in 1 million vaccinees) and is seen almost exclusively in people with impaired immune responses. Three such cases (two fatal) in severely immunocompromised infants were reported in Canada between 1993 and 1998; one was associated with HIV infection. Severe osteitis/osteomyelitis can also occur very rarely.

Contraindications

BCG immunization is contraindicated for people with immune deficiency diseases, including HIV infection, altered immune status due to malignant disease, and impaired immune function secondary to treatment with corticosteroids, chemotherapeutic agents or radiation. Extensive skin disease or burns are also contraindications. BCG is contraindicated for individuals with a positive tuberculin skin test, although immunization of tuberculin reactors has frequently occurred without incident.

Immunization of pregnant women should preferably be delayed until after delivery, although harmful effects on the fetus have not been observed.

The vaccine should not be administered to individuals receiving drugs with anti-tuberculous activity, since these agents may be active against the vaccine strain.

Other Considerations

It is impossible to differentiate between a positive tuberculin reaction due to BCG immunization and one that is the result of infection. The following is an extract from the *Canadian Tuberculosis Standards*, 5th edition[1], which provides assistance in interpretation:

"BCG vaccination may have been received by several population groups, including immigrants from many European countries and most developing countries. In Canada, many Aboriginal Canadians and persons born in Quebec and Newfoundland from the 1940s until the early 1980s have been vaccinated.

From studies conducted in Canada and in several other countries, if BCG is received in infancy (the first year of life), it is very unlikely to cause tuberculin reactions of 10 mm or more after the age of 2 or 3. Therefore, a history of BCG vaccination received in infancy can be ignored in all population groups when interpreting a tuberculin reaction of 10 mm or greater.

If the BCG vaccination was received between the ages of 2 and 5, persistently positive tuberculin reactions will be seen in 10% to 15% of subjects even 20 to 25 years later. Among subjects vaccinated at the age of 6 or older (i.e. during school age years), up

BCG Vaccine

---

[1] Reprinted with kind permission from *Canadian tuberculosis standards*, 5th edition. Ottawa: Canadian Lung Association, 2000.

to 25% will have persistent positive reactions. BCG-related reactions may be as large as 25 mm or even greater. Therefore if BCG vaccination was received after the first year of life, it can be an important cause of false-positive tuberculin reactions, particularly in populations in which the expected prevalence of TB infection (i.e. true-positive reactions) is less than 10%. This means that in the general population of non-Aboriginal Canadians or immigrants from industrialized countries who received BCG vaccinations after the age of 2, this would be the more likely cause of a positive test than true infection.

On the other hand, in populations with a high prevalence of TB infection, such as immigrants from TB-endemic countries, Aboriginal Canadians, or close contacts of an active case, the likelihood of true infection would be greater than the likelihood of a false-positive reaction, and BCG vaccination should be ignored. An additional group in whom the history of BCG vaccination should be ignored are those with high risk of development of active disease if infected, such as immunocompromised individuals, those with renal failure, diabetes, or HIV, or patients with abnormal chest radiograph consistent with inactive TB."

Selected References

Brewer TF, Colditz GA. *Relationship between bacille Calmette-Guérin (BCG) strains and the efficacy of BCG vaccine in the prevention of tuberculosis.* Clin Infect Dis 1995;20:126-35.

Canadian Lung Association. *Canadian tuberculosis standards, 5th ed.* Ottawa, 2000.

Ciesielski SC. *BCG vaccination and the PPD test: what the clinician needs to know.* J Fam Pract 1995;40:76-80.

Colditz GA, Berkey CS, Mosteller F et al. *The efficacy of bacillus Calmette-Guérin vaccination of newborns and infants in the prevention of tuberculosis: meta-analyses of the published literature.* Pediatrics 1995;96:29-35.

Colditz GA, Brewer TF, Berkey CS et al. *Efficacy of BCG vaccine in the prevention of tuberculosis.* JAMA 1994;271:698-702.

Fine PE. *Bacille Calmette-Guérin vaccines: a rough guide.* Clin Infect Dis 1995;20:11-14.

Global tuberculosis programme and global programme on vaccines. Statement on BCG revaccination for the prevention of tuberculosis. Wkly Epidemiol Rec 1995;70:229-31.

Houston S, Fanning A, Soskoline C et al. *The effectiveness of bacillus Calmette-Guérin (BCG) vaccination against tuberculosis: a case-control study in treaty Indians, Alberta, Canada.* Am J Epidemiol 1990;131:340-48.

Lotte A, Wasz-Hockert O, Poisson N et al. *BCG complications.* Adv Tuberc Res 1984;21;107-93.

O`Brien KL, Ruff AJ, Louis MA et al. *Bacille Calmette-Guérin complications in children born to HIV-1 infected women with a review of the literature.* Pediatrics 1995;95:414-18.

Pabst HF, Godel J, Grace M et al. *Effect of breast-feeding on immune response to BCG vaccination.* Lancet 1989;1:295-97.

Roche PW, Triccas JA, Winter N. *BCG vaccination against tuberculosis: past disappointments and future hopes.* Trends Microbiol 1995;3:397-401.

Watson JM. *BCG — mass or selective vaccination?* J Hosp Infect 1995;30 (June suppl):508-13.

Cholera Vaccine

Cholera is an acute bacterial infection that presents as profuse, watery diarrhea. It is associated with rapid dehydration and occasionally hypovolemic shock, which may be life threatening. The disease is caused by an enterotoxin produced by *Vibrio cholerae*. Two serogroups, 01 and 0139 (Bengal), have been implicated in human epidemics. Within the serogroup 01 are the classical and El Tor biotypes.

Mortality ranges from 50% or more without treatment to < 1% among adequately treated patients. Treatment consists mainly of oral or parenteral rehydration. Cholera infection is associated with poor sanitation and is generally acquired from contaminated water or food, particularly undercooked or raw shellfish and fish.

The spectrum of disease is wide, with mild and asymptomatic cases occurring more frequently than severe ones. The ratio of symptomatic to asymptomatic cases varies from strain to strain. In El Tor infections, this ratio (1:50) is much lower than in cholera infection due to the classical biotype (1:5). Humans are the only known natural host.

Cholera is a quarantinable disease subject to international health regulations. It must be reported to the World Health Organization (WHO) within 24 hours through Health Canada's Division of Quarantine, Travel and Migration Health. The Division must be contacted immediately in the event of a suspected case, at 613-957-3236 (after hours, telephone the medical officer on call at 613-545-7661).

Epidemiology

The seventh cholera pandemic began in 1961, when *V. cholerae* of the El Tor biotype spread through southern Asia, the Middle East, Eastern Europe and, in 1970, Africa. In 1991, the El Tor biotype caused an outbreak in Peru, which led to an extensive epidemic in other Amazonian and Central American countries.

During the 1990s, a new strain of cholera, serogroup 0139 (Bengal), caused an epidemic that began in India and Bangladesh, around the Bay of Bengal. This epidemic spread to other countries in Asia, but not outside the region.

In Canada, three cholera cases were reported in 1998; preliminary surveillance data indicate that there were none in 1999 and five (unconfirmed) in 2000. Between 1993 and 1997 there were 23 reported cases of the biotype El Tor or Ogawa. Although travel history was not given for all cases, the reported destinations included El Salvador, Mexico, the Dominican Republic, India and Pakistan. Many of these people had travelled to private homes. No secondary transmission was noted, which is as expected in countries such as Canada that have modern sanitation, good hygiene and clean water supplies, and a low risk of transmission.

For travellers, prevention relies primarily on care in the choice of food and water supply and in the use of good hygienic measures rather than on immunization.

Preparations Licensed for Immunization

Oral, live attenuated cholera vaccine, CVD 103-HgR (Mutacol®), is licensed in Canada for use in adults and children > 2 years. Cloned strains of *V. cholerae* are used in its preparation. The vaccine also contains aspartame (a phenylalanine derivative), which is added as a sweetener. The buffer solution contains sodium bicarbonate, ascorbic acid and lactose, which serve to neutralize gastric acid.

There is no cholera vaccine currently available that has been shown to protect against the 0139 Bengal strain in South Asia.

CVD 103-HgR has **not** been shown to offer protection against enterotoxigenic *Escherichia coli* (ETEC)-associated diarrhea, which is a common cause of diarrhea in travellers. An experimental oral vaccine containing cholera toxin B-subunit and whole inactivated cholera bacteria (BS-WC), which is **not** currently licensed in Canada, may offer some protection against ETEC-associated diarrhea as well as against cholera.

A combined, live attenuated oral cholera/typhoid vaccine (Colertif Berna®) is licensed but not currently distributed in Canada.

Parenteral, inactivated cholera vaccine offers short, limited effectiveness and is **not** recommended for Canadians travelling to endemic areas.

Note: This chapter will deal only with the oral cholera CVD 103-HgR vaccine.

Efficacy and Immunogenicity

Seroconversion rates over 90% have been reported after a single, oral dose of the vaccine, occurring as early as 8 days after administration and lasting for 6 months. Efficacy studies have been carried out in volunteers challenged with pathogenic *V. cholerae* of both biotypes and serotypes. Protection against the classic biotype was demonstrated among 82% to 100% of subjects, and protection against the El Tor biotype among 62% to 67% of subjects exposed. However, even when the vaccine did not provide complete protection, no volunteer lost > 1 litre of diarrheal fluid in 24 hours.

Of note is the observation that there is no efficacy against the 0139 Bengal strain.

Recommended Usage

Travellers should take all the necessary precautions to avoid contact with or ingestion of potentially contaminated food or water since not all recipients of the vaccine will be fully protected against cholera. This is particularly true for travellers to areas where 0139, for which there is no vaccine, is endemic.

The WHO indicates that since 1992 no country or territory has required a certificate of immunization against cholera. Cholera immunization is no longer required or recommended for the vast majority of Canadian travellers. People following the usual tourist itineraries in countries affected by cholera are at virtually no risk of acquiring infection.

Travellers who may be at increased risk (e.g., health professionals working in endemic areas or workers in refugee camps) may benefit from immunization. A detailed, individual risk assessment should be made in order to determine likely candidates.

Route of Administration

The oral cholera vaccine is administered as a single dose with the provided buffer solution, mixed as a drink in cold or lukewarm water. It should be taken 1 hour before food or drink.

Booster Doses and Re-Immunization

An optimal booster dose or interval has not yet been established. The manufacturer recommends a repeat dose every 6 months, if indicated.

Serologic Testing

There is no indication for pre- or post-immunization serologic testing.

Storage Requirements

CVD 103-HgR should be stored at a temperature between 2° and 8° C in a dry place and be protected from light; it should not be frozen. The reconstituted vaccine should be ingested as soon after mixing as possible.

Simultaneous Administration with Other Vaccines

The administration of oral typhoid vaccine (Ty21a) capsules and oral cholera vaccine should be separated by at least 8 hours. The newer form of the same oral typhoid vaccine available in a sachet form does not need to be separated from the oral cholera vaccine, and the two can be given together, mixed with a single sachet of buffer.

There is no problem anticipated with the concomitant administration of oral cholera vaccine with killed vaccines. The concomitant administration of oral polio vaccine (no longer used in Canada) or yellow fever vaccine does not interfere with the immune response to oral cholera vaccine.

Adverse Reactions

Randomized controlled trials involving several thousand subjects have been carried out in a number of cholera-endemic and non-endemic areas, and have demonstrated good safety of the CVD 103-HgR (Mutachol®) vaccine. The side effect profile was

Cholera Vaccine

similar in the placebo and vaccine groups and included nausea, abdominal cramps and diarrhea, all of which were mild in nature and of short duration.

Contraindications and Precautions

Hypersensitivity to the vaccine or the buffer components is a contraindication to further doses. Patients with phenylketonuria must be aware that the vaccine contains aspartame (a phenylalanine derivative), at 17 mg of phenylalanine per double-chamber sachet. The vaccine should not be given during an acute febrile illness or to any person with acute gastrointestinal disease.

Excretion of vaccine organisms is minimal, and spread to contacts of vaccinees is unlikely.

Pediatric use: Because the safety of the oral cholera vaccine has not been established in children < 2 years of age, the product is not recommended for this age group.

Use in pregnant women and nursing mothers: There are no data on the safety of the vaccine in pregnancy. Since it is a live vaccine, it should be used with caution in pregnant and nursing women. A risk/benefit analysis should be carried out to determine whether an individual in these groups should be immunized. It is not known if the vaccine is excreted in human milk.

Use in immunocompromised hosts: There are no data on the safety of the vaccine in such groups, and the vaccine should be used with caution in the immunocompromised or immunosuppressed. An individual risk assessment should be carried out to determine the indications for immunization.

Other Considerations

Simultaneous administration with antibiotics or antimalarials: Antibiotics may interfere with the effectiveness of the vaccine. People receiving therapy with antibiotics should wait 7 days after the completion of therapy before taking the oral cholera vaccine.

Antimalarial prophylaxis, specifically chloroquine and doxycycline, may interfere with the effectiveness of the vaccine, and therefore antimalarial prophylaxis with these medications should start no sooner than 7 days after administration of the oral cholera vaccine.

Antimalarial prophylaxis with mefloquine or proguanil does not interfere with the effectiveness of the oral cholera vaccine and therefore can be administered simultaneously.

Summary of Recommendations

1. Oral cholera vaccine (CVD 103 HgR) offers protection against serogroup 01. It does not protect against serogroup 0139 (Bengal strain).

2. The use of CVD 103 HgR is not routinely recommended for the prevention of cholera in the majority of travellers to endemic areas, and a detailed, individual risk assessment should be used to detect a traveller at increased risk of acquiring cholera (e.g., aid workers or health care professionals working in endemic areas).

3. CVD 103 HgR has not been shown to offer protection against ETEC-associated travellers' diarrhea.

4. Travellers are advised to follow the CATMAT recommendations for the prevention and treatment of travellers' diarrhea.

Selected References

Committee to Advise on Tropical Medicine and Travel and the National Advisory Committee on Immunization. *Statement on oral cholera vaccination*. CCDR 1998;24(ACS-5).

Committee to Advise on Tropical Medicine and Travel. *Statement on traveller's diarrhea*. CCDR 2001;27(ACS-3).

Cyrz SJ, Levine MM, Kaper JB et al. *Randomized, double-blind, placebo-controlled trial to evaluate the safety and immunogenicity of the live cholera vaccine strain CVD-HgR in Swiss adults*. Vaccine 1990;8:577-80.

Drug monograph. *Mutachol Berna® vaccine – cholera vaccine live oral attenuated CVD 103-HgR manufactured by Swiss Serum and Vaccine Institute Berne*. Distributed by Berna Products Corporation, March 1, 2000.

Kotloff KL, Wasserman SS, O'Donnell S et al. *Safety and immunogenicity in North Americans of a single dose of live oral cholera vaccine CVD 103-HgR: results of a placebo-controlled, double-blind crossover trial*. Infect Immun 1992;60:4430-32.

MacPherson DW, Tonkin M. *Cholera vaccination: a decision analysis*. Can Med Assoc J 1992;146:1947-52.

Peltola H, Siitonen A, Kyronseppa H et al. *Prevention of traveller's diarrhea by oral B-subunit/ whole-cell cholera vaccine*. Lancet 1991;338:1285-89.

Sack DA, Cadoz M. *Cholera vaccines*. In Plotkin SA, Orestein WA. *Vaccine*. 3rd edition. Philadelphia: W.B. Saunders, 1999:639-49.

Cholera Vaccine

Diphtheria Toxoid

Diphtheria is a serious communicable disease caused by toxigenic strains of *Corynebacterium diphtheriae*. The case-fatality rate remains at 5% to 10%, the highest death rates occurring in the very young and the elderly. The organism may be harboured in the nasopharynx, skin and other sites of asymptomatic carriers, making eradication of the disease difficult.

Epidemiology

Routine immunization against diphtheria in infancy and childhood has been widely practised in Canada since 1930. In 1924, there were 9,000 cases reported, the highest annual number ever recorded in Canada (see Figure). At the same time, diphtheria was one of the most common causes of death in children from 1 to 5 years of age. By the mid-1950s, routine immunization had resulted in a remarkable decline in the morbidity and mortality of the disease. Only one or two cases have been reported annually in recent years, and classic diphtheria is a rarity.

Toxigenic strains of diphtheria bacilli are still detected each year in carriers (in the pharynx, skin and ear), sometimes associated with mild clinical symptoms. Asymptomatic carriage of *C. diphtheriae* is far more common than clinical diphtheria. The disease occurs most frequently in unimmunized or partially immunized individuals. Although occasional cases of mild clinical diphtheria do occur in apparently fully immunized people, antitoxin stimulated by immunization is believed to persist at protective levels for 10 years or more. Recent serosurveys of healthy adult populations in Canada indicate that approximately 20% of those surveyed (higher in some age groups) do not have protective levels of antibody to diphtheria. The actual levels of

Diphtheria – Reported Cases, Canada, 1924-2000

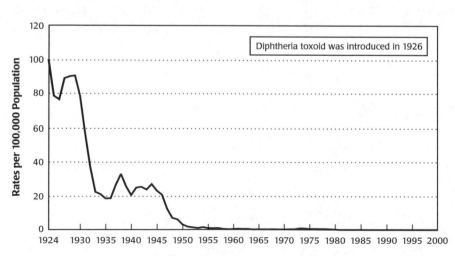

serosusceptibility in the general adult population may be even higher. The potential for disease re-emergence if immunization levels are allowed to fall has been demonstrated most recently in the Commonwealth of Independent States (former Soviet Union), where tens of thousands of cases and substantial mortality have been reported.

Preparations Licensed for Immunization

Diphtheria toxoid is a cell-free preparation of diphtheria toxin detoxified with formaldehyde. It is highly immunogenic, but two to three primary doses are necessary to ensure reliable seroconversion and sufficiently high concentrations of protective antibody. Titres decline slowly with time but can be boosted by additional doses. In terms of protection against diphtheria, the significance of loss of antitoxin in adequately immunized people is not clear. The immunity conferred is antitoxic, not antibacterial, and thus protects against the potentially lethal systemic effects of diphtheria toxin but not directly against local infection. However, carriage of *C. diphtheriae* has been observed to be lower in immunized populations.

Diphtheria toxoid is available as a preparation adsorbed with aluminum phosphate and combined with other toxoids or vaccines (e.g., tetanus, poliomyelitis or pertussis, see Appendix III). The amount of toxoid present is measured in flocculating units (Lf). It should be noted that the amount of diphtheria toxoid in combined preparations of diphtheria and tetanus toxoids varies widely with the specific product and manufacturer. Preparations containing only 2 Lf of diphtheria toxoid (commonly designated Td) are intended for use in people ≥ 7 years of age.

Recommended Usage

Routine immunization against diphtheria is recommended for everyone, regardless of age at which immunization is begun. Adsorbed vaccines must be injected intramuscularly.

Primary immunization of children < 7 years of age

It is preferable to use products in which diphtheria toxoid is combined with acellular pertussis vaccine and tetanus toxoid (DTaP), with or without inactivated poliomyelitis vaccine (DTaP-IPV) and *Haemophilus influenzae* type b (Hib) conjugate vaccine. The primary immunizing course of diphtheria toxoid alone or in combination consists of four doses and should ideally begin at 2 months of age. Diphtheria toxoid is most conveniently given as part of the recommended routine immunization schedule (see Part 2: Recommended Immunization Schedules). If the routine schedule is not adhered to, the following guidelines should be observed.

The recommended time interval between the initial three doses is normally 8 weeks. Longer intervals do not compromise the final level of antibody achieved, but the interval between doses should not be < 4 weeks. The fourth dose should be given 6 to 12 months after the third. A further booster dose is recommended 30 to 54 months after the fourth dose, most commonly at 4 to 6 years (school entry). This booster dose is not necessary if the fourth dose in the primary series was given on or after the fourth birthday. Although diphtheria toxoid is not essential for the fifth dose, a fifth dose of pertussis vaccine *is* strongly recommended and is most easily given combined with diphtheria and tetanus toxoids. An additional booster dose of adult-type preparation (Td) should be given at 14-16 years of age (school leaving booster) and at least once again during adult life (see below).

Primary immunization of persons ≥ 7 years of age

The recommended agent is a combined adsorbed tetanus and diphtheria preparation (Td, adult-type) containing less diphtheria toxoid than preparations given to younger children. This reduced amount is less likely to cause reactions in older people. Two doses are given 4 to 8 weeks apart, with a further dose 6 to 12 months later to complete the course.

Booster Doses

The need for regular boosters during adult life has never been established. In Canada and the U.S., diphtheria rarely develops in adults who have completed a primary series of immunizations, despite a general failure to observe the recommendation for 10-year boosters. At the same time, the relation between limited compliance with this recommendation and the current favourable disease control status is unknown. Consequently, there are few firm data on which to base a recommendation for less frequent boosters; moreover, antitoxin levels are known to decline with time.

Ensuring that children receive the recommended series of doses, *including the school leaving dose* at 14 to 16 years of age, and that adults have completed primary immunization should be the first priority.

The acceptable options for adult booster doses are

■ to continue to offer boosters of Td at 10-year intervals, or

■ as a minimum, to review immunization status at least once during adult life, e.g., at 50 years of age, and offer a single dose of Td to everyone who has not received one within the previous 10 years.

In addition,

■ People who are travelling to areas where they are likely to be exposed to diphtheria may be offered a booster dose of Td if > 10 years have elapsed since their most recent booster.

■ If a case of diphtheria occurs, close contacts (household, classroom or similar) should be given a dose of a toxoid preparation appropriate for their age unless they are known to have been fully immunized and the last dose was given in the previous 10 years. The remaining doses required to provide full immunization should be given to any contacts who were previously unimmunized or incompletely immunized. Patients convalescent from diphtheria should be given a complete primary course of toxoid, unless serologic testing indicates protective levels of antitoxin, since diphtheria infection does not always confer immunity.

People requiring a booster dose of tetanus toxoid for wound management should receive Td as a convenient means of reinforcing their diphtheria protection.

Adverse Reactions

Diphtheria toxoid may cause severe but transient local and febrile reactions in children and adults, the frequency increasing with age, the dose of toxoid and the number of doses given. A large proportion of children receiving a booster dose of DTaP vaccine at 4 to 6 years of age experience local redness and/or swelling of $\geq$ 5 cm or more in diameter. When a booster dose of Td is given at 14 to 16 years of age, only 10% experience marked local reactions.

Contraindications and Precautions

Individuals $\geq$ 7 years of age should be given only those preparations formulated for older children and adults (Td or dTap). Before a combined vaccine is given, it is very important to ensure that there are no contraindications to the administration of any of the other components.

When a combined diphtheria-tetanus preparation is being considered, care should be taken to avoid administration of tetanus toxoid more frequently than is recommended (see section on Tetanus Toxoid), or adverse reactions may result.

It is important to ensure that adsorbed products are given intramuscularly, since subcutaneous injection of adsorbed products produces a much higher rate of local reactions.

Combined Vaccines Against Diphtheria, Pertussis, Tetanus and Poliomyelitis

It is recommended that diphtheria and tetanus toxoids, and acellular pertussis and poliomyelitis vaccines always be administered in a combined formulation appropriate for age.

Local and systemic reactions associated in the past with the primary series of DPT or DPT-Polio containing whole cell pertussis vaccine appear to have been due primarily to the pertussis component. Reaction rates of the combined vaccines were similar to those of pertussis vaccine alone. Vaccines containing acellular pertussis vaccine have much lower rates of adverse reaction, but local reactions have been observed with the fourth and fifth doses of vaccine.

Combined adsorbed preparations of diphtheria and tetanus toxoid formulated for adults (Td or dTap) are the preferred immunizing agents for people ≥ 7 years of age. They are recommended as follows:

1. primary immunization of older children and adults against diphtheria and tetanus;

2. regular booster doses for children at 14 to 16 years of age, and for adults; and

3. management of wounds when tetanus toxoid is indicated.

A combined adsorbed preparation containing diphtheria and tetanus toxoids, and inactivated poliomyelitis vaccine (Td-Polio) is available for immunization of older children ≥ 7 years and selected adults. For details of usage and precautions to be taken, see relevant sections of the *Guide*.

Discussion of control of cases and outbreaks in the community is beyond the scope of this *Guide*.

Selected References

Galazka AM, Robertson SE. *Immunization against diphtheria with special emphasis on immunization of adults*. Vaccine 1996;14:845-57.

Galazka AM, Robertson SE, Oblapenko GP. *Resurgence of diphtheria*. Eur J Epidemiol 1995;11:95-105.

Gupta RK, Griffin Jr. P, Xu J et al. *Diphtheria antitoxin levels in US blood and plasma donors*. J Infect Dis 1996;173:1493-7.

Larsen K, Ullberg-Olsson K, Ekwall E et al. *The immunization of adults against diphtheria in Sweden*. J Biol Stand 1987;15:109-16.

Maple PA, Efstratiou A, George RC et al. *Diphtheria immunity in UK blood donors*. Lancet 1995;345:963-5.

Plotkin SA, Orenstein WA. *Vaccines*. 3rd edition. Philadelphia: W.B Saunders Company, 1999.

Simonsen O, Kjeldsen K, Vendborg H-A et al. *Revaccination of adults against diphtheria. 1: Responses and reactions to different doses of diphtheria toxoid in 30-70-years-old persons with low serum antitoxin levels*. Acta Pathol Microbiol Immunol Scand [C] 1986;94:213-18.

Yuan L, Lau W, Thipphawong J et al. *Diphtheria and tetanus immunity among blood donors in Toronto*. Can Med Assoc J 1997;156:985-90.

Haemophilus Vaccine

Haemophilus influenzae type b (Hib) was the most common cause of bacterial meningitis and a leading cause of other serious invasive infections in young children before the introduction of Hib vaccines. About 55% to 65% of affected children had meningitis, the remainder suffering from epiglottitis, bacteremia, cellulitis, pneumonia or septic arthritis. The case-fatality rate of meningitis is about 5%. Severe neurologic sequelae occur in 10% to 15% of survivors and deafness in 15% to 20% (severe in 3% to 7%).

H. influenzae is also commonly associated with otitis media, sinusitis, bronchitis and other respiratory tract disorders. However, since type b organisms seldom cause these disorders, Hib vaccines have not affected their incidence.

Epidemiology

Before the introduction of Hib conjugate vaccines in Canada in 1988, there were an estimated 2,000 cases of Hib disease annually. Since then the overall incidence has fallen by more than 99%. The majority of cases occur now in children too old to have received primary immunization. In 1998, 15 cases were reported in children < 5 years of age. The incidence was 2 cases/100,000 children < 1 year of age and 0.5 cases/100,000 children between the ages of 1 and 5 years. In 2000, only four cases were detected by the 12 centres involved in the IMPACT (Immunization Monitoring Program, Active) enhanced surveillance program across the country. Two of these cases occurred in infants < 8 months of age who had not yet received the three-dose

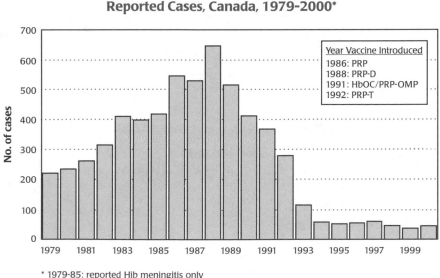

Haemophilus influenzae **type b (Hib) Disease – Reported Cases, Canada, 1979-2000***

Year Vaccine Introduced
1986: PRP
1988: PRP-D
1991: HbOC/PRP-OMP
1992: PRP-T

* 1979-85: reported Hib meningitis only
  1986-2000: all invasive forms (meningitis and septicemia)

primary immunization series, and two cases were considered vaccine failures. Over the few years preceding 2000 there had been several cases in unvaccinated children, which were considered to have been preventable.

The risk of Hib meningitis is at least twice as high for children attending full-time day care as for children cared for at home. The risk is also greater among children with splenic dysfunction (e.g., sickle cell disease, asplenia) or antibody deficiency, and among Inuit children.

Preparations Licensed for Immunization

All Canadian provinces and territories include Hib conjugate vaccine in their immunization program for children. Hib conjugate vaccines are the second generation of vaccines against Hib disease, having replaced an earlier polysaccharide product. Polysaccharide-protein conjugate antigens have the advantage of producing greater immune response in infants and young children than purified polysaccharide vaccine. The latter stimulates only B-cells, whereas the former activates macrophages, T-helper cells and B-cells, resulting in greatly enhanced antibody responses and establishment of immunologic memory.

As of 1997, there are three Hib conjugate vaccines licensed for use in Canada in infants ≥ 2 months of age: HbOC (HibTITER™), PRP-OMP (PedvaxHIB™) and PRP-T (Act-HIB™). A fourth Hib conjugate vaccine, PRP-D (ProHIBIT™), is licensed for use only in children ≥ 18 months of age. PRP-D is currently not recommended in Canada because it induces antibody responses that are suboptimal compared with other Hib conjugate vaccines.

The Hib conjugate vaccines differ in a number of ways, including the protein carrier, polysaccharide size and types of diluent and preservative. As of 1997, all Canadian provinces and territories use the PRP-T vaccine because it is the only Hib conjugate vaccine currently licensed for use that is combined with acellular pertussis vaccine and diphtheria and tetanus toxoids, with or without inactivated polio vaccine.

The protein carriers in Hib conjugate vaccines should not be considered as immunizing agents against diphtheria, tetanus or meningococcal disease.

Efficacy and Immunogenicity

HbOC, PRP-OMP and PRP-T stimulate good antibody responses after primary immunization in infants starting at 2 to 3 months of age and prime them for an excellent booster response at 15 to 18 months. The booster response can be elicited by any of the conjugate Hib vaccines.

Across Canada, the *H. influenzae* conjugate vaccine is now given in combination with diphtheria, tetanus, pertussis and polio as Pentacel™. Several studies have demonstrated reduced antibody response to the Hib component when it is given as a combination vaccine, although the Hib responses are not reduced with Pentacel™. As well, since the switch to Pentacel™ there has only been one breakthrough case of invasive Hib disease in Canada after completion of the primary immunization series.

When given as a single dose to previously unimmunized children $\geq$ 15 months of age, HbOC, PRP-OMP and PRP-T stimulate excellent antibody responses (> 1 µg/mL) in 80% to 100% of children. The duration of immunity following completion of age-appropriate immunization is unknown and warrants ongoing study. Current data suggest that protection will be long lasting.

Capsular polysaccharide antigen can be detected in the urine of vaccinees for up to 2 weeks after immunization with conjugate vaccine. This phenomenon could be confused with antigenuria associated with invasive Hib infection.

Hib conjugate vaccine failure, defined as onset of confirmed invasive Hib infection more than 28 days after completion of the primary immunization series, can occur but is rare with the products in current use.

Recommended Usage

Routine immunization with Hib conjugate vaccine is recommended for all infants beginning at 2 months of age. It is preferable, when possible, to use the same product for all doses in the primary series. However, available data suggest that a primary immunization series consisting of three doses of different Hib conjugate vaccine product results in adequate antibody responses. When use of a different product is unavoidable, for instance, when a child moves from a jurisdiction using a different Hib vaccine, the specific vaccine given for each of the primary series injections should be carefully documented.

Children in whom invasive Hib disease develops before 24 months of age should still receive vaccine as recommended, since natural disease may not induce protection.

Infections due to encapsulated bacteria, including *H. influenzae,* occur more commonly in those with primary and secondary disorders of the humoral immune system, including disorders of antibody production or function, lymphoreticular or hematopoietic malignancies, antibody dyscrasias, protein wasting syndromes, anatomic or functional asplenia, bone marrow transplantation and HIV infection. For previously unimmunized adults and children > 5 years who have these underlying conditions, the efficacy of Hib immunization is unknown. Despite limited efficacy data, Hib vaccine is commonly given to those with anatomic or functional asplenia and may be considered in other immunocompromised people at increased risk of invasive Hib infection. Consultation with an infectious disease expert may be helpful in these cases.

Schedule and Dosage

The recommended schedule for PRP-T vaccine is shown in the Table along with the schedules for other licensed products. The dose of each Hib conjugate vaccine is 0.5 mL. Infants and children starting a primary series of Hib vaccine after 2 months

Detailed Vaccination Schedule for *Haemophilus* b Conjugate Vaccines

Vaccine	Age at 1st dose (months)	Primary series	Age at booster dose* (months)
PRP-T† (Aventis Pasteur)	2-6	3 doses, 2 months apart	15-18
	7-11	2 doses, 2 months apart	15-18
	12-14	1 dose	15-18
	15-59	1 dose	
HbOC‡ (Wyeth Ayerst)	2-6	3 doses, 2 months apart	15-18
	7-11	2 doses, 2 months apart	15-18
	12-14	1 dose	15-18
	15-59	1 dose	
PRP OMP** (Merck-Frosst)	2-6	2 doses, 2 months apart	12
	7-11	2 doses, 2 months apart	15-18
	12-14	1 dose	15-18
	15-59	1 dose	

* The booster dose should be given at least 2 months after the previous dose.

† Supplied as lyophilized powder that can be reconstituted with any of the following Aventis Pasteur products: the supplied diluent, DPT adsorbed, DPT polio adsorbed or Quadracel™

‡ Supplied as a solution (HibTITER™) for injection in a seperate limb from other vaccines or as a pre-mixed liquid formulation in combination with Wyeth Ayerst DPT adsorbed (TETRAMUNE™)

** Supplied as lyophilized powder that must be reconstituted only with the supplied Merck Frosst diluent

of age should be immunized as soon as possible according to the schedules shown in the Table.

Previously unimmunized children 15 to 59 months of age should be given a single dose of PRP-T, HbOC or PRP-OMP.

Preparation and Route of Administration

Hib conjugate vaccines that are supplied as a lyophilized powder should be reconstituted only with products supplied by the same manufacturer, as recommended in product monographs. Conjugate vaccines should be administered intramuscularly.

Rifampin or other appropriate chemoprophylaxis is not required for household contacts of index cases of invasive Hib infection when the contacts are completely immunized against Hib. Complete immunization is defined as receipt of the primary Hib vaccination series and booster dose as presented in the Table. When contacts < 48 months of age are not completely immunized, consultation with the local public health unit is advised.

Booster Doses and Re-immunization

Protective serum antibody (anti-PRP) concentrations are achieved in 99% of children after completion of the primary PRP-T immunization series of three doses. Antibody levels subsequently decline, and at present a booster dose is given at 15 to 18 months of age with any of the Hib conjugate vaccines approved for use in infants. Recent data from the United Kingdom, however, reveal that vaccine efficacy remains high without the booster dose, despite declining antibody titres. This has led to the conclusion that the 15-18 month booster dose may not be necessary if there is continued high uptake of primary immunization.

For children who have conditions that predispose them to infection with encapsulated bacteria and who have already received the primary Hib immunization series plus booster, it is not known whether additional doses of Hib vaccine are beneficial.

Storage Requirements

Hib conjugate vaccines should be stored at a temperature between $2°$ and $8°$ C and should not be frozen. Vaccines that require reconstitution should be used immediately thereafter.

Simultaneous Administration with Other Vaccines

PRP-T and HbOC may be combined with vaccines produced by other manufacturers. Combined vaccine products allow the administration of multiple antigens with the use of a single needle and have safety profiles similar to those of separately administered vaccines.

Any of the four Hib conjugate vaccines may be given simultaneously with polio, measles, mumps, rubella, hepatitis B, pneumococcal and meningococcal vaccines, but at a different site. There are no data on administration of Hib conjugate vaccines at the same time as influenza vaccine.

Adverse Reactions

A temperature of $> 38.3°$ C has been reported in a minority of infants given Hib conjugate vaccine either alone or in combination with other vaccines. A local reaction at the site of injection, including pain, redness and swelling, occurs in 25% of immunized children. These symptoms are mild and usually resolve within 24 hours. No severe adverse reactions have been noted in clinical trials, although a few temporally associated allergic reactions have been reported in older children receiving the vaccine as part of their routine immunization program.

Contraindications

Immunization is contraindicated for people who are allergic to any component of the vaccine.

Selected References

Anderson EL, Decker MD, Englund JA et al. *Interchangeability of conjugated Haemophilus influenzae type b vaccines in infants.* JAMA 1995;273:849-53.

Committee on Infectious Diseases. *Haemophilus influenzae infections.* In: American Academy of Pediatrics. *Report of the Committee of infectious Diseases (Red Book),* 25th ed. Elk Grove Village, IL: American Academy of Pediatrics, 2000:262-74.

Eskola J. *Analysis of Haemophilus influenzae type b conjugate and diphtheria-tetanus-pertussis combination vaccines.* Infect Dis 1996;174:S302-5.

Friede A, O'Carroll PW, Nicola RM et al, eds. Centers for Disease Control and Prevention. *CDC prevention guidelines. A guide to action.* Baltimore: William and Wilkins, 1997:394-492.

Immunization Monitoring Program, Active (IMPACT) of the Canadian Paediatric Society and the Laboratory Centre for Disease Control. *Recent trends in pediatric Haemophilus influenzae type b infections in Canada.* Can Med Assoc J 1996;154:1041-47.

LCDC. *Canadian national report on immunization, 1996.* CCDR 1997;23S4:13-4.

Scheifele D, Halperin S. *Haemophilus influenzae type B disease control using PENTACEL™, Canada, 1998-1999.* CCDR 2000;26(11):93-6.

Heath PT, Booy R, Slack MPE et al. *Are Hib booster vaccinations redundant?* Lancet 1997;349(9060):1197-202.

Hepatitis A Vaccine

Hepatitis A virus (HAV) is an RNA virus of a single serotype. Infection usually causes clinical hepatitis in adults and school-aged children but is often asymptomatic in younger children. Typical symptoms of illness include anorexia, nausea, fatigue, fever and jaundice. The severity of the illness increases with age. Recovery often takes 4 to 6 weeks but may take months. Recurrent hepatitis for up to a year occurs in about 15% of cases, but longer chronic infection is not known to occur. About 25% of reported adult cases require hospitalization. Fulminant disease with liver necrosis is rare but can be fatal. Individuals with pre-existing chronic liver disease are at increased risk of serious complications from HAV infection. The overall estimated mortality rate associated with hepatitis A is 0.1% to 0.3%, but this rises to 1.8% over the age of 50.

Epidemiology

HAV is transmitted by the fecal-oral route, through direct contact with infected people or indirectly through ingestion of contaminated water or foods, especially uncooked shellfish. The virus may persist for days or weeks in the environment. Shedding of the virus in feces and thus maximum infectiousness occurs during the latter part of the incubation period with peak levels in the 2 weeks before clinical illness. Infectiousness diminishes rapidly thereafter and ends shortly after the onset of jaundice. Although humans are the principal reservoir for HAV, persistent infection does not occur. The incubation period ranges from 15 to 50 days with an average of 20 to 30 days. Lifelong immunity usually follows infection.

In Canada, between 1990 and 1999, the annual number of cases of HAV infection reported to the National Notifiable Disease Registry varied from 890 to 3,020, with corresponding rates from 3.0 to 10.8 per 100,000 population. Given under- reporting and asymptomatic infection, however, the actual number of cases is considerably higher. In 1999, the reported rate was 1.6 times higher among males than females. Age-specific incidence rates were highest among those 25 to 59 years of age and lowest among those < 5 years or > 59 years; 18% of all cases were < 15 years old, an age group in which the disease is often asymptomatic. Although representative data are not available for the general Canadian population, a study in a cohort of women of child-bearing age by the British Columbia Centre for Disease Control shows that age-specific prevalence rates of anti-HAV, indicating past infection, increased consistently from age 15 and 16 (13.5%) to age 40 to 44 (40.6%).

Immunity to HAV infection increases with age. About 3% of children < 13 years old are immune to HAV, as compared with more than 60% of adults > 60. The difference in levels of immunity reflects progressive accumulation of immunity over time and the greater likelihood of exposure in the past, when the infection was more common.

Risk factors for HAV infection in Canada include the following:

- residence in certain communities in rural or remote areas lacking adequate sanitation or a secure supply of potable water;

- residence in certain institutions, such as correctional facilities and those for developmentally challenged individuals;

- oral or intravenous illicit drug use;

- sexual behaviours involving anal contact, particularly between men;

- travel to or residence in countries with inadequate sanitation.

Overall, the most commonly identified risk factor for HAV infection is household or sexual exposure to a recent case. Twenty-five percent of cases have no identifiable risk factor. In Canada, unlike in the U.S., outbreaks of HAV have not occurred in children or staff of child day care facilities in the absence of community outbreaks.

Cases in returned travellers and contacts of travellers, including children, account for a large proportion of reported cases; some cases have occurred in people who spent < 2 weeks in an endemic area. The risk for susceptible travellers to developing countries has been estimated at 3 to 5 cases per 1,000 travellers per month, increasing in people who eat or drink under poor hygienic conditions. Risk also increases in proportion to the relative incidence of HAV in different countries, related possibly to the likelihood of consuming food prepared by an infectious person.

Preparations Licensed for Immunization

Four inactivated monovalent hepatitis A vaccines are licensed in Canada. There is some evidence that these four vaccines may be used interchangeably, despite different schedules and systems of measuring antigen content. Two combined hepatitis A and hepatitis B vaccines, one for adults and one for children, are also licensed in Canada (see the Table and the chapter Hepatitis Vaccines Combined).

In three of the HAV vaccines (Havrix™, Vaqta® and Avaxim®) various strains of cell culture adapted virus are propagated in human fibroblasts, purified from cell lysates, inactivated with formalin and adsorbed to an aluminum hydroxide adjuvant. In the fourth (Epaxal Berna®), immunopotentiating reconstituted influenza virosomes are used as an adjuvant. Complete and detailed descriptions of these vaccines have been published previously in the *Canada Communicable Disease Report*.

Immune globulin (IG) may be used for short-term protection against HAV in infants and in people who are immunocompromised (who may not respond fully to HAV vaccine), and in people for whom HAV vaccine is contraindicated (see Passive Immunizing Agents).

Recommended Doses of Currently Licensed Hepatitis A Vaccine

Vaccine	Antigen*	Volume	Schedule (Booster)	Age**
Avaxim®	160 antigen units HAV	0.5 mL	0, (6-12) months	12 years and older
Avaxim™ Pediatric	80 antigen units HAV	0.5 mL	0, (6-12) months	1 to 15 years
Expaxal Berna®	Minimum 500 radio-immunoassay units HAV	0.5 mL	0, (12) months	1 year and older
Havrix™ 1440	1440 ELISA units HAV	1.0 mL	0, (6-12) months	19 years and older
Havrix™ 720 Junior	720 ELISA units HAV	0.5 mL	0, (6-12) months	1 to 18 years
Twinrix™	720 ELISA units HAV 20 µg HBsAg	1.0 mL	0, 1, 6 months	19 years and older
Twinrix™ Junior	360 ELISA units HAV 10 µg HBsAg	0.5 mL	0, 1, 6 months	1 to 18 years
Vaqta®	50 units HAV	1.0 mL	0, (6-18) months	18 years and older
Vaqta® Pediatric/ Adolescent	25 units HAV	0.5 mL	0, (6-18) months	2 to 17 years

* There is no international standard for HAV antigen measurement. Each manufacturer uses its own units of measurement.

** Ages for which the vaccine is licensed.

Efficacy and Immunogenicity

All the HAV vaccines have shown high levels of immunogenicity and at least 85% to 90% efficacy in preventing clinical illness. Epidemiologic studies of hepatitis A outbreaks have shown repeatedly that the use of vaccine in the susceptible population interrupts the outbreak, suggesting that receipt of vaccine before exposure is almost invariably protective. This conclusion is also supported by an Italian study, in which the use of vaccine in household contacts prevented secondary cases effectively. Protection appears to occur rapidly within 3 weeks after immunization.

In serologic studies of all HAV vaccines, 95% to 100% of individuals consistently developed protective levels of serum antibody against HAV 4 weeks after a single dose of any inactivated hepatitis A vaccine.

Hepatitis A Vaccine

Recommended Usage

Pre-exposure prophylaxis

Hepatitis A vaccine is recommended for pre-exposure prophylaxis of individuals at increased risk of infection. Candidates for the vaccine are

- travellers to countries where hepatitis A is endemic, especially when there is travel to rural locations or places with inadequate sanitary facilities; the risk of acquiring HAV increases with the duration and frequency of travel, but most travel-related cases have occurred in people who spent ≤ 2 weeks in an endemic area;

- residents of communities that have high endemic rates of HAV or are at risk of HAV outbreaks;

- members of the armed forces, emergency relief workers and others likely to be posted abroad at short notice to areas with high rates of HAV infection;

- residents and staff of institutions for the developmentally challenged in which there is evidence of sustained HAV transmission;

- inmates of correctional facilities in which there is evidence of sustained HAV transmission;

- people with life-style risks of infection, including people engaging in oral or intravenous illicit drug use in unsanitary conditions, and males having sexual contact with other males, particularly when there is a likelihood of oral-anal contact;

- people with chronic liver disease who may not be at increased risk of infection but are at increased risk of fulminant hepatitis A, should infection occur;

- people with hemophilia A or B receiving plasma-derived replacement clotting factors; the solvent-detergent method used to prepare all the present plasma-derived factor VIII and some factor IX concentrates does not reliably inactivate HAV, since the virus does not have an envelope;

- zoo-keepers, veterinarians and researchers who handle non-human primates;

- workers involved in research on hepatitis A virus or production of hepatitis A vaccine who may be exposed to HAV;

- any person who wishes to decrease his or her risk of acquiring HAV.

Outside the aforementioned risk groups, the probability of becoming infected in Canada is low.

Post-exposure prophylaxis

HAV vaccine has been shown in one study to be at least as effective as IG for the prevention of HAV. Although more studies of its use in post-exposure prophylaxis are needed to document its effect fully, HAV vaccine used in the first week after exposure appears to be highly effective as a post-exposure measure to prevent infection in identified contacts. It is recommended for this use in preference to IG. Therefore, one dose of HAV vaccine should be given to contacts of HAV within 1 week of exposure. It should also be considered if > 1 week has elapsed since exposure, since there are no data on the outer limit of efficacy.

Post-exposure immunoprophylaxis should be undertaken for household and other intimate contacts of proved or suspected cases of HAV. It should be considered when hepatitis A occurs in day care centres, and especially in those that have diapered children. Post-exposure prophylaxis is not necessary for other contacts, such as school, workplace or health care workers caring for HAV cases unless an outbreak is suspected (see Outbreak Control, next section).

If HAV vaccine is unavailable or unaffordable for post-exposure prophylaxis, IG may be used as a substitute. IG is still the recommended immunoprophylactic agent for infants < 1 year of age, immunocompromised people, who may not respond fully to the vaccine, and those for whom vaccine is contraindicated (see Passive Immunizing Agents for dosages).

Outbreak control

There have been several outbreaks in which HAV vaccine has been used to arrest the transmission of the virus in communities. This observation supports its use in outbreak control. The outbreaks in which the vaccine has been used successfully for this purpose include three Canadian outbreaks — in Kitchener-Waterloo in 1997, in Montreal in 1997-98 and on Vancouver Island in 1995-96 — and a U.S. outbreak in Alaska. In accordance with the data and experience documented in these reports, HAV vaccine should be considered as an important control measure in a coordinated public health response to hepatitis A outbreaks in the community and in institutions.

Universal immunization

Universal immunization programs against HAV are possible because of the availability of safe and effective vaccines. In the United States, programs exist in states in which the incidence of HAV exceeds the national average. The WHO, however, recommends targeted programs for countries with low endemicity, such as Canada. There are several pros and cons of universal hepatitis programs in Canada:

Pros

- the vaccine is highly effective;
- the illness may be moderately severe, and deaths occur; greater numbers of older adults are now susceptible because they are less likely than previous generations to have been exposed as children, and if they do become infected they are more likely than younger people to have severe disease;
- the illness has social and economic costs to those affected;

- more travellers would be immunized before travel to endemic areas, thereby preventing illness after their return and the potential for secondary cases in Canada;

- there would be fewer outbreaks and consequently lower costs for control and intervention;

- targeted programs have not been evaluated and may not be cost-effective, and some of those at risk may be missed in targeted programs.

Cons

- the vaccine is expensive, although competitive pricing may reduce costs;

- the illness has low prevalence in the general population;

- there are significant costs to deliver the vaccine to recipients;

- there are other vaccines competing for public funding;

- public acceptance of a vaccine program for an infection with low incidence may itself be low.

A universal immunization program against HAV should be considered in Canada, but the decision to implement such programs will depend on circumstances in each jurisdiction. Further discussion is needed nationally, possibly through a consensus conference, and cost-benefit analysis should be undertaken before implementation. The establishment of programs would benefit people who may be at risk but who do not seek pre-exposure immunization, such as unimmunized travellers to endemic areas and their close contacts. Although the lifetime risk of HAV changes with time and population cohort and is therefore difficult to quantify, over half of those now > 60 have had this disease. The current lifetime risk is likely to be lower, but may still be significant with increased travel.

People who do not need routine HAV immunization

- Children and staff of child-care facilities. Outbreaks in this type of setting have not been frequently reported in Canada. In addition, serologic testing has not indicated an increased risk of infection for workers or children.

- Health care workers are not considered to be at increased risk if standard infection control techniques can be exercised. Data from serosurveys of health care workers have not shown a greater prevalence of HAV infection in that segment of the population.

- Sewage workers may be at increased risk of infection during community outbreaks, but the data are insufficient to make a recommendation for routine immunization.

- Food handlers may be a source of food-borne outbreaks of hepatitis A but are not themselves at increased risk of infection occupationally. It has not been determined to what extent immunization of such workers would be practical or effective in reducing food-borne outbreaks.

Schedule and Dosage

The dosage schedules for adults and children of the four HAV vaccines are listed in the Table, along with antigen content and volumes of doses.

If the second dose in the hepatitis A vaccine series is missed, it can be given at a later time without the need to repeat the first dose.

Because each of the HAV vaccines licensed in Canada has similar HAV antigen and because each vaccine alone has been shown to induce high levels of protective antibody, it is likely that any HAV vaccine will provide an effective second dose after a different HAV vaccine. Lack of availability of the identical product, therefore, should not be considered an impediment to administering the second dose of HAV vaccine, nor is there a need to repeat the primary dose of vaccine in these circumstances. The timing of the dose in this situation should be based on the vaccine used for that dose.

Route of Administration

Hepatitis A vaccines should be administered intramuscularly.

Booster Doses and Re-immunization

Although the duration of protection and thus the need for additional booster doses after two doses of HAV vaccine is unknown, kinetic models of antibody decline suggest that protective levels of antibody will likely persist for at least 20 years. Should future study indicate the need for booster doses, recommendations will be made at that time.

Serologic Testing

Pre-immunization

Some studies have indicated that pre-immunization serologic testing is only cost-effective in populations that have a significant level of immunity. Variations in the cost of testing and vaccine will affect these analyses and the specific level of population immunity at which testing will become cost-effective. Nevertheless, pre-immunization testing for immunity against HAV should be considered in populations with the potential for higher levels of pre-existing immunity. Older Canadians and people from HAV endemic areas of the world are examples of these populations. In addition, people with a history of hepatitis or jaundice that may have been caused by HAV should be considered for assessment of immunity before immunization is undertaken.

Post-immunization

The high response rate to immunization makes routine serologic testing afterwards unnecessary. Moreover, commercial assay kits are not universally reliable for detecting vaccine-induced antibody.

Storage Requirements

Hepatitis A vaccine should be stored at a temperature between 2° C and 8° C and should not be frozen. Opened vials of Vaqta® should be used promptly since they contain no preservative.

Simultaneous Administration with other Vaccines

Concomitant administration of other vaccines at other injection sites is unlikely to interfere with the immune response to HAV vaccine. There have been studies on concomitant administration of some of the HAV vaccines with various other vaccines, such as yellow fever, typhoid and cholera, which demonstrated no immune interference; however, complete data on all HAV vaccines are not available.

Combined vaccines against hepatitis A and B are licensed in Canada for adults and children (see the Table). Clinical trials have not demonstrated any increase in side effects or clinically significant reduction in protection against either infection — rather, there is possibly increased efficacy — when the combined vaccine is used.

Adverse Reactions

Side effects reported in vaccine recipients are generally mild and transient, and limited to soreness and redness at the injection site. Other less frequent side effects include headache, malaise, fever, fatigue, and gastrointestinal symptoms. Local side effects in children appear to be less frequent than in adults. No significant difference in reactions is evident between initial and subsequent doses or in the presence of pre-existing immunity. Rare cases of anaphylaxis have been reported.

Contraindications

HAV vaccine should not be given to any person who has had an anaphylactic reaction to any component of the vaccine preparation. Since each HAV vaccine has different components, it is important to ascertain the specific cause of previous anaphylaxis, if possible, and refer to the manufacturer's description of the vaccine.

Precautions

The safety of HAV vaccine given during pregnancy has not been studied in clinical trials. Since the vaccine is prepared from inactivated virus, however, the risk to the developing fetus is likely to be negligible. Therefore, HAV vaccine may be given to pregnant women when indicated. HAV vaccine can be used safely in breast-feeding women.

HAV vaccine can also be used safely in those with chronic illnesses or immunosuppression. Although the efficacy of HAV vaccine may be reduced in those who are immunosuppressed, the vaccine still provides some protection against HAV in these populations and should be considered for pre-exposure use when there is an

indication for the vaccine. IG is still recommended for the immunosuppressed for post- exposure immunoprophylaxis.

Selected References

Bryan JP, Henry CH, Hoffman AG et al. *Randomized, cross-over, controlled comparison of two inactivated hepatitis A vaccines.* Vaccine 2001;19:743-50.

De Serres G, Laliberte D. *Hepatitis A among workers from a waste water treatment plant during a small community outbreak.* Occup Environ Med 1997;54:60-2.

Deshaies MD, Dion R, Valiquette L et al. *Immunization against hepatitis A during an outbreak in a Jewish orthodox community Quebec 1997-1998.* CCDR 1998;24:145-51.

Dumas R, Forrat R, Lang J et al. *Safety and immunogenicity of a new inactivated hepatitis A vaccine in concurrent administration with a typhoid fever or a typhoid fever and yellow fever vaccine.* Adv Ther 1997;14(4):160-67.

Hockin J, Isaacs S, Kittle D et al. *Hepatitis A outbreak in a socially contained religious community in rural southern Ontario.* CCDR 1997;23:161-66.

McMahon BJ, Beller M, Williams J et al. *A programme to control an outbreak of HAV in Alaska by using an inactivated hepatitis A vaccine.* Arch Pediatr Adolesc Med 1996;150:733-39.

National Advisory Committee on Immunization. *Supplementary statement on hepatitis A vaccine.* CCDR 2000;26(ACS-4, ACS-5):12-19.

National Advisory Committee on Immunization. *Statement on combination vaccines against hepatitis A and hepatitis B.* CCDR 1999;25(ACS-3):1-2.

National Advisory Committee on Immunization. *Supplementary statement on hepatitis prevention – hepatitis A and hepatitis B combination vaccine for children.* CCDR 1999;25:(ACS-4):3-4.

National Advisory Committee on Immunization. *Supplementary statement on hepatitis prevention.* CCDR 1997;23 (ACS-4):1-3.

National Advisory Committee on Immunization. *Supplementary statement on hepatitis A prevention.* CCDR 1996;22:1-3.

National Advisory Committee on Immunization. *Statement on the prevention of hepatitis A infections.* CCDR 1994;20:133-36, 139-43.

Poovorawan Y, Tieamboonlers A, Chumdermpadetsuk S et al. *Control of a hepatitis A outbreak by active immunisation of high-risk susceptibles.* J Infect Dis 1994;169:228-29.

Prikazsky V, Olear V, Cernoch A et al. *Interruption of an outbreak of hepatitis A in two villages by vaccination.* J Med Virol 1994;44:457-59.

Sagliocca L, Amoroso P, Stroffolini T et al. *Efficacy of hepatitis A vaccine in prevention of secondary hepatitis A infection: a randomised trial.* Lancet 1999;353(9159):1136-39.

Vento S, Garofano T, Renzini C et al. *Fulminant hepatitis associated with hepatitis A virus superinfection in patients with chronic hepatitis.* N Engl J Med 1998;388:286-90.

Werzberger A, Kuter B, Shouval D et al. *Anatomy of a trial: a historical view of the Monroe inactivated hepatitis A protective efficacy trial.* J Hepatol 1993;18(Suppl. 2):S46-S50.

Wu J, Zou S, Giulivi A. *Hepatitis A and its control.* In: Bloodborne Pathogens Division, Health Canada. *Viral hepatitis and emerging bloodborne pathogens in Canada.* CCDR 2001;27S3:7-9.

Hepatitis B Vaccine

Hepatitis B virus (HBV) is one of several viruses that cause hepatitis. HBV is a double stranded DNA virus with three major antigens, known as hepatitis B surface antigen (HBsAg), hepatitis B e antigen (HBeAg), and hepatitis B core antigen (HBcAg). HBsAg can be detected in serum 30 to 60 days after exposure and persists until the infection resolves. Any person positive for HBsAg is considered infectious. In most cases, anti-HBs appears after the infection has resolved and confers long-term immunity, although in a proportion, which varies inversely with age, infection persists and this protective antibody is not produced.

HBcAg never appears in serum. Anti-HBc develops in all HBV infections, is not protective and persists indefinitely as a marker of infection. Anti-HBc IgM is a marker of recent HBV infection. HBeAg is associated with viral replication and high infectiousness. Anti-HBe indicates loss of replicating virus and lower infectiousness. Recently, methods of quantification of HBV DNA in serum have become available to assist in determining both infectiousness and prognosis.

Initial infection with HBV may be asymptomatic in up to 50% of adults and 90% of children. When symptoms occur, they include an insidious onset of anorexia, vague abdominal pain, nausea, vomiting and jaundice. Acute illness may last up to 3 months and has a case fatality rate of 1% to 2%, which increases with age. Fulminant hepatitis and death may also occur in pregnant women and in infants born to infected mothers.

An individual with either acute symptomatic or asymptomatic HBV infection may become a chronic carrier. A chronic carrier is an individual from whom serum samples taken 6 months apart are HBsAg positive or a single serum sample is HBsAg positive and anti-HBc IgM negative. The risk of becoming a chronic carrier varies inversely with the age at which infection occurs (infants: 90% to 95%; children < 5 years: 25% to 50%; adults: 6% to 10%). The risk of becoming a chronic carrier is also greater in immunocompromised patients. Chronic carriers often do not have overt disease but over time are at increased risk of developing hepatic cirrhosis and hepatocellular carcinoma. Chronic carriers are likely the major source of infection, and all carriers should be considered infectious.

Epidemiology

HBV infection is usually associated with exposure to infected blood or other bodily fluids. Common means of transmission include sexual contact, injection drug use and perinatal transmission. The risk of transfusion-related hepatitis B is extremely low because of routine HBsAg screening of donated blood and rejection of donors at risk of infection. Infections also occur in settings of close personal contact through unrecognized contact with infectious bodily fluids. The incubation period for hepatitis B is 45 to 160 days, with an average of 120 days.

Although there are no national data on the prevalence of chronic HBV infection for the whole Canadian population, Canada is considered an area of low endemicity. It is

estimated that < 5% of residents have markers of past infection and < 1% are HBsAg carriers. There are, however, specific segments of the population that are at increased risk of HBV infection and consequently have a higher prevalence of infection. These segments include populations with

- life-style risk factors, such as sexual contact between males, and injection drug use;

- geographic risk factors, including infection acquired in certain parts of the world where the prevalence of HBV is higher than in Canada, and in some native populations;

- occupational risk factors, such as health care workers' frequent exposure to blood.

In some of these populations, such as health care workers, the risk of infection has been reduced with the use of HBV vaccine.

The interpretation of HBV incidence rates in Canada has been confounded by inconsistencies in reporting acute versus chronic infections. According to data from the National Enhanced Sentinel Surveillance in 1998-1999, the overall incidence rate of clinically recognized acute hepatitis B has been estimated to be 2.3 per 100,000. The rate is higher among males (3.0 per 100,000) than females (1.5 per 100,000). The age-specific rates are low for people < 15 years of age, rising rapidly to a peak for those 30 to 39 years (6.1 per 100,000) followed by those aged 15-29 (2.7 per 100,000) and 40-59 (1.8 per 100,000), and then declining to low rates for people > 59 years of age. Injection drug use accounts for 34% of acute HBV cases, multiple sexual partners for 24% and sex with HBV-infected individuals for 12%. In Canada, as in other countries, almost a third of infections have no identified risk factors.

Preparations Licensed for Immunization

Two monovalent recombinant DNA hepatitis B vaccines are licensed in Canada: Recombivax HB™ and Engerix-B™. Both vaccines contain purified HBsAg produced from a genetically engineered yeast strain. Recombivax HB™ vaccine contains 10 µg/mL and Engerix B™ vaccine 20 µg/mL of purified HBsAg. A preparation of Recombivax HB™ containing 40 µg/mL is available for use in hemodialysis patients and others in whom hyporesponsiveness is likely. Trace amounts of yeast antigens are present in the vaccines, but no increase in yeast antibody titres has been observed following administration of either vaccine.

For hepatitis B vaccine, the required dose in micrograms should be established and that dose administered using any appropriate formulation (see the Table and the section Schedule and Dosage).

In most preparations, the antigen is adsorbed onto aluminum hydroxide with thimerosal as preservative. A preparation of Recombivax HB™ is available without thimerosal and contains 5 µg of HBsAg in 0.5 mL. It is recommended for the immunization of infants. If thimerosal-free vaccine is not available, post-exposure immunoprophylaxis for infants born to infected mothers should still be undertaken without delay, because of the high risk of long-term complications if infection

Doses and Schedules for Hepatitis B Vaccines Pre-exposure Usage

Recipients	Recombivax Hb™			Engerix-B™		
	μg	mL	Schedule (months)	μg	mL	Schedule (months)
Infants of HBV-negative mothers or children <11*	2.5	0.25	0, 1, >2	10	0.5	0, 1, 6 or 0, 1, 2, 12
Children 11 to 15	10	1.0	0, 4-6	N/A	N/A	N/A
Children 11 to 19	5	0.5	0, 1, >2	10†	0.5	0, 1, 6 or 0, 1, 2, 12
Adults	10	1.0	0, 1, >2	20	1.0	0, 1, 6 or 0, 1, 2, 12 or 7, 14, 21 and 365 days
Adults who may be hyporesponsive	40	1.0‡ or 2.0‡	0, 1, 6	40	2.0	0, 1, 2, 6

Children who may be hyporesponsive: double the μg dose for the age and use the three or four dose schedule only.

* The thimerosal free preparation is recommended. For the post-exposure schedule for children of HBV infected mothers, please refer to the Figure and the text section on post-exposure prophylaxis.

† The manufacturer recommends the standard adult dosage (20 μg, 1.0 mL) if it is unlikely that there will be compliance with this schedule.

‡ 1.0 mL of the dialysis formulation, 2.0 mL of the standard formulation.

occurs. With regard to other indications for immunization in infants, immunization should be deferred until 2 months of age unless a thimerosal-free vaccine is used. As this vaccine becomes more available and sufficient supplies for neonates are assured, it should become the vaccine preparation of choice against hepatitis B.

Hepatitis B vaccines induce anti-HBs production, which confers immunity to hepatitis B. A protective level of anti-HBs is 10 international units per litre. Antigenic subtypes of HBV exist, but immunization confers immunity to all subtypes because of the presence of a common antigen. Hepatitis B vaccines are licensed in Canada for pre-exposure and post-exposure prophylaxis.

Plasma-derived hepatitis B vaccine has not been available in Canada since the early 1990s.

Hepatitis B immune globulin (HBIG) is prepared from pooled human plasma from selected donors who have a high level of anti-HBs and are seronegative for bloodborne infections. It provides immediate short-term passive immunity. HBIG administered concurrently with vaccine, but at a different site, does not interfere with the antibody response of the vaccine.

Formulations combining antigen against both HAV and HBV are also licensed in Canada for adults and children (see Hepatitis Vaccines Combined).

Efficacy and Immunogenicity

Use of the recommended schedule and routes of immunization results in seroconversion rates of 90% to 99% in immunocompetent individuals, depending on age. The antibody response is lower in patients with diabetes mellitus (70% to 80%), renal failure (60% to 70%) and chronic liver disease (60% to 70%) as well as in immunocompromised patients, such as those infected with HIV (50% to 70%). Immunization of obese people, smokers and those with alcoholism also produces lower antibody titres.

Antibody response in general decreases with age. Children between age 2 and 19 years have the highest response rate (99%), and children < 2 have a 95% response rate. The response rate for older individuals is as follows: 20 to 29: 95%; 30 to 39: 90%; 40 to 49: 86%; 50 to 59: 71%; and > 60: 50% to 70%. The immune mechanisms for suboptimal response to hepatitis B vaccine are not well understood.

Studies in areas of the world where HBV is endemic have consistently shown decreases in HBV incidence when hepatitis B vaccine is used in infant immunization programs. These studies also show persistence of protection until at least age 5, the highest risk period of transmission from infected mother to child. As well, hepatitis B vaccine reduces the incidence of hepatocellular carcinoma and liver cirrhosis by preventing chronic HBV carriage.

Recommended Usage

Hepatitis B prevention should include programs for universal immunization of children, universal screening of all pregnant women for HBsAg, pre-exposure immunization of high-risk groups, and post-exposure intervention for those exposed to disease, particularly infants born to HBV infected mothers.

Universal immunization

Universal immunization against HBV is now part of the publicly funded vaccine programs offered in all provinces and territories. The age at which children and adolescents are offered hepatitis B vaccine varies from jurisdiction to jurisdiction. Should effective combination vaccines, including hepatitis B and other childhood vaccines, become available in Canada for infants, NACI would support their use.

If childhood immunization against HBV is given in infancy, the level and duration of protection may be better if the last dose is given after the first birthday. Because of the possibility of persistence of maternal antibody, an unimmunized child who is positive for either anti-HBs or anti-HBc should still receive hepatitis B vaccine.

Pre-exposure prophylaxis

Health care and emergency service workers and other occupational exposure

Immunization with hepatitis B vaccine is recommended for those people who are at increased risk of occupational infection, namely, those exposed frequently to blood, blood products and bodily fluids that may contain the virus. This group includes all health care workers and others who will be or may be exposed to blood or are at risk of injury by instruments contaminated by blood. For these workers, a series of hepatitis B immunizations should be initiated at the first opportunity. Students in these occupations should complete their vaccine series before possible occupational exposure to blood or sharps injuries. Emergency service workers, such as police and firefighters, may also be at higher risk of exposure, although there are currently no data to quantify their risk. Workers who have no contact with blood or blood products are at no greater risk than the general population.

Others at increased risk

- residents and staff of institutions for the developmentally challenged;
- males having sexual contact with other males;
- others with multiple sexual partners or with a recent history of a sexually transmitted disease;
- injection drug users;
- hemophiliacs and others receiving repeated infusions of blood or blood products;
- hemodialysis patients (40 µg of vaccine antigen per dose should be used);
- staff and inmates of long-term correctional facilities;
- household and sexual contacts of acute HBV cases and HBV carriers;
- populations or communities in which HBV is highly endemic;
- children < 7 years of age whose families have immigrated to Canada from areas where there is a high prevalence of hepatitis B and who may be exposed to HBV carriers through their extended families;
- travellers to hepatitis B endemic areas;
- children in child care settings in which there is an HBV infected child;
- any person who wishes to decrease his or her risk of acquiring HBV.

Post-exposure prophylaxis

Infants

Because of the importance of preventing hepatitis B infection in infants, all pregnant women should be routinely tested for HBsAg. All infants born to infected mothers should be given the initial dose of HBV vaccine within 12 hours of birth. The second and third dose of the vaccine series should be given 1 and 6 months after the first. An intramuscular dose of 0.5 mL HBIG should also be given immediately after birth, since its efficacy decreases sharply after 48 hours. Vaccine and HBIG may be given at the same time but at different sites. If exceptional circumstances prevent immediate administration of vaccine and HBIG, they should be given at the first possible opportunity. Their administration, however, should never be delayed unnecessarily.

Neonates weighing less than 2000 g born to infected mothers should have an individualized schedule that includes at least four doses of vaccine, HBIG and assessment of antibody response after the series has been completed.

If maternal testing has not been done during pregnancy, it should be done on an urgent basis at the time of delivery. If maternal HBV status is not available within 12 hours of delivery, serious consideration should be given to administering vaccine and HBIG while the results are pending, *taking into account the mother's risk factors* and erring on the side of providing vaccine and HBIG if there is any suspicion that the mother could be infected. If the mother is ultimately shown to have HBV infection, a series of vaccine should also be given to the infant, as described earlier. Should the mother's infection be recognized during lactation, the infant's HBV status should be assessed urgently and the infant started immediately on full immunoprophylaxis, which should be completed if the infant is found not to be already infected or immune.

When a mother is infected with HBV, testing of the infant for HBsAg and anti-HBs is recommended 1 month after completion of the vaccine series to monitor the success of immunoprophylaxis. If HBsAg is found, the child is likely to become a chronic carrier. If the infant is negative for both HBsAg and anti-HBs (i.e., a non-responder), additional doses up to a second full course of vaccine should be given, with repeated serologic testing for antibody response.

Accountability mechanisms should be in place to ensure that every infant born to an infected mother receives a full course of vaccine and HBIG expeditiously as well as testing for serologic response to the vaccine (see Serologic Testing).

Percutaneous (needlestick) or mucosal exposure

Figures 1 and 2 outline the management of vaccinated or unvaccinated individuals after potential exposure to hepatitis B, including injury by needles found on the street. The management of potential percutaneous or mucosal exposure to HBV should be based on the immunization and antibody status of the injured person and the infectious status, if known, of the source. It is critically important to ascertain whether the exposed individual has received a full and properly administered course of hepatitis B vaccine and to assess the post-vaccination anti-HBs antibody level. Therefore, all health care workers and health care students should have their antibody status assessed and documented after immunization.

– Figure 1* –
Infected (HBsAg +) or High Risk Source[1]

Hepatitis B Vaccine

1. A known source is high risk if the person comes from a highly endemic region for HBV, has a partner infected with HBV or at high risk of being so, is in close family contact with an infected person, uses injection drugs, or received blood or blood products prior to 1970. Wherever possible, the source should be tested. In the case of an unknown source, background circumstances may provide some indication of the degree of risk, e.g. syringe found in the street, attendance at an STD, detoxification or well baby clinic.

2. Responder known to have ≥ 10 IU/L anti-HBs. No measures are required if the person has developed an immunity following an infection.

3. Anti-HBs titre should be determined as soon as possible to avoid needless administration of HBIG and because efficacy is unknown if given after 7 days.

4. The administration of HBIG can be omitted if the high risk source can be tested within 48 hours and the result is negative. In that case, the non-infected source algorithm is followed.

5. The second dose of HBIG should be given 1 month after the first.

6. This test does not change the continuation of vaccination, but may reassure the exposed individual about the immediate risk of becoming infected.

7. If it is possible to quickly obtain anti-HBs titre confirming ≥10 IU/L, administration of HBIG should be omitted.

8. Determination of anti-HBs titre should be delayed for 6 months to allow HBIG antibodies to wane.

9. Test for anti-HBs 1 to 6 months after the course of vaccine.

• **This figure has been adapted from *Protocole d'immunisation du Québec*, 3ᵉ édition, 1999, and published with the kind permission of the Ministère de la santé et des services sociaux.**

– Figure 2* –
Uninfected Source (HBsAg –) or at Low Risk

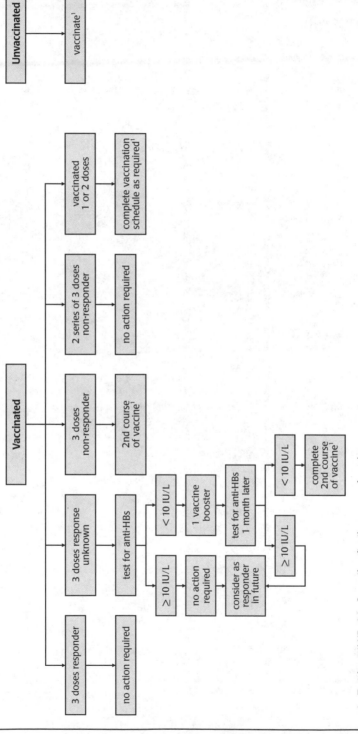

1. Test for anti-HBs 1 to 6 months after the course of vaccine.

* **This figure has been adapted from *Protocole d'immunisation du Québec*, 3e édition, 1999, and published with the kind permission of the Ministère de la santé et des services sociaux.**

Testing of the source should be conducted according to Health Canada guidelines (CCDR 1997;23S2) with informed consent and respect for confidentiality. If the assessment results of the injured person and the source are not available within 48 hours, management of the injured person should assume possible exposure.

Sexual and household contacts of hepatitis B

All sexual and household contacts of acute cases and chronic carriers should be immunized with hepatitis B vaccine. If prophylaxis can be started within 14 days of the last sexual contact with the HBV infected person, a single dose of HBIG (0.06 mL/kg) should also be given. Unimmunized sexual assault victims should be managed in the same manner if the assailant is infected with HBV or cannot be assessed.

All sexual partners of people with HBV infection should be counselled that protection from infection cannot be ensured until the course of vaccine has been completed and protective levels of anti-HBS demonstrated. Counselling on the use of condoms and their ability to reduce but not eliminate the risk of transmission should be completed.

HBIG is not indicated for household contacts of an acute HBV case; exceptions are infants < 12 months of age when the mother or primary care giver is acutely or chronically infected, sexual contacts as described above, and people with identifiable exposure to the infected person's blood, as occasioned by shared toothbrushes or razors.

People who do not routinely require hepatitis B vaccine

- Social contacts of HBV cases and carriers who do not live in the same household and are not sexual contacts
- Workers whose jobs do not normally involve exposure to infectious blood, bodily fluids or items potentially contaminated with HBV

Schedule and Dosage

A variety of schedules that provide long-term protection and are used in Canada and throughout the world are valid for any potential vaccine recipient. The standard recommended schedule for hepatitis B vaccine is three doses given at 0, 1 and > 2 months. If the vaccine is given in a more condensed schedule, earlier protection will be provided. Engerix-B™ may be used in a rapid schedule at 7, 14, 21 and 365 days.

The last dose should be given as closely as possible to 12 months after the first, since there is evidence that the antibody response will be greater and more durable. There is no benefit in giving the last dose later than 12 months after the first, with the possible exception of infants. If Engerix-B™ is used at 0, 1 and 2 months, the manufacturer recommends a fourth dose at 12 months.

Recombivax HB™ has been licensed for a two-dose schedule in 11 to 15 year olds, using the adult formulation of 10 µg at 0 and 4-6 months.

For infants born to HBsAg infected mothers, for those who may have a diminished response to the vaccine and for the two-dose adolescent schedule, the timing of doses should be carefully respected.

Vaccines produced by different manufacturers can be used interchangeably when three or more doses are given, despite different levels of antigen. The dosage used should be that recommended by the manufacturer. The exception to interchangeability is the two-dose adolescent schedule.

Interruption of the immunization schedule does not require that any dose be repeated if the minimum intervals between doses are respected. If any dose has not been given according to an approved schedule, it should be given at the first opportunity. If years have elapsed between the first and second dose, it may be prudent to assess antibody response when the series is complete, especially if the patient is at significant risk of infection.

The dose of vaccine administered varies with age, the product used and with some medical conditions. In general, higher doses of antigen, more frequent doses and a greater number of total doses may assist in improving the antibody response in people likely to respond poorly. Doses of 40 µg are recommended for adult hemodialysis patients and others listed in Recommended Usage in whom response may be less than optimal. A specific formulation for dialysis patients and others is available (Recombivax HB™), which contains 40 µg per mL, to be given at 0, 1 and 6 months. When the required dose is achieved using two adult vials of Engerix B™ (20 µg per mL each), the manufacturer recommends a series of four immunizations at 0, 1, 2 and 6 months. If patients will be at continued risk of exposure to HBV, post-immunization testing should be carried out to assess antibody levels and additional doses of vaccine given to those not adequately protected.

For children undergoing hemodialysis, the common practice is to double the dose for the child's age and assess the antibody response when the series is complete.

Route of Vaccine Administration

All hepatitis B vaccine should be injected into the deltoid muscle of children and adults, and into the anterolateral thigh muscle of infants. Gluteal administration should not be used because of poor immune response, possibly the result of inadvertent deposition into fatty tissue. Vaccine administered that has been frozen or inadequately mixed has also led to poor antibody responses and should not be used.

Immune responses following intradermal injection have been variable, and this route of vaccine administration is not recommended.

Booster Doses and Re-immunization

Routine boosters in immunocompetent people are not needed since protection has been shown to last for at least 15 years. In addition, people who have had protective antibody level previously demonstrated will not develop markers of infection when exposed to HBV, whether or not antibody has waned. This observation is likely due to an anamnestic response to HBV challenge. Thus, absence of detectable anti-HBs in a person who has been previously demonstrated to have anti-HBs does not mean lack of protection, because immune memory persists. Booster doses in this situation are not indicated. Studies of long-term protective efficacy, however, will determine whether booster doses of vaccine are ever needed.

Additional doses of vaccine up to three doses will produce a protective antibody response in 50% to 70% of otherwise healthy people who fail to mount a response after the first series of vaccines. Administration of additional doses with testing for response after each dose should be undertaken when the response to vaccine needs to be ensured. Individuals who fail to respond to three additional doses of vaccine are unlikely to benefit from further immunization.

Immunocompromised people often respond suboptimally to the vaccine and may need additional antigen to mount a response. Should protection be achieved and then wane, however, subsequent HBV exposure in these individuals can result in acute disease or the carrier state. Therefore, in this population boosters may be necessary for those who have mounted an initial response. The optimal timing of booster doses for immunocompromised individuals *who are at continued risk of HBV exposure and have mounted an initial response* is not known. Periodic monitoring for the presence of anti-HBs should be considered, taking into account the severity of the compromised state and whether the risk for HBV is still present. Should antibody testing show subsequent suboptimal protection, a booster dose and re-testing should be undertaken as necessary.

Serologic Testing for Hepatitis B Antigen and Antibody

Pre-immunization

Pregnancy

All pregnant women should be routinely tested for HBsAg at the first prenatal visit. If testing has not been done during pregnancy, it should be done at the time of delivery. A pregnant woman who has no markers of acute or chronic HBV infection but who is at high risk of acquiring HBV should be offered the vaccine at the first opportunity and tested for antibody response. Repeat testing before delivery may be considered in uninfected and unimmunized women with continuing high-risk behaviour. Infants born to HBsAg positive mothers should receive post-exposure prophylaxis.

Adopted children at high risk

Children adopted from countries, geographic regions or family situations in which there is a high prevalence of HBV infection should be screened for HBsAg, and if they are positive the household contacts should be immunized before adoption.

Others at high risk for HBV infection

Routine pre-immunization serologic testing for hepatitis B, including HBsAg, anti-HBs or anti-HBc, is recommended for people at high risk of having been infected. This testing will identify those already infected or immune, for whom vaccine will confer no benefit. Testing will also assist in the medical management and contact follow-up of those individuals found to be already infected, and will prevent the mistaken belief that they pose no risk to others. The cost of such testing may or may not be less than the cost of immunization, depending on the HBV prevalence in the high-risk population. Routine pre-immunization serologic screening, however, is not practical for universal immunization programs.

Post-immunization

The seroconversion rate in healthy people is usually 90% or more, and in children 98% or more. Thus, post-immunization testing for universal programs is not necessary.

Post-immunization testing is recommended, however, if it is important to ensure protection against a continual known or repeated potential exposure to hepatitis B. People included in these circumstances are infants born to infected mothers, sexual partners and household contacts of chronic carriers, and those who have been immunized because of occupational exposure. If anti-HBs is shown not to be protective, re-immunization should be conducted as described above (see Boosters and Re-immunization).

In particular, post-immunization testing for anti-HBs should be conducted on all health care workers and students in health care disciplines to establish antibody response and the need for re-immunization should the first course of vaccine fail to provide protection. Ideally, testing should be undertaken at least 1 month but no later than 6 months after the last dose of vaccine. If a health care worker has completed immunization against HBV more than 6 months previously, testing for anti-HBs should still be done as part of the routine occupational health assessment or when a potential exposure occurs (see Figure 1). This type of routine assessment will be even more important as new professionals, immunized as adolescents, begin their training.

The results of post-immunization testing should be recorded in the individual's medical file and provided to the tested person. If protective antibody is documented, testing need not be repeated nor should further immunization be undertaken, even when a definite exposure occurs. If a health care worker never before tested is found not to have protective antibody, re-immunization with a second course of vaccine is indicated. If testing is done beyond the recommended 6-month window, a negative test may indicate primary vaccine failure or waning antibody but with an anamnestic response to challenge with virus or vaccine. In either case, re-immunization is indicated, as it is impossible to differentiate between these two possibilities.

Testing for protective levels of anti-HBs after each dose of a second series may eliminate the need for further doses, once a protective level has been achieved.

Determination of antibody response *after re-immunization is complete* will identify those who do not respond to two courses of vaccine and who will need passive immunization after potential exposure to hepatitis B.

In addition, those who are immunocompromised should also be tested after the vaccine course is complete. If protective antibody is not present, the vaccine course should be repeated, and if protective antibody is still not present, the individual should receive counselling on alternative risk reduction measures. If an antibody response ultimately occurs in an immunocompromised person, periodic reassessment of antibody and booster doses may be indicated, as noted above.

Storage Requirements

Hepatitis B vaccine should be stored at a temperature between $2°$ C and $8°$ C and should not be frozen.

Simultaneous Administration with Other Vaccines

Hepatitis B vaccine may be administered simultaneously with other vaccines at different sites. A separate needle and syringe should be used for each vaccine.

Adverse Reactions

Hepatitis B vaccines are well tolerated and safe to administer to adults and children. Reported side effects are usually mild, transient and generally limited to soreness at the injection site and temperature no greater than $37.7°$ C. Pain occurs no more frequently, however, than with placebo.

As with all vaccines, anaphylaxis is very rare but can occur. Cases of rheumatoid arthritis and demyelinating diseases of the central nervous system have been reported rarely, but a causative link to hepatitis B vaccine has not been identified despite exhaustive and ongoing research. It is likely that any temporal association is coincidental.

Adverse reactions have not been observed when hepatitis B vaccines have been given to people who are immune to hepatitis B or who are hepatitis B carriers.

Contraindications

The only contraindication to hepatitis B vaccine is a previous anaphlyactic reaction to any component of the vaccine.

Precautions

Hepatitis B vaccine can be used safely in pregnancy and during breast-feeding for women in whom immunization is recommended. Since acute hepatitis B in a pregnant woman may result in severe disease for the mother and chronic infection of the infant, it should not be withheld when indicated. Although data are not available on the safety of these vaccines for the fetus, the risk is expected to be negligible since the vaccines consist of noninfectious subunits.

Selected References

Ascherio A, Zhang SM, Hernan MA et al. *Hepatitis B vaccination and the risk of multiple sclerosis.* N Engl J Med 2001;344:327-32.

Banatvala J, VanDamme P, Oehen S et al. *Lifelong protection against hepatitis B: the role of vaccine immunogenicity in immune memory.* Vaccine 2001;19:877-85.

Belloni C, Pistorio A, Tinelli C et al. *Early immunisation with hepatitis B vaccine: a five-year study.* Vaccine 2000;18:1307-11.

Confavreau C, Suissa S, Saddier P et al. *Vaccinations and the risk of relapse of multiple sclerosis.* N Engl J Med 2001;344:319-26.

Duval B, Boulianne G, De Serres G. *Should children with isolated anti-HBs or anti-HBc be immunized against hepatitis B virus?* JAMA 1997;287:1064.

Health Canada. *An integrated protocol to manage health care workers exposed to bloodborne pathogens.* CCDR 1997;23S2.

Health Canada. *Proceedings of the Consensus Conference on Infected Health Care Workers: Risk for Transmission of Bloodborne Pathogens.* CCDR 1998;24S4.

Monteyne P, Andre F. *Is there a causal link between hepatitis B vaccine and multiple sclerosis?* Vaccine 2000;18:1994-2001.

Salisbury D, Begg, N. *Immunisation against infectious disease.* HMSO 1996.

Watson B, West DJ, Chilkatowsky A et al. *Persistence of immunologic memory for 13 years in recipients of a recombinant hepatitis B vaccine.* Vaccine. 2001;19:3164-68.

Zhang J, Zou S, Giulivi A. *Hepatitis B in Canada.* CCDR 2001;27S3:10-12.

Zou S, Zhang J, Tepper M et al. *Enhanced surveillance of acute hepatitis B and acute hepatitis C in four health regions in Canada 1998-1999.* Can J Infect Dis 2001;12(6):357-63.

Hepatitis Vaccines Combined

There are now vaccine formulations for adults and children that protect against both hepatitis A and hepatitis B.

Preparations Licensed for Immunization

Bivalent vaccine for adults (Twinrix™) and a reduced dose format for children aged 1 to 18 (Twinrix Junior™) are licensed for protection against both hepatitis A and hepatitis B. Each Twinrix™ dose contains 20 μg of purified hepatitis B surface antigen (HbsAg) protein and 720 ELISA units of inactivated hepatitis A viral antigen (HM 175 strain) in 1 mL. Twinrix Junior™ contains 10 μg of purified HBsAg and 360 ELISA units of inactivated hepatitis A antigen in 0.5 mL. These vaccines are made from the same bulk vaccines as are used in the monovalent formulations.

Efficacy and Immunogenicity

All recipients show protective antibody against hepatitis A and close to 100% against hepatitis B 1 month after the third dose. If both vaccines are required, there is no reduction and possibly even an increase in protective antibody when the combined vaccine is used. Refer to the hepatitis chapters for additional information on the efficacy of the two monovalent vaccines.

Recommended Usage

Bivalent hepatitis vaccine is the preferred vaccine for people with indications for immunization against both hepatitis A and hepatitis B. People who should be considered for bivalent hepatitis vaccine are as follows:

- travellers to certain areas of Africa, Asia and the Americas where both hepatitis A and hepatitis B are endemic;

- users of illicit drugs, taken both orally and by injection;

- males who have sexual contact with other males;

- hemophiliacs receiving plasma-derived replacement clotting factors;

- populations and communities in which both hepatitis A and hepatitis B are endemic;

- people who have previously received hepatitis A vaccine and hepatitis B vaccine, and who require additional doses of both;

- people with clinically significant chronic liver disease, including chronic hepatitis due to hepatitis C virus.

There are also situations in which different indications may apply for the two vaccine components. Under these circumstances, bivalent vaccine is an efficient way to protect against both diseases. Examples include

- children who are scheduled to receive hepatitis B vaccine routinely in a universal program and who also have an indication for hepatitis A vaccine;

- inmates who have not already received hepatitis B vaccine and who are in a prison in which there is uncontrolled transmission of hepatitis A.

Monovalent vaccine should be used when protection against only one of these diseases is required.

Schedule and Dosage

The recommended schedule for Twinrix™ formulations is 0, 1, and 6 months. The dose for Twinrix™ is 1.0 mL and for Twinrix Junior™ 0.5 mL.

Route of Administration

Combined hepatitis vaccines should be given intramuscularly.

Booster Doses

Booster doses are not needed for individuals who have completed a course of Twinrix™ or its equivalent in the form of monovalent hepatitis vaccine.

Storage Requirements

Twinrix™ should be stored at a temperature between 2° C and 8° C and should not be frozen.

Simultaneous Administration with Other Vaccines

Either monovalent vaccine may be given at the same time as other vaccines but at different sites using separate needles and syringes. It may be assumed that the same is true when the bivalent vaccines are used.

Adverse Reactions

There is no increase in adverse events when combined vaccine is compared with monovalent vaccine. For further information, please refer to the hepatitis chapters.

Contraindications

The only contraindication to bivalent hepatitis vaccines is previous anaphylaxis demonstrated to any component of the bivalent vaccine.

Please refer to the other hepatitis vaccine chapters in this guide for a complete discussion of the epidemiology of hepatitis A and B, indications for and uses of hepatitis vaccines, recommendations for pre-immunization screening and post-immunization serologic testing, and information on adverse events for hepatitis vaccines. Further details on bivalent hepatitis vaccines are also contained in the product monographs.

Selected References

National Advisory Committee on Immunization. *Canadian immunization guide*, 5th edition. Ottawa: Canadian Medical Association, 1998.

National Advisory Committee on Immunization. *Supplementary statement on hepatitis prevention*. CCDR 1997;23:ACS-4.

Hepatitis Vaccines Combined

Influenza Vaccine

NACI produces a Statement on Influenza Vaccination each year that contains specific information and recommendations regarding the vaccine to be used in the forthcoming season. It is published in the Canada Communicable Disease Report (CCDR), and it can also be accessed through the Health Canada Website (http://www.hc-sc.gc.ca). The reader is referred to the latest annual CCDR statement for a more in-depth discussion of selected topics and for recommendations that have been updated after publication of this book.

Influenza is caused by influenza A and B viruses and occurs in Canada every year, generally during late fall and the winter months. Influenza A viruses, which periodically undergo antigenic changes, are the most common cause of epidemic influenza. Outbreaks of influenza B are generally more localized and in any one year may be restricted to one region of the country. An association between influenza outbreaks, especially those caused by type B virus, and cases of the rare, but serious, Reye syndrome has been noted.

The annual incidence of influenza varies widely, and it is difficult to predict the impact of a particular virus strain on disease during an inter-pandemic period. People at greatest risk of serious disease and death are those with chronic medical conditions (especially cardiopulmonary diseases) and the elderly. Although many other respiratory viruses can cause influenza-like illness during the year, influenza virus is usually the predominant cause of serious respiratory disease in a community.

Influenza A viruses are classified into subtypes based on their hemagglutinin (H) and neuraminidase (N) antigens. Recently circulating strains have possessed one of three H and one of two N antigens, and the subtypes are designated accordingly (e.g., H3N2, H1N1). Antibodies to these antigens, particularly to H antigen, can protect an individual against a virus carrying the same antigen. During inter-pandemic periods, minor H antigen changes ("drift") are common, and the greater the change the less will be the cross-immunity to the new strain conferred by the previously circulating virus. It is this antigenic variation from one influenza virus subtype to another that is responsible for continued outbreaks of influenza and that necessitates annual reformulation and administration of the influenza vaccine. The antigens of influenza B viruses are much more stable than those of influenza A viruses and, although antigenic variation does occur, it is less frequent.

Pandemic influenza is usually associated with a major antigenic change or "shift" and the rapid global spread of influenza A virus with a different H and often a different N antigen from strains circulating previously. Canada, like other countries, has been affected by major influenza pandemics, e.g., in 1889-90, 1918-19, 1957-58 and 1968-69.

Preparations Licensed for Immunization

Three influenza vaccines are licensed for use in Canada, two produced by Aventis Pasteur (Fluzone® and Vaxigrip®) and one by Shire Biologics (Fluviral S/F®). All three are sterile suspensions prepared from influenza viruses propagated in chicken embryos. The virus is inactivated, purified and treated with an organic solvent to remove surface glycoproteins, producing a "split-virus" preparation that is intended to reduce vaccine reactogenicity. One dose (0.5 mL) of vaccine contains 15 µg of hemagglutinin of each of three antigens. The antigens are selected from two strains of influenza A and one strain of influenza B. The virus strains chosen for inclusion in influenza vaccine are reviewed annually to ensure that they include antigens that are expected to provide the best protection during the following winter.

All three licensed vaccines use thimerosal (0.01%) as a preservative. Gelatin (0.05%) is used as a stabilizer in Fluzone®. Vaxigrip® may contain undetectable traces of neomycin, used during production.

Influenza vaccines derived from tissue culture and live attenuated vaccines are in development, but at the time of printing of this book they are not licensed in Canada.

Efficacy and Immunogenicity

Intramuscular administration of inactivated influenza vaccine results in the production of circulating IgG antibody to the viral hemagglutinin as well as a cytotoxic T lymphocyte response. Both humoral and cell-mediated responses are thought to play a role in immunity to influenza. Anti-hemagglutinin serum antibody is a predictor of total protection (acquisition of infection) and partial protection (disease after infection). The production and persistence of antibody after vaccination depends on several factors, including the age of the recipient, prior and subsequent exposure to antigens, and the presence of immunodeficiency states. Humoral antibody levels, which correlate with vaccine protection, are generally achieved 2 weeks after immunization, and immunity usually lasts less than 1 year. However, antibody levels in the elderly may fall below protective levels in 4 months or less. Data are not available at this time to support the administration of a second dose of influenza vaccine in elderly individuals in order to boost immunity.

Repeated annual administration of influenza vaccine has not been demonstrated to impair the immune responsiveness of the recipient.

The effectiveness of influenza vaccine varies, depending upon the age and immunocompetence of the vaccine recipient, the endpoint studied, the incidence of infection, and the degree of similarity ("match") between the vaccine viral strain and the circulating viral strain during influenza season. With a good match, influenza vaccination has been shown to prevent influenza illness in approximately 70% to 90% of healthy children and adults, whereas a vaccine efficacy of 30% to 60% has been demonstrated when there are significant antigenic differences between circulating and vaccine viral strains. During 8 of the past 10 years, there has been a good to excellent match between the predominant seasonal viral strain and the chosen vaccine strain.

A double-blind placebo controlled trial involving people > 60 years of age demonstrated vaccine efficacy of 58% in the prevention of laboratory-proven influenza illness. Pooled estimates from a meta-analysis of 20 cohort studies of influenza vaccine among the elderly demonstrated 56% effectiveness in preventing respiratory illness, 50% in preventing hospitalization for pneumonia and 68% in preventing death. Among residents of long-term care facilities, effectiveness in preventing influenza illness may be relatively low (30% to 40%), but vaccination may be 50% to 60% effective in preventing hospitalization and pneumonia, and up to 85% to 95% in preventing death.

Recommended Usage

As is the case with other vaccines, recommendations for usage may change over time, as new research becomes available. Recommended recipients for the influenza vaccine at the time of this publication are outlined below, but the reader is referred to the annual CCDR influenza statement for up-to-date information.

Recommended recipients

Influenza vaccine may be administered to any healthy child, adolescent or adult for whom contraindications are not present. To reduce the morbidity and mortality associated with influenza and the impact of illness in our communities, immunization programs should focus on those at high risk of influenza-related complications, those capable of transmitting influenza to individuals at high risk of complications, and those who provide essential community services. However, significant morbidity and societal costs are also associated with seasonal interpandemic influenza illness and its complications occurring in healthy children and adults. For this reason, healthy adults and their children who wish to protect themselves from influenza should be encouraged to receive the vaccine.

People at high risk for influenza-related complications

- Adults and children with chronic cardiac or pulmonary disorders (including bronchopulmonary dysplasia, cystic fibrosis and asthma) severe enough to require regular medical follow-up or hospital care.

- People of any age who are residents of nursing homes and other chronic care facilities.

- People ≥ 65 years of age.

- Adults and children with chronic conditions, such as diabetes mellitus and other metabolic diseases, cancer, immunodeficiency, immunosuppression (due to underlying disease and/or therapy), renal disease, anemia and hemoglobinopathy.

- Children and adolescents (age 6 months to 18 years) with conditions treated for long periods with acetylsalicylic acid. This therapy might increase the risk of Reye syndrome after influenza.

- People at high risk of influenza complications embarking on travel to destinations where the virus is likely to be circulating.

People capable of transmitting influenza to those at high risk of influenza-related complications

People who are potentially capable of transmitting influenza to those at high risk should receive annual immunization, regardless of whether the high-risk person(s) has been immunized.

- Health care workers (HCWs) and other personnel who have significant contact with people in the high-risk groups previously described. The following groups should be immunized: HCWs in long-term care facilities, hospitals, and outpatient settings; employees of long-term care facilities who have patient contact; and those who provide services within relatively closed settings to people at high risk (e.g., providers of home care services, crews on ships that cater to those at high risk).

- Household contacts (including children) of people at high risk who either cannot be immunized or may respond inadequately to immunization.

People who provide essential community services

Immunization may be considered for these individuals in order to minimize the disruption of routine activities in epidemics. Employers and their employees should consider yearly influenza immunization for healthy working adults, as this has been shown to decrease work absenteeism due to respiratory and other illnesses.

Other potential recipients

Immunization of healthy people

Anyone who wishes to protect him/herself from influenza should be encouraged to receive the vaccine, even if that individual is not in one of the aforementioned priority groups. Several studies have suggested that influenza immunization of healthy adults and children may be cost-effective under selected circumstances. Assessment of the potential benefits of influenza immunization in healthy adults and children depends on numerous factors, including seasonal viral virulence and attack rates, the match between vaccine and circulating viral strains, protective immunity in previously infected individuals, vaccine side effects, and the costs of immunization and of influenza-associated morbidity. Among children, the effects of co-circulating viruses such as respiratory syncytial virus must be separated from those of influenza. Policy decisions regarding public funding of influenza vaccine for healthy adults and children depends on modelling of these factors within populations, as well as assessment of health priorities, resources and pragmatic programmatic issues.

Immunization of pregnant women

Influenza vaccine is considered safe for pregnant women at all stages of pregnancy and for breast-feeding mothers. Immunization is recommended for pregnant and breastfeeding women who are characterized by any of the conditions listed under "Recommended Recipients". Any pregnant woman who wishes to decrease her risk of developing influenza may be safely immunized. However, NACI concludes that there is insufficient evidence at this time to recommend a public health program to routinely immunize healthy Canadian women who are pregnant during influenza season.

Schedule and Dosage

The recommended dosage schedule and type of influenza vaccine are presented in the Table. Split-virus vaccines are available in Canada. Previously unvaccinated children < 9 years require two doses of the split-virus influenza vaccine, with an interval of 4 weeks. The second dose is not needed if the child has received one or more doses of vaccine during a previous influenza season.

In infants < 6 months of age, influenza vaccine is less immunogenic than in infants and children aged 6 to 18 months. **Therefore, immunization with currently available influenza vaccines is not recommended for infants < 6 months of age**.

Route of Administration

The vaccine should be administered intramuscularly. The deltoid muscle is the recommended site in adults and older children, and the anterolateral thigh in infants and young children.

Recommended Influenza Vaccine Dosage, by Age, for the 2001-2002 Season

Age	Vaccine Type	Dose (mL)	No. of Doses
6-35 months	split-virus	0.25	1 or 2*
3-8 years	split-virus	0.5	1 or 2*
≥ 9 years	split-virus	0.5	1
* See text for criteria			

Storage Requirements

The vaccine should be refrigerated at a temperature between 2° C and 8° C. The vaccine should not be frozen.

Simultaneous Administration of Other Vaccines

Influenza vaccine may be given at the same time as other vaccines, provided different sites and administration sets (needle and syringe) are used.

The target groups for influenza and pneumococcal immunization overlap considerably. Health care providers should take the opportunity to immunize eligible people against pneumococcal disease when influenza vaccine is given. *Pneumococcal vaccine, however, is usually given only once, whereas influenza vaccine is given annually.*

Adverse Reactions

Influenza immunization cannot cause influenza because the vaccine does not contain live virus. Soreness at the injection site lasting up to 2 days is common but rarely interferes with normal activities. Fever, malaise and myalgia may occur within 6 to 12 hours after vaccination and last 1 to 2 days, especially in young adults who have received the whole-virus vaccine and those receiving vaccine for the first time. Prophylactic acetaminophen may decrease the frequency of some side effects in adults. Healthy adults receiving the split-virus vaccine have shown no increase in the frequency of fever or other systemic symptoms compared with those receiving placebo. In children aged 2 to 12 years, fever and local reactions are no more frequent after administration of split-virus vaccine than after placebo injections. In those < 24 months of age, fever occurs more often but is seldom severe.

Allergic responses are rare and are probably a consequence of hypersensitivity to some vaccine component, most likely residual egg protein, which is present in minute quantities.

Rare cases of systemic vasculitis have been reported to occur in individuals within 2 weeks of influenza immunization. Influenza antigens have not been identified in circulating immune complexes or in vessel walls, and a causal relationship has not been proven.

Guillain-Barré syndrome (GBS) associated with influenza immunization has been observed in a minority of influenza seasons over the last two decades. Apart from the 1976-1977 swine flu season, the risk of GBS associated with influenza immunization is small. In a retrospective study of the 1992-93 and 1993-94 seasons in four U.S. states, the relative risk of GBS occurring within 6 weeks after influenza immunization, adjusted for age and sex, was 1.7 (95% confidence interval 1.0-2.8, $p = 0.04$), suggesting slightly more than one additional case of GBS per million people vaccinated against influenza. In comparison, the morbidity and mortality associated with influenza are much greater.

In Canada, a study carried out in Ontario and Quebec estimated the background incidence of GBS to be just over 20 cases per million population. A variety of infectious agents, such as *Campylobacter jejuni*, have been associated with GBS. It is not known whether influenza virus infection itself is associated with GBS, or whether influenza immunization is causally associated with increased risk of recurrent GBS in people with a previous history of this syndrome. Avoiding subsequent influenza immunization of people known to have developed GBS within 6 to 8 weeks of a previous influenza vaccination appears prudent at this time.

Influenza vaccine is not known to predispose to Reye syndrome.

An increased number of influenza vaccine-associated adverse events, primarily characterized by oculorespiratory symptoms, were reported in Canada during the 2000-2001 influenza season. Although the number of these reported adverse events was higher than in the past, conjunctivitis and/or respiratory symptoms following influenza immunization have been reported previously in Canada, the United States and Europe. A case definition for what was called "oculorespiratory syndrome (ORS)" was devised, and enhanced surveillance was initiated. The majority of reported cases of ORS were associated with Fluviral S/F®, one of the three influenza vaccines licensed for use in Canada. The syndrome was noted to be mild and self-resolving within several days.

Electron microscopic studies revealed a higher proportion of unsplit (whole) virus as well as aggregated virus particles in Fluviral S/F® than in other influenza vaccines used in Canada during the 2000-2001 season. The reader is referred to the July 2001 CCDR *Annual Statement on Influenza Vaccination for the 2001-2002 Season* for more in-depth information and a discussion of potential pathophysiologic mechanisms underlying this syndrome. Subsequent CCDR reports will provide further updates and recommendations, and should be consulted by health care providers. At the time of writing (May 2001), manufacturers are investigating improved methods of virus splitting in the preparation of influenza vaccines. Evidence of a satisfactory safety profile will be required before vaccine licensure. **The benefits of influenza immunization in recommended recipients continue to greatly outweigh the risks associated with the vaccine.**

Contraindications and Precautions

Influenza vaccine should not be given to people who had an anaphylactic reaction to a previous dose, or those with known anaphylactic hypersensitivity to eggs manifested as hives, swelling of the mouth and throat, difficulty in breathing, hypotension and shock. (See Part 1 – General Considerations: Anaphylactic Hypersensitivity to Egg and Egg-related Antigens).

Individuals with acute febrile illness should not usually be immunized until their symptoms have abated.

Although influenza immunization can inhibit the clearance of warfarin and theophylline, clinical studies have not shown any adverse effects attributable to these drugs in people receiving influenza vaccine.

Strategies for Reducing the Impact of Influenza

Immunization is recognized as the single most effective way of preventing or attenuating influenza for those at high risk of serious illness or death. Influenza vaccine programs should aim to vaccinate at least 90% of eligible recipients. Nevertheless, only 70% to 91% of residents of long-term care facilities and 20% to 40% of adults and children with medical conditions listed previously receive vaccine annually. Studies of HCWs in hospitals and long-term care facilities have shown immunization rates of 26% to 61%.

This low rate of utilization is due both to failure of the health care system to offer the vaccine and to immunization refusal by people who fear adverse reactions or mistakenly believe that the vaccine is either ineffective or unnecessary. The reader is referred to the current annual *CCDR Statement on Influenza Vaccination* for a discussion of strategies to increase vaccination coverage of target groups, as well as guidelines regarding the prophylactic use of licensed antiviral medication in outbreak settings.

Selected References

CDC. *Prevention and control of influenza: recommendations of the Advisory Committee on Immunization Practices (ACIP).* MMWR 2001;50(RR-4):1-44.

Demicheli V. *Mass influenza vaccination in Ontario: Is it worthwhile?* Can Med Assoc J 2001;164(1):38-9.

Kilbourne ED, Arden NH. *Inactivated influenza.* In: Plotkin SA, Orenstein WA, eds. *Vaccines.* Philadelphia: W.B. Saunders, 1999:531-51.

McArthur MA, Simor AE, Campbell B et al. *Influenza vaccination in long-term-care facilities: structuring programs for success.* Infect Control Hosp Epidemiol 1999;20:499-503.

Nichol KL. *Cost-benefit analysis of a strategy to vaccinate healthy working adults against influenza.* Arch Intern Med 2001;161:749-59.

McIntosh K, Lieu T. *Is it time to give influenza vaccine to healthy infants?* N Engl J Med 2000;342(4):275-6.

Potter J, Stott DJ, Roberts MA et al. *Influenza vaccination of health-care workers in long-term-care hospitals reduces the mortality of elderly patients.* J Infect Dis 1997;175:1-6.

Japanese Encephalitis Vaccine

Japanese encephalitis (JE) virus is the leading cause of viral encephalitis in Asia, where more than 50,000 cases occur each year. Clinically apparent infection with JE virus is seen only rarely in travellers. Countries where the disease occurs are listed in the Table. Although the incidence of JE varies widely from year to year and between regions within countries, it has been decreasing in China, Korea and Japan but holding steady or even increasing in areas of South and Southeast Asia.

JE virus is an arthropod-borne flavivirus, a group that also includes yellow fever virus and St. Louis encephalitis virus. Although subtle serologic differences between isolates obtained in different geographic regions have been described, recent genotyping suggests that JE virus is essentially monotypic. The principal vectors are *Culex* mosquitoes, which breed mainly in rice fields. Swine and certain species of wild birds are intermediate hosts in the transmission cycle. Conditions that support transmission of JE virus are primarily rural agricultural ones, but occasionally cases are reported from urban areas. *Culex* mosquitoes tend to bite in the evening and night, but day-biting species predominate in some regions.

The disease occurs in epidemic form in temperate and northern tropical regions and is endemic in southern tropical regions of Asia. Cases occur chiefly during the summer and autumn in temperate zones and during the rainy season in tropical zones. In areas where irrigation is the main factor affecting the abundance of vector mosquitoes, transmission may occur year round. For this reason, the periods of greatest

Countries Where Japanese Encephalitis Has Been Recognized and Season of Epidemic Risk

Zone	Country
Temperate regions (Risk greatest July to October)	Bangladesh China Northern India Japan Kampuchea Korea Laos Myanmar Nepal Far Eastern Russia Northern Thailand Northern Vietnam
Tropical regions (Risk greatest during the rainy season. Note that the rainy season varies somewhat from region to region but is typically May to November)	Southern India Pakistan Indonesia Malaysia Philippines Sri Lanka Taiwan Southern Thailand Southern Vietnam

risk for JE virus transmission to travellers are highly variable and depend on such factors as season, location, duration of stay and the type of activities undertaken. Crude estimates for North Americans travelling to Asia place the overall risk of JE illness at less than 1 per million. However, for travellers to rural areas during the transmission season, the risk per month of exposure can be as high as 1 per 5,000. Rare case reports suggest that even short-term, resort-based travellers can occasionally contract JE.

Most JE infections do not result in obvious illness. Between 50 and 300 infections occur for each clinical case identified. However, when encephalitis does occur, it is usually severe, with 10% to 25% mortality rates and residual neuropsychiatric problems in 50% of survivors.

The disease usually affects children, but in countries where it has been recently introduced all age groups may be affected. In addition to children < 10 years of age, the elderly are a group in which increased incidence has been observed in the developed countries of Asia.

Limited data indicate that JE acquired during the first or second trimester of pregnancy causes intrauterine infection and miscarriage. Infections that occur during the third trimester of pregnancy have not been associated with adverse outcomes in newborns.

Since JE begins with an infected mosquito bite and only a small proportion (< 3%) of mosquitoes carry the virus, even in areas of intense transmission, the risk to travellers can be significantly reduced by the appropriate use of bed-nets, repellants and protective clothing.

Preparation Licensed for Immunization

A highly purified, formalin-inactivated vaccine derived from mouse brain has been licensed in Canada. The vaccine is based upon the Beijing-1 strain; it is produced by the Research Institute of Osaka University (Biken) and distributed by Aventis Pasteur (Canada). The vaccine contains thimerosal as a preservative and other minor components.

A live-attenuated JE vaccine developed in China (SA14-14-2) appears to be both safe and efficacious. This vaccine is currently available only in China but may soon become more widely available in Southeast Asia. Of particular interest is its capacity to elicit good serologic responses with fewer doses. A number of tissue culture-based vaccines (e.g., Vero cell) and recombinant or subunit vaccines for JE are also under development.

Efficacy and Immunogenicity

The vaccine has been widely used in Asia. In Japan, where JE vaccine has been licensed since 1954, countrywide immunization for children was introduced between 1965 and 1968. In a study of children in Northern Thailand, JE vaccine was demonstrated to have an efficacy of 91% (95% confidence interval 70%-97%). In this trial, immunization consisted of two subcutaneous 1.0 mL doses of vaccine, except in children < 3 years of age who received two 0.5 mL doses. A single dose of a similar vaccine did not generate significant antibody titres.

Immunogenicity studies in the United States and Britain indicate that three doses are needed to provide protective levels of antibody in a suitable proportion of vaccinees. Less than 80% of vaccinees developed neutralizing antibody after two doses of vaccine, as compared with 99% after three doses. After two doses of vaccine, antibody levels declined substantially in most vaccinees within 6 to 12 months (protective titres in < 29%). The response in Asian subjects after only two doses may reflect prior exposure to JE or other flaviviruses circulating in Asia. Although seroconversion rates (i.e., ≥ four-fold increases in antibody titres) are similar in Asian and non-Asian subjects who receive a primary series of immunizations over 2 weeks (day 0, 7, 14) or 3 weeks (day 0, 7, 30), the geometric mean titres are uniformly higher in the Asians. The duration of protection after a complete primary series is unknown, but titres > 1:10 persist in 94% of healthy young adults for at least 3 years. Although neutralizing antibody titres after immunization are highest against homologous strains, sufficient cross-reactivity exists to provide adequate protection against a range of heterologous strains.

Recommended Usage

Immunization is indicated for active immunization against JE for people ≥1 year of age who will spend 1 month or more in endemic or epidemic areas during the transmission season, especially if travel will include rural areas. However, there have been several reports of JE in short-term travellers to endemic regions. Immunization should therefore be considered for some people spending < 30 days in endemic areas, e.g., travellers to areas where there is an epidemic, travellers making repeated short trips, or those with extensive outdoor rural exposure. *All travellers should be advised to take personal precautions against mosquito bites.*

Immunization is recommended for all laboratory personnel working with JE virus.

Schedule and Dosage

A series of three 1.0 mL doses is given subcutaneously on days 0, 7 and 30. When time does not permit, they may be administered 5 to 7 days apart, but the antibody response to this accelerated schedule is lower and may not be as durable. Two doses of vaccine 7 to 14 days apart can provide reasonable protection (80% efficacy) for short periods of time (< 1 year).

Booster Doses

No definitive recommendation can be made regarding the timing of booster doses in travellers. In a study of a small number of adults, protective titres of neutralizing antibodies persisted for 3 years after primary immunization. No pediatric data are currently available. Booster doses of 1.0 mL (0.5 mL for children < 3 years) may be considered at intervals of 2 to 3 years. There are no data on use of the vaccine in infants < 1 year of age. Wherever possible, immunization of infants should be deferred until they are 1 year of age.

Storage Requirements

The lyophilized preparation should be stored at the temperature recommended by the manufacturer (2° C to 8° C) until it is reconstituted with diluent. After reconstitution, the vaccine should be stored at a temperature between 2° C and 8° C and used within 8 hours.

Simultaneous Administration of Other Vaccines

There are only limited data on the effect of concurrent administration of other vaccines, drugs (e.g., chloroquine, mefloquine) or biologics on the safety and immunogenicity of JE vaccine. As a general rule, JE vaccine can be given simultaneously with any other vaccine. However, if live virus vaccines need to be administered (e.g., MMR) and time permits, it would be ideal to administer at least two doses of JE vaccine before administration of the live viral agents. Theoretically, serologic responses may be diminished if JE vaccine is administered while chloroquine is being taken for prophylaxis against malaria.

Adverse Reactions

JE vaccine has been associated with injection site tenderness, redness and swelling. Other local effects have been reported in an average of 20% of vaccinees (range < 1% to 31%). Systemic side effects, principally fever, headache, malaise, rash and other reactions such as chills, dizziness, myalgia, nausea, vomiting and abdominal pain, are reported in 5% to 10% of vaccinees.

In an immunization program for U.S. military personnel in Okinawa, an overall reaction rate of 62.4 per 10,000 vaccinees occurred, including reports of urticaria, angioedema, generalized itching and wheezing. These reactions were generally mild to moderate in severity. Nine out of 35,253 people who had been immunized were hospitalized, primarily to allow administration of intravenous steroids for refractory urticaria. None of these reactions was considered life threatening. A more recent study of 14,249 U.S. military personnel (36,850 doses of vaccine) demonstrated overall reaction rates of 16/10,000 for the first two doses and only 2/10,000 for the third dose. A Danish case control study in travellers suggests an overall risk of about 1/10,000 doses for allergic-type responses.

Since 1989, an apparent increase in the incidence of late systemic hypersensitivity reactions has been reported in several developed countries. The reactions are characterized by urticaria, often in a generalized distribution, and/or angioedema of the extremities, face and oropharynx, especially of the lips. Distress or collapse due to hypotension or other causes has led to hospitalization in several cases. Most of the reactions reported have been treated successfully with antihistamines and steroids given either orally or parenterally. Some individuals have complained of generalized itching without evidence of a rash. An important feature of these reactions is the interval between immunization and onset of symptoms. Reactions after a first dose of vaccine occur a median of 12 hours after immunization; 88% of reactions occurred within 3 days. The interval between a second dose and onset of symptoms is generally longer (median 3 days) and as long as 2 weeks. Reactions can occur after a second or third dose when preceding doses were received uneventfully.

Data on U.S. military personnel and Danish travellers suggest that the risk of developing a systemic allergic reaction is greater in younger subjects, women and those with a history of allergy (e.g., urticaria, allergic rhinitis, asthma), particularly to other immunizing agents. Recent post-marketing surveillance suggests that such late reactions continue to occur at a rate of approximately 6.3/100,000 doses in the United States. The vaccine constituents responsible for the late hypersensitivity syndrome have not been identified, although reactions to gelatin have been implicated in some cases.

Severe neurologic adverse effects such as encephalitis or encephalopathy have been reported after JE immunization but are rare (approximately 0.2/100,000 doses in Japanese vaccine recipients and possibly fewer in North American vaccinees).

Contraindications and Precautions

Allergic reactions (generalized urticaria or angioedema) to a previous dose of vaccine are contraindications to further doses. JE vaccine should not be given to people with known hypersensitivity to proteins of rodent or neural origin or JE vaccine excipients (e.g., gelatin, thimerosal).

Epinephrine (1:1000) must be immediately available should an acute anaphylactic reaction occur to any component of the vaccine.

Possible allergic reactions exhibited as generalized urticaria and angioedema may occur from minutes to as long as 9 days after immunization. Vaccinees should be observed for 30 minutes after immunization and warned against the possibility of delayed urticaria and angioedema of the head and airway.

Vaccinees should not embark on international travel within 10 days of immunization because of the possibility of delayed allergic reactions; they should be advised to remain in an area with ready access to medical care for 10 days after immunization.

A history of urticaria or angioedema after other immunizing agents, hymenoptera venom, drugs, or physical or other provocations, or a history of idiopathic hypersensitivity responses should be considered when weighing the risks and benefits of the vaccine for an individual patient. There are no data supporting the use of prophylactic antihistamines or steroids in preventing JE vaccine-related allergic reactions.

Use in pregnancy and breast-feeding

The vaccine has not been assessed in pregnancy or in breast-feeding women. It is not known whether JE vaccine can cause fetal harm when administered to a pregnant woman. Pregnant women who must travel to areas where the risk of JE infection is high should be immunized when the theoretic risks of immunization are outweighed by the risk of infection to the mother and developing fetus. There are no contraindications to the use of JE vaccine in breast-feeding women.

Use in immunocompromised hosts

People undergoing immunosuppressive therapy are likely to have a poor immune response to vaccines in general and killed vaccines in particular. JE immunization should be deferred, if possible, while patients are receiving such therapy. If travel must be undertaken, such patients may be immunized as already outlined, with the understanding that the antibody response may be suboptimal. A recent study of Thai children with HIV infection suggests that in up to 50% routine immunization can be expected to be ineffective.

Selected References

Andersen MM, Ronne T. *Side-effects with Japanese encephalitis vaccine.* Lancet 1991;337:1044.

Berg SW, Mitchell BS, Hanson RK et al. *Systemic reactions in US Marine Corps personnel who received Japanese encephalitis vaccine.* Clin Infect Dis 1997;24:265-66.

CDC. *Inactivated Japanese encephalitis virus vaccine: recommendations of the Immunization Practices Advisory Committee (ACIP).* MMWR 1993;(RR- l):1-15.

Chambers TJ, Tsai TF, Pervikov Y et al. *Vaccine development against dengue and Japanese encephalitis: report of a World Health Organization meeting.* Vaccine 1997;15:1494-1552.

Defraites RF, Gambel JM, Hoke CH et al. *Japanese encephalitis vaccine (inactivated, Biken) in US soldiers: immunogenicity and safety of vaccine administered in two dosing regimens.* Am J Trop Med Hyg 1999;61:288-93.

Gambel JM, DeFraites R, Hoke C Jr et al. *Japanese encephalitis vaccine: persistence of antibody up to 3 years after a three-dose regimen.* J Infect Dis 1995;171:1074.

Hoke CH, Nisalak A, Sangawhipa N et al. *Protection against Japanese encephalitis by inactivated vaccines.* N Engl J Med 1988;319:608-14.

Jelinek T, Northdurft HD. *Japanese encephalitis vaccine in travellers. Is wider use prudent?* Drug Safety 1997;16:153.

Kurane I, Takasaki T. *Immunogenicity and protective efficacy of the current inactivated Japanese encephalitis vaccine against different Japanese encephalitis virus strains.* Vaccine 2000;18:33-5.

Liu Z-L, Hennessy S, Strom BL et al. *Short-term safety of live attenuated Japanese encephalitis vaccine: results of a randomized trial with 26,239 subjects.* J Infect Dis 1997;176:1366-69.

Plesner A, Ronne T, Wachmann H. *Case-control study of allergic reactions to Japanese encephalitis vaccine.* Vaccine 2000;18:1830-36.

Plesner AM, Arlien-Soborg P, Herning M. *Neurological complications to vaccination against Japanese encephalitis.* Eur J Neurol 1998;5:479-85.

Japanese Encephalitis Vaccine

Poland JD, Cropp CB, Craven RB et al. *Evaluation of the potency and safety of inactivated Japanese encephalitis vaccine in U.S. inhabitants*. J Infect Dis 1990;161:878-82.

Robinson HC, Russell ML, Csokoney WM. *Japanese encephalitis vaccine and adverse effects among travellers*. CDWR 1991;17:173-77.

Rojanasuphot S, Shaffer N, Chotpitayasundondh T et al. *Response to JE vaccine among HIV-infected children, Bangkok, Thailand*. Southeast Asian J Trop Med Public Health 1998;29:443-50.

Ruff TA, Eisen D, Fuller A et al. *Adverse reactions to Japanese encephalitis vaccine*. Lancet 1991;338:881-82.

Sakaguchi M, Yoshida M, Kuroda W et al. *Systemic immediate-type reactions to gelatin included in Japanese encephalitis vaccines*. Vaccine 1997;15:121-2.

Takahashi H, Pool V, Tsai TF et al. and the VAERS Working Group. *Adverse events after Japanese encephalitis vaccination: review of post-marketing surveillance data from Japan and the United States*. Vaccine 2000;18:2963-69.

Tsai TF. *New initiatives for the control of Japanese encephalitis by vaccination: minutes of a WHO/CVI meeting, Bangkok, Thailand, 13-15 October 1998*. Vaccine 2000;18:1-25.

Tsarev SA, Sanders ML, Vaughn DW et al. *Phylogenetic analysis suggests only one serotype of Japanese encephalitis virus*. Vaccine 2000;18:36-43.

Vaughn DW, Hoke CH. *The epidemiology of Japanese encephalitis: prospects for prevention*. Epidemiol Rev 1992;14:197-221.

Lyme Disease Vaccine

Lyme disease is a tick-borne zoonosis caused by the spirochete *Borrelia burgdorferi*. The consequences of infection with *B. burgdorferi* are highly variable, ranging from asymptomatic infection to death. The most common manifestations include the development of a characteristic, slowly expanding rash called *erythema migrans*, as well as nonspecific symptoms such as fever, malaise, fatigue, headache, myalgia and arthralgia. The presence of *erythema migrans* in an individual with exposure to appropriate tick vectors has an excellent predictive value for Lyme disease. If the infection is not recognized and treated, a number of those infected with *B. burgdorferi* go on to develop musculoskeletal, cardiac or central nervous system complications that can be debilitating and, in rare circumstances, fatal.

Epidemiology

In North America, Lyme disease is mostly localized to the northeastern, mid-Atlantic, upper north-central and northwestern regions of the U.S. In the U.S., roughly 12,500 cases are reported to the Centers for Disease Control and Prevention annually. Lyme disease is rare in Canada, an average of 24 cases being reported annually between 1993 and 1999. During this period, 60% were epidemiologically linked to exposure in endemic areas of the U.S., although cases in British Columbia appear to have acquired the disease locally.

Ticks competent to transmit *B. burgdorferi* can be found in the southern regions of Canada, and surveillance activities in Ontario and Quebec have demonstrated that a small proportion (< 10%) of these ticks are infected. The large majority of such isolations are believed to represent adventitious introductions (i.e., nymphal forms dropped by migratory birds) rather than indigenous replicating populations of infected ticks.

At the current time, vector ticks are known to be established in only two localized regions of southern Canada: 1) *Ixodes pacificus* is present in regions of the Fraser delta, the Gulf Islands and Vancouver Island, and 2) reproducing populations of *I. scapularis* are established in some areas along the northern shore of Lake Erie and eastern shore of Lake Ontario. In some of these areas, up to 20% of the nymphal forms (the form most likely to transmit Lyme disease) and 50% of adult ticks may be infected. However, even in high transmission regions of the U.S., such as New York and Connecticut (annual incidence rates of 25 to 55 per 100,000 in 1998), Lyme disease remains very focal in nature, and the risk of infection varies greatly from county to county and even within individual counties. There are no such regions of high transmission in Canada. For example, the incidence rates of Lyme disease in Ontario (including cases acquired outside of the province) and in the region that includes the northern shore of Lake Erie were approximately 0.2 per 100,000 in 1999.

In the U.S., most *B. burgdorferi* infections result from peri-residential exposure to ticks in endemic areas. Thus, individuals who live or work in residential areas surrounded by woods or overgrown brush infested with vector ticks are at risk of acquiring Lyme disease. In addition, people who participate in recreational activities such as hiking, camping, fishing and hunting in tick habitat or engage in outdoor occupations, such as landscaping, brush clearing, forestry, and wildlife and parks management in endemic areas are at risk of acquiring Lyme disease.

Personal Protection

The first line of defence against Lyme disease and other tick-borne illnesses includes the avoidance of tick-infested habitats, use of personal protective measures such as repellents and protective clothing, and checking for and removing attached ticks. The daily inspection for attached ticks is particularly important. Animal studies suggest that transmission of *B. burgdorferi* from infected ticks usually requires at least 24 hours and often as long as 48 hours. These data have recently been corroborated by documentation that the state of nymphal tick engorgement (a surrogate for length of attachment) is a significant factor in the risk of transmission. As a result, daily inspection and prompt removal of ticks can prevent transmission.

Ticks can be deterred to some extent by insect repellents containing n,n-diethyl-m-toluamide (DEET). Permethrin (a synthetic pyrethroid) kills ticks on contact and is available as a spray in animal care stores for application on clothing and cloth only (e.g., tent screens).

Preparations Licensed for Immunization

Two Lyme disease vaccines have been developed using recombinant *B. burgdorferi* lipidated outer surface protein A (rOspA) as immunogen (LYMErix™, GlaxoSmith-Kline; ImuLyme®, Aventis Pasteur). Only LYMErix™ has been licensed for use in Canada. Each dose of this vaccine contains 30 µg of recombinant OspA produced in *Escherichia coli* adsorbed onto aluminum hydroxide adjuvant (0.5 mg). Each dose of the vaccine preparation also contains 10 mmol of phosphate buffered saline and 2.5 mg of 2-phenoxyethanol as a bacteriostatic agent.

The protection afforded by LYMErix™ is dependent on the development of a humoral immune response to rOspA. Antibodies are ingested by the tick from the immunized host during feeding and are active against the *Borrelia* spirochetes in the gut of the tick. Expression of OspA is rapidly downregulated by the spirochete in response to the blood meal. As a result, the protection conferred by the vaccine depends entirely upon the delivery of high titres of preformed antibodies to the gut of the tick during feeding. Antigenic differences in OspA occur between and within *B. burgdorferi* genospecies (e.g., *B. burgdorferi sensu stricto*, *B. afzelii*, *B. garinii*) in both North America and Europe. Although a wide range of mutations, frameshifts and recombination events in OspA have been documented, the greatest diversity occurs in European strains; North American isolates are more homogeneous. As a result, the currently available vaccines may not provide protection against European strains (or equal protection against all North American strains).

Efficacy and Immunogenicity

The licensure of LYMErix™ was based primarily on data from a large, randomized controlled trial (RCT) of 10,936 subjects aged 15 to 70 years. Efficacy in preventing "definite" Lyme disease (e.g., either *erythema migrans* or objective neurologic, musculoskeletal or cardiovascular manifestations of Lyme disease, plus laboratory confirmation of infection by cultural isolation, PCR positivity, or Western blot seroconversion) was 49% (95% confidence interval [CI] 15%-69%) after two doses and 76% (95% CI 58%-86%) after three doses. Efficacy in protecting against asymptomatic infection (no recognized symptoms, but with Western blot IgG seroconversion) was 83% (95% CI 32%-97%) in year 1 and 100% (95% CI 26%-100%) in year 2. Comparable efficacy data have been generated in a second large RCT using a very similar, recombinant OspA vaccine. Although the immune correlates of protection against Lyme disease are not yet fully understood, 400 ELISA units (EIU) are believed to represent a minimum protective titre. Titres in the 700-1400 EIU range are believed to confer protection with a sensitivity of 70%-95%.

Recommended Usage

Lyme disease vaccine does not protect all recipients against infection with *B. burgdorferi*, has unknown efficacy for exposures to *B. burgdorferi* outside of North America and offers no protection against other tick-borne diseases (e.g., babesiosis, ehrlichioses, rickettsioses). The vaccine should be considered an adjunct or supplement to personal protective measures against ticks, and early diagnosis and treatment of suspected tick-borne infections. Decisions regarding the use of vaccine should be based on individual assessment of the risk of exposure to infected ticks, and on careful consideration of the relative risks and benefits of immunization compared with other protective measures, including early diagnosis and treatment of Lyme disease.

Risk assessment in the U.S. is determined on a county-by-county basis. Risk classification (high, moderate, low, minimal/no) is based upon detailed epidemiologic information, including the presence of the tick vectors (*I. scapularis, I. pacificus*), the predicted prevalence of infection in these ticks AND the incidence of clinically recognizable disease. Although vector-competent tick populations are established in many regions of southern Canada and adult tick infection rates of up to 10% have been documented, no residential areas in Canada would be classified as "high" or even "moderate" risk.

People at high risk

People at high risk of *B. burgdorferi* infection are those who reside in or visit areas of high or moderate risk AND engage in activities (e.g., recreational, property maintenance, occupational, leisure) that result in *frequent or prolonged exposure* to tick-infested habitat. Lyme disease vaccine should only be considered for people >15 years of age since the product is not currently licensed for younger children.

People at moderate risk

People at moderate risk of *B. burgdorferi* infection are those who reside in or visit areas of high or moderate risk AND are exposed to tick infested habitat, but whose *exposure is neither frequent nor prolonged*. For those at moderate risk of *B. burgdorferi* infection, Lyme disease vaccine may be considered, but the benefit of immunization beyond that provided by basic personal protection and early diagnosis and treatment of infection is uncertain.

People at low or no risk

People at low or no risk of *B. burgdorferi* infection are those who reside in areas of low or no risk as well as those who reside in or visit areas of high or moderate risk BUT have minimal or no exposure to Lyme disease vector ticks (*I. scapularis* or *I. pacificus*). Lyme disease vaccine is not recommended for those who are at low or no risk of *B. burgdorferi* infection. The vast majority of Canadians are considered to be at low or no risk of acquiring Lyme disease.

Schedule and Dosage

Currently, the standard schedule comprises a single 30 µg/0.5 mL dose given intramuscularly at 0, 1 and 12 months. Administration should be timed to provide maximum protection in advance of the peak tick transmission season (spring and early summer) in 2 successive years. Several studies have recently demonstrated that accelerated schedules (either 0, 1 and 6 months or 0, 1 and 2 months) can also result in antibody titres believed to be protective. Antibody titres fall steadily after immunization, and vaccine failures have occurred in subjects as titres fall. The vaccine is limited for use in people ≥ 15 years of age.

Laboratory Diagnosis of Lyme Disease

Clinicians and laboratory directors should be alert to the fact that vaccine-induced antibodies routinely cause false positive EIA results for Lyme disease. Immunization can also alter the appearance of some commercial immunoblots leading to uncertainties in diagnosis. Other immunoblotting protocols are less subject to misinterpretation and can be used to distinguish between the immune response to immunization and the response to natural infection.

Booster Doses

As already explained, the protection afforded by immunization is entirely dependent upon the presence of preformed antibodies at the time of the infected bite. Under conditions of "natural" exposure to *B. burgdorferi*, there is no opportunity for a protective anamnestic response. A substudy included in the large clinical trial outlined earlier examined the development and durability of OspA antibodies at months 2, 12, 13 and 20. At month 2, 1 month after the second injection, the geometric mean antibody titre (GMT) was 1227 EIU/mL. Ten months later, the GMT had declined to

116 EIU/mL. At month 13, 1 month after the third injection, a marked booster response resulted in a GMT of 6006 EIU/mL. At month 20, the mean response had fallen to 1991 EIU/mL. Although insufficient data are available to make firm long-term predictions, booster doses once every 2 years after a primary series would be likely to maintain protective levels of circulating antibody.

Simultaneous Administration With Other Vaccines

The safety and efficacy of the simultaneous administration of rOspA vaccine with other vaccines has not been established. If LYMErix™ must be given concurrently with other vaccines, each vaccine should be administered in a separate syringe at a separate injection site.

Adverse Reactions

Several large placebo-controlled studies involving more than 20,000 study subjects have been performed with rOspA vaccines in recent years to assess both safety and efficacy. Soreness at the injection site is the most frequently reported adverse event (about 24% of vaccine recipients versus 7%-8% of placebo recipients). Redness and swelling at the injection site were reported by less than 2% of both groups but were more frequent among vaccine recipients than among those who received placebo. Myalgia, influenza-like illness, fever and chills were significantly more common among vaccine than placebo recipients, but none of these effects was reported by more than 3% of subjects. Reports of arthritis were not significantly different between vaccine and placebo recipients, but vaccine recipients tended to report more transient arthralgia and myalgia following each dose of vaccine.

To date, there has been no excess of vaccine-attributable serious adverse events or hypersensitivity responses. In one study, subjects with a self-reported history of prior Lyme disease had a higher rate of musculoskeletal complaints within 30 days of receiving the vaccine than vaccinees without a previous history of Lyme disease. This difference in the rate of musculoskeletal complaints disappeared at 30 days after administration. Although a number of theoretical concerns have been raised about OspA epitopes, cross-reacting T cells and autoimmune disorders, there is no evidence to date that the incidence of neurologic or rheumatologic disorders is increased after Lyme disease immunization.

Precautions

Vaccine use in pregnancy or nursing mothers

There is no evidence that pregnancy increases either the risk of Lyme disease or its severity. Acute Lyme disease in pregnancy responds well to antibiotic therapy, and adverse fetal outcomes have not been reported in pregnant women receiving standard courses of treatment. Since the safety of rOspA vaccines administered during pregnancy has not been established, immunization of women who are known to be pregnant is not recommended. There is every reason to believe that rOspA vaccines can be given safely to breast-feeding women if immunization is indicated.

People with immunodeficiency

People with immunodeficiency were excluded from the large Phase III trials, and there are no safety or efficacy data on the use of Lyme disease vaccine in this group. However, since it is a recombinant vaccine, there is every reason to believe that immunocompromised individuals at significant risk for Lyme disease can be immunized without undue risk.

People with previous history of Lyme disease

People with a history of treated *erythema migrans* may become re-infected and are appropriate candidates for immunization if they remain at risk of infection. These subjects may have a higher incidence of musculoskeletal complaints in the first month after immunization than those without such a history. However, their risk of late musculoskeletal and other adverse events from the vaccine does not appear to be elevated. People with a history of Lyme arthritis generally have high antibody titres directed against a range of *B. burgdorferi* antigens and do not appear to be susceptible to re-infection.

People with rheumatologic or neurologic conditions

Individuals with serious medical conditions, including chronic rheumatologic and neurologic diseases, have been excluded from all trials to date. As a result, no data are available to determine the safety and efficacy of rOspA vaccine in these people, and the risks and benefits of immunization need to be evaluated on a case-by-case basis.

Children and adolescents

At the current time, immunization against *B. burgdorferi* is not recommended for children < 15 years of age. However, a recently completed randomized, placebo controlled trial in 4,090 children 4-18 years of age demonstrates that rOspA vaccines are both safe and immunogenic in healthy children and adolescents. Indeed, these study subjects attain much higher anti-OspA antibodies than adult vaccinees (mean titre 27,485 EIU versus 8216 EIU in adults during the first month after a series of three doses). Side effects in this population are similar to those in adults. Even younger children (2-5 years of age) also respond well to rOspA-containing vaccines, but insufficient data are currently available to establish safety or efficacy in this age range.

Other Considerations

Although Lyme disease can be prevented in many instances with the use of prophylactic antibiotics, the routine administration of such prophylaxis is not currently recommended. Most tick bites in North America are not attributable to species that transmit Lyme disease. Furthermore, in all but hyperendemic areas (there are very few such areas in Canada) the large majority of deer ticks are NOT infected with *B. burgdorferi*. The risk of infection after a documented deer tick bite is quite low (1.5% to 3.0%), even in areas with intense transmission. Most individuals infected with *B. burgdorferi* in North America (65%-80%) develop *erythema migrans*, which is readily recognized and treated. The risk of developing late sequelae from Lyme disease without *erythema migrans* following a recognized bite is thought to be very low. In extremely anxious individuals, paired early and late (e.g., 4-6 weeks) sera can be used to confirm the absence of seroconversion.

Selected References

American Academy of Pediatrics. *Prevention of Lyme disease: policy statement.* Pediatrics 2000;105:142-47.

Banerjee SN, Banerjee M, Fernando K et al. *Presence of spirochete causing Lyme disease, **Borrelia burgdorferi** in the blacklegged tick, **Ixodes scapularis**, in southern Ontario.* Can Med Assoc J 2000;162:1567-69.

Barker IK, Lindsay LR. *Lyme borreliosis in Ontario: determining the risks.* Can Med Assoc J 2000;162:1573-4.

Centers for Disease Control and Prevention. *Recommendations for the use of Lyme disease vaccine. Recommendations of the Advisory Committee on Immunization Practices (ACIP).* MMWR 1999;48:1-25.

Dennis DT. *Epidemiology, ecology, and prevention of Lyme disease.* In: Rahn DW, Evans J, eds. *Lyme disease.* Philadelphia: American College of Physicians, 1998;7-34.

Fawcett PT, Rose CD, Budd SM et al. *Effect of immunization with recombinant OspA on serologic tests for Lyme borreliosis.* Clin Diag Lab Microbiol 2001;8:79-84.

Lindsay LR, Artsob H, Barker I. *Distribution of **Ixodes pacificus** and **Ixodes scapularis** re concurrent babesiosis and Lyme disease.* CCDR 1998; 24:121-2.

Morshed MG, Scott JD, Banerjee SN et al. *First isolation of Lyme disease spirochete, **Borrelia burgdorferi**, from black-legged tick, **Ixodes scapularis** removed from a bird in Nova Scotia.* CCDR 1999;25:153-5.

Morshed MG, Scott JD, Banerjee SN et al. *First isolation of Lyme disease spirochete, **Borrelia burgdorferi**, from black-legged tick, **Ixodes scapularis** collected at Rondeau Provincial Park, Ontario.* CCDR 2000;26:42-5.

Nadelman RB, Nowakowski J, Fish D et al. and the Tick Bite Study Group. *Prophylaxis with single-dose doxycycline for the prevention of Lyme disease after an **Ixodes scapularis** tick bite.* N Engl J Med 2001;345:79-84.

Shapiro ED. *Doxycycline for ticks bites – not for everyone.* N Engl J Med 2001;345:133-4.

Sikand VK, Halsey N, Krause PJ et al. and the Pediatric Lyme Vaccine Study Group. *Safety and immunogenicity of a recombinant **Borrelia burgdorferi** outer surface protein A vaccine against Lyme disease in healthy children and adolescents: a randomized controlled trial.* Pediatrics 2001;1-8:123-8.

Sigal LH, Zahradnik JM, Lavin P et al. *A vaccine consisting of recombinant **Borrelia burgdorferi** outer-surface protein A to prevent Lyme disease.* N Engl J Med 1998;339:216-22.

Lyme Disease Vaccine

Steere AC, Sikand VK, Meurice F et al. *Vaccination against Lyme disease with recombinant Borrelia burgdorferi outer-surface lipoprotein A with adjuvant.* N Engl J Med 1998;339:209-16.

Steere AC. *Lyme disease.* N Engl J Med 2001;345:115-25.

Thanassi WT, Schoen RT. *The Lyme disease vaccine: conception, development and implementation.* Ann Intern Med 2000;132:661-8.

Van Hoecke C, Lebacq E, Beran J et al. *Alternative vaccination schedules (0, 1 and 6 months versus 0, 1 and 12 months) for a recombinant OspA Lyme disease vaccine.* Clin Infect Dis 1999;28:1260-4.

Lyme Disease Vaccine

Measles Vaccine

Measles (rubeola) is the most contagious vaccine-preventable infection of humans. There has been a marked reduction in incidence in countries where vaccine has been widely used, but measles remains a serious and common disease in many parts of the world. Complications such as otitis media and bronchopneumonia occur in about 10% of reported cases, even more commonly in those who are poorly nourished and chronically ill, and in infants < 1 year of age. Measles encephalitis occurs in approximately 1 of every 1,000 reported cases and may result in permanent brain damage. In countries like Canada, death is estimated to occur once in 3,000 cases. Furthermore, prior measles infection is associated with subacute sclerosing panencephalitis (SSPE), a rare but fatal disease.

Epidemiology

Before the introduction of the vaccine, measles occurred in cycles with an increasing incidence every 2 to 3 years. At that time, an estimated 300,000 to 400,000 cases occurred annually. Since the introduction of vaccine, the incidence has declined markedly in Canada (see Figure). Between 1989 and 1995, in spite of the very high vaccine coverage, there were many large outbreaks involving mainly children who had received one dose of measles vaccine. It was estimated that 10% to 15% of immunized children remained unprotected after a single dose given at 12 months of age, a proportion large enough to allow circulation of the virus. These vaccine failures were mainly caused by the interference of persisting maternal antibody. To eliminate measles, it was thus necessary to change to a two-dose schedule to further decrease the proportion of susceptible children.

Measles – Reported Cases, Canada, 1979-2000

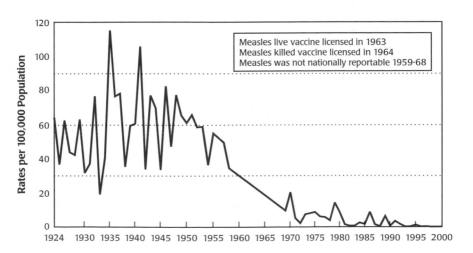

Measles live vaccine licensed in 1963
Measles killed vaccine licensed in 1964
Measles was not nationally reportable 1959-68

In 1996 and 1997, every province and territory added a second dose to its routine schedule, and most conducted catch-up programs in school-aged children in order to protect those left susceptible after their first dose. These interventions achieved vaccine coverage for the second dose in excess of 85%, reducing the proportion of vulnerable children to a negligible level that will not sustain transmission of the virus.

Because an effective vaccine is available and there is no non-human reservoir or source of infection, measles elimination within a population should be possible. During the XXIV Pan American Sanitary Conference in September 1994, representatives from Canada and other nations resolved to eliminate measles by the year 2000. In Canada, sustained transmission has been eliminated by our current schedule and high vaccine coverage. However, as expected, some clusters due to imported cases continue to occur. Secondary spread from these imported cases is self-limited and involves the few Canadians who are still vulnerable. In 23 incidents resulting from importation between 1998 and 2000, only six led to secondary transmission, with up to 200 cases reported in 1 year.

Most other countries in North, Central and South America have also succeeded in eliminating sustained transmission, but the situation in other continents is evolving at a slower pace.

The great challenge for future years will be to continue achieving vaccine coverage rates of 95% or more as measles becomes increasingly unfamiliar to Canadian parents. Immunization against measles will continue to be necessary in Canada until global elimination of the disease has been achieved.

Preparations Licensed for Immunization

Live measles virus vaccines are prepared from Edmonston B "further attenuated" strains (e.g., Moraten, Edmonston-Zagreb, Schwarz, Connaught strains). They are available alone, in combination with live rubella vaccine (MR) or with mumps and rubella vaccines (MMR). Measles vaccines are generally prepared in chick fibroblast cell cultures, except for MoRu-Viraten Berna®, which is grown in human fibroblasts. All preparations may contain traces of antibiotics (e.g., neomycin) and stabilizer such as gelatin. Consult the product monograph for details.

Efficacy

The efficacy of the measles vaccine increases with age at immunization. The main mechanism explaining poor efficacy in children immunized at an early age is the interference by maternal antibody. These antibodies are transferred from the mother to the fetus in utero, and their levels slowly decrease after birth. Most infants have lost their maternal antibody by 12 months of age, but studies have shown that immunization at 15 months of age gives higher protection. Maternal antibodies are not the unique factor in vaccine failure, as the protection appears to reach a plateau after 15 months of age. The efficacy of a single dose given at 12 or 15 months is estimated to be 85% to 95%. With a second dose, almost 100% of children are protected.

Recommended Usage

Infants and children

For routine immunization, two doses of measles vaccine should be given. Infants should receive a first dose combined with mumps and rubella vaccines (MMR) shortly after their first birthday; the second dose should be given at least 4 weeks after the first and before school entry. It is convenient to link this dose with other routinely scheduled immunizations. Options include giving it with the next scheduled immunization at 18 months of age, with school entry immunization at 4 to 6 years, or at any intervening age that is practicable (such as entry to day care). For routine second doses, MMR vaccine is preferred because a proportion of children will also benefit from enhanced protection against rubella and mumps.

Two doses of vaccine given 4 weeks apart are recommended for children who

- are out of step with the routine schedule;

- are without an immunization record;

- are without reliable records of measles immunization (e.g., immigrants);

- were given live measles vaccine and immune globulin (IG) simultaneously or live measles vaccine within 5 months of receiving IG;

- received an inadequate vaccine dosage.

Vaccine may be recommended for children < 12 months of age if they are at high risk of exposure to measles or are travelling abroad to an area where measles is common; measles vaccine alone or as MMR may be given as early as 6 months of age. Under these circumstances, or if vaccine was inappropriately given before the child's first birthday, such children should receive two additional doses of MMR after the first birthday.

Post-exposure use: Susceptible individuals > 12 months of age who are exposed to measles may be protected from disease if measles vaccine is given within 72 hours after exposure. There are no known adverse effects of vaccine given to people incubating measles. IG given within 6 days after exposure can modify or prevent disease and may be used for this purpose in infants < 12 months of age, people for whom vaccine is contraindicated, or those for whom more than 72 hours but less than 1 week have elapsed since exposure (for IG dose see page 33). Unless it is contraindicated, individuals who receive IG should receive measles vaccine later, at the intervals specified in Table 7 on page 34.

Adults

Routine immunization is recommended for adults born after 1970 without a history of disease. In the 1998 edition of the *Canadian Immunization Guide*, this cut-off was changed from 1957 to 1970 because the epidemiology of measles in Canada since 1989 has demonstrated that cases are very rare in adults born before that year.

Measles Vaccine

This observation is explained by the relatively free circulation of measles virus in Canada up until the early 1970s, which allowed most people born before then to acquire measles. Although the vaccine was licensed for use in both Canada and the U.S. in 1963, it was used on a large scale in Canada only in the early 1970s, as compared with the mid 1960s in the U.S. Furthermore, in 1976, age at immunization was raised to 15 months in the U.S. while it remained at 12 months in Canada. The greater proportion of primary vaccine failures associated with a younger age at immunization permitted the large outbreaks of measles observed until the recent introduction of the two-dose schedule.

A small proportion of adults born since 1970 are still vulnerable, and this proportion is greater among younger adults. Epidemiologic data show that settings with large concentrations of young adults, such as colleges and universities, permit transmission of measles. Thus, vaccine should be administered to adults born since 1970 who attend such institutions or who are expected to be at higher risk of measles exposure than the general population, for example, during travel or outbreaks. Although two doses of vaccine or documented proof of disease are generally needed as evidence of complete protection, the administration of a single dose of vaccine to adults without such proof appears satisfactory. In fact, most adults without proof of immunity are already immune, and a single dose of vaccine will raise that proportion close to 100%. The benefit of a second dose 1 month later is limited, because the main cause of vaccine failure (anti-measles maternal antibody) is not a problem in adults.

One additional dose of vaccine should be offered only to adults born since 1970 who are at the greatest risk of exposure and who have not already received two doses or had natural measles infection. These people include

- travellers to a measles endemic area
- health care workers
- students at post-secondary institutions
- military recruits
- adults who are aware that they were never immunized.

Dosage

The dose of measles vaccine, either alone or in combination with rubella and mumps vaccine (MMR), is 0.5 mL. For unidose vials, the whole content of the vial should be injected after reconstitution (0.5-0.7 mL).

Route of Administration

The vaccine should be administered subcutaneously.

Storage Requirements

Measles-containing vaccine should be stored in the refrigerator at a temperature of 2° C to 8° C. Once reconstituted, the vaccine should be administered promptly.

Simultaneous Administration with Other Vaccines

Measles-containing vaccine can be given concurrently with other childhood vaccines such as combined diphtheria, pertussis, tetanus, polio or *Haemophilus influenzae* type b vaccines. Separate injections are required at different anatomic sites. When administered with other live vaccines, like varicella vaccine, measles-containing vaccine should be given at the same time or separated by a minimum 4-week interval.

Adverse Reactions

Measles vaccine produces a mild, non-transmissible and usually subclinical infection. Fever, with or without rash, may be seen in about 5% to 10% of individuals 7 to 10 days after administration. Fever may occasionally trigger a seizure in susceptible children, such as those who have previously had convulsions or whose siblings or parents have a history of convulsions. However, the risk is low, and the benefit of immunizing children greatly outweighs any potential risk associated with febrile seizures. Transient thrombocytopenia occurs, rarely, during the month after immunization. Adverse reactions are less frequent after the second dose of vaccine and tend to occur only in those not protected by the first dose.

Encephalitis has been reported in association with administration of live attenuated measles vaccine at a frequency of approximately 1 per million doses distributed in North America, which is so rare that it is uncertain whether vaccine is the cause. Nevertheless, the reported incidence is much lower than that observed with the natural disease (approximately 1 per 1,000 cases).

There has been a dramatic decline in the incidence of SSPE since the introduction of widespread measles immunization. To date, no cases from whom measles virus was isolated had a vaccine strain.

If MMR is used, reactions to the mumps and rubella components may be encountered (see pages 167 and 203). Despite reports of an association between MMR vaccine and autism or inflammatory bowel disease, rigorous studies have confirmed the lack of causality (see General Cautions and Contraindications, page 7). Therefore, separate administration of the different components of MMR is strongly discouraged, as it will give no health benefit, will increase the proportion of children who fail to receive all three antigens and/or delay achieving complete protection against all three diseases, and will cause unnecessary pain and distress to children.

Measles Vaccine

Contraindications

Measles vaccine (or MMR) is contraindicated in individuals with a previous anaphylactic reaction to a measles-containing vaccine. If there is a compelling reason to re-immunize such individuals, MMR skin testing and graded challenge in an appropriately equipped facility can be considered. However, the possibility of a hypersensitivity reaction to the MMR skin test or during the graded challenge must be considered.

Administration of measles vaccine or MMR should be deferred if there is any severe acute illness. However, immunization should not be delayed because of minor acute illness, with or without fever.

Although there is no known risk from measles vaccine administered during pregnancy, it should not be given to pregnant women.

Since measles vaccine may contain trace amounts of neomycin, people who have experienced anaphylactic reactions to topically or systemically administered neomycin should not receive measles vaccine. Measles vaccine may also contain gelatin as a stabilizer, and so those who have had severe allergic reactions to gelatin or gelatin-containing products should be immunized with great caution.

Measles vaccine is contraindicated in most people whose immune system is impaired as a result of disease or therapy (for HIV, see the section below and Vaccination in Immunocompromised Hosts, on page 20).

Precautions

Tuberculosis may be exacerbated by natural measles infection, but there is no evidence that measles vaccine has such an effect. Measles immunization can suppress a positive tuberculin skin test for several weeks. If skin testing for tuberculosis is required, it should be done on the same day as immunization or delayed for 6 or more weeks.

MMR is indicated for most infants infected with HIV whose immune function at 12 to 15 months of age is compatible with safe MMR immunization (1994 Pediatric HIV Classification categories E, N1, A1). Consultation with an expert is required in the case of HIV-infected children to determine the presence or absence of significant immunodeficiency in individual cases. Measles re-vaccination may still be appropriate for HIV-infected people with moderate immunodeficiency if there is a high risk of measles in the local community or travel to an area where measles is endemic. Consultation with local public health authorities will help determine the local level of measles activity and risk to travellers abroad.

Because the response to prior immunization may be impaired, HIV-infected children should receive IG after recognized exposures to measles. When other susceptible people with immune deficiencies are exposed to measles, passive immunization with IG should be given as soon as possible (see page 33). It is desirable to immunize close contacts of immunocompromised individuals in order to minimize the latter's risk of exposure to measles.

Clinical studies have demonstrated that egg allergy should no longer be considered a contraindication to immunization with MMR. In people who have a history of anaphylactic hypersensitivity to hens' eggs (urticaria, swelling of the mouth and throat, difficulty in breathing or hypotension), measles vaccine can be administered in the routine manner without prior skin testing. However, this should take place where adequate facilities are available to manage anaphylaxis. Those at risk should be observed for 30 minutes after immunization for any sign of allergic reaction. No special precautions are necessary for children with minor egg hypersensitivity who are able to ingest small quantities of egg uneventfully or who are given measles-rubella vaccine free of avian protein. No special measures are necessary for children who have never been fed eggs before MMR immunization. Prior egg ingestion should not be a prerequisite for MMR immunization (see Anaphylaxis section, page 14).

For travellers, care must be taken in the timing of immunization when IG is also required (see Table 7, page 34).

Outbreak Control

A full discussion of measles outbreak control is beyond the scope of this chapter. Readers are referred to the statement on outbreak control issued by the Advisory Committee on Epidemiology.

With the current two-dose schedule for measles vaccine, large outbreaks of measles are not expected to recur. However, because many countries have lower immunization coverage, measles will continue to be imported into Canada. Imported cases will result in limited transmission of measles, usually among unvaccinated children and young adults who have not received two doses of vaccine.

Control interventions in schools or other facilities had little impact when Canada was using a single-dose program. With the two-dose strategy and high vaccine coverage, the benefits of control interventions are likely to be negligible except in settings where vaccine coverage is known to be low. Thus, before any intervention is started, suspected measles cases should be promptly confirmed by culture or serology. If cases are confirmed, contacts should be informed that measles is circulating and advised to update their immunization status if necessary. For practical purposes, all students attending the same school or facility should be considered contacts. Immunization within 72 hours of exposure will usually prevent measles and is not known to produce adverse effects. Should an individual already be immune or infected by measles virus, there is no increased risk of adverse reactions from immunization with live measles vaccine or with MMR.

Selected References

Advisory Committee on Epidemiology. *Guidelines for control of measles outbreaks in Canada.* CCDR 1995;21:189-95.

Bell A, King A, Pielak K et al. *Epidemiology of measles outbreak in British Columbia — February 1997.* CCDR 1997;23:49-51.

Measles Vaccine

De Serres G, Boulianne N, Meyer F et al. *Measles vaccine efficacy during an outbreak in a highly vaccinated population: incremental increase in protection with age at vaccination up to 18 months*. Epidemiol Infect 1995;115:315-23.

De Serres G, Gay NJ, Paddy C et al. *Epidemiology of transmissible diseases after elimination*. Am J Epidemiol 2000;151(1):1039-48.

De Serres G, Sciberras J, Naus M et al. *Protection after two doses of measles vaccine is independent of interval between doses*. J Infect Dis 1999;180:187-90.

Gay NJ, De Serres G, Farrington CP et al. *Elimination of measles from the United States: an assessment through basic surveillance data*. J Infect Dis 2002, in press.

Halsey NA, Hyman SL. *Measles-mumps-rubella vaccine and autistic spectrum disorder: report from the New Challenges in Childhood Immunizations Conference convened in Oak Brook, Illinois, June 12-13, 2000*. Pediatrics 2001;107:E84

Institute of Medicine, Immunization Safety Review Committee (Stratton K, Gable A, Shetty P et al, eds.). *Measles-mumps-rubella vaccine and autism*. Washington DC: National Academy Press, 2001.

King A, Varughese P, De Serres G et al. *The epic of measles in Canada: from endemic to epidemic to elimination: measles in Canada*. J Infect Dis 2002, in press.

Markowitz L, Albrecht P, Orenstein WA et al. *Persistence of measles antibody after revaccination*. J Infect Dis 1992;166:205-08.

McLean ME, Walsh PJ, Carter AO et al. *Measles in Canada — 1989*. CCDR 1990;16:213-18.

Osterman JW, Melnychuk D. *Revaccination of children during school-based measles outbreaks: potential impact of a new policy recommendation*. Can Med Assoc J 1992;146:929-36.

Ratnam S, Chandra R, Gadag V. *Maternal measles and rubella antibody levels and serologic response in infants immunized with MMRII vaccine at 12 months of age*. J Infect Dis 1993;168:1596-98.

Ratnam S, West R, Gadag V et al. *Immunity against measles in school aged children: implications for measles revaccination strategies*. Can J Public Health 1996;87:407-10.

Strauss B, Bigham M. *Does measles-mumps-rubella (MMR) vaccination cause inflammatory bowel disease and autism?* CCDR 2001;27:65-72.

Wong T, Lee-Han H, Bell B et al. *Measles outbreak in Waterloo area, Ontario, 1990-1991*. CCDR 1991;17:219-24.

Meningococcal Vaccine

In light of the recent licensure of meningococcal C conjugate vaccines, this chapter has been completely revised.

Epidemiology

Invasive meningoccocal disease (IMD) is endemic in Canada, and periods of increased activity occur roughly every 10 to 15 years but with no consistent pattern. The last major epidemic of serogroup A meningococcal disease occurred in 1940-43, when the peak incidence was close to 13 per 100,000 population per year. Since then, outbreaks have been uncommon and localized, and the overall incidence of disease has remained at or below 2 per 100,000 per year (range 0.5 to 2.1). The incidence of IMD has varied considerably with different serogroups, age groups, geographic locations and time.

Serogroups A and C *Neisseria meningitidis* were the groups most frequently identified from 1971 to 1974. From 1975 to 1989, serogroup B predominated, the majority being serotype 2b, 4 and 15 and the most common subtype P1.2. In 1986, a new clone of serogroup C, serotype 2a, characterized as electrophoretic type 15 (ET-15), was identified in Canada for the first time. Since then serogroups B and C have been responsible for most of the cases of endemic disease in Canada. However, serogroup C isolates have almost exclusively been responsible for clusters or outbreaks in schools and communities.

Overall, the incidence has been highest among children < 1 year of age and has declined with age, except for a smaller peak in the 15 to 19 year age group. Age-specific incidence rates (per 100,000 population per year) during the period 1985 to 2000 were 14.8 among infants < 1 year old, 4.2 among children 1 to 4 years, 2.3 among those 15 to 19 years and 0.5 among adults ≥ 20 years. Children < 1 year of age accounted for 18% of cases (mean of 50 cases per year), those 1 to 4 accounted for 21% (mean of 58 cases per year), those 5 to 9 accounted for 7% (mean of 20 cases per year) and adolescents 15 to 19 years of age accounted for 14% (mean of 41 cases per year). One-third of cases occurred in people ≥ 20 years. The overall case fatality rate (CFR) varied from 9% in 1985 to 12% in 1993 with the emergence of the more virulent ET-15.

Serogroup C

The emergence of the ET-15 clone was initially associated with an increase in localized outbreaks and in the proportion of endemic disease caused by serogroup C. The features of serogroup C disease for the period 1985 to 2000 have included the occurrence of clusters in schools, a high incidence among adolescents and young adults (median age 15 years), a higher proportion of cases presenting as septicemia (88% vs 79%), and a high CFR as compared with group B disease (14% vs 6%). A retrospective study in Quebec of cases presenting during 1990 to1994 showed that 15% of survivors of serogroup C disease had sequelae (skin scars 12%, amputations 5%, hearing loss 2%, renal problems 1% and other sequelae 4%), and the 20-59 year age group suffered the most in terms of illness and death.

From January 2000 to June 2001, there has been a resurgence of group C disease with localized clusters or outbreaks, mainly affecting adolescents and young adults, in five provinces (Alberta, British Columbia, Manitoba, Quebec and Ontario).

Immunization campaigns, generally targeting high school-aged children and extending to a varying degree to include younger children and young adults, have been launched in different provinces.

Other serogroups

There has been less fluctuation in the incidence of serogroup B than of serogroup C disease over time. Children < 5 years account for the majority of serogroup B cases (average 54%, range 47%-60%) and the highest incidence (median age, 2 years).

An increasing trend in serogroup Y disease has been observed in the United States during the past decade, although no such trends have been observed in Canada over this time. In this country, from 1993 to 2000, serogroup Y represented approximately 1% to 15% of isolates characterized, and serogroup-specific incidence remained relatively stable at 0.05 to 0.1 per 100,000 population per year (mean 24 confirmed cases per year, range 16 to 47). Of note, however, is a recent increase in the incidence of serogroup Y disease in Ontario, accounting for 30% of laboratory confirmations (10 of 33 isolations) from this province during the first 4 months of 2001. Serogroup Y disease has tended to affect older adults (median age 25 years 1985-2000) and is associated with a CFR between that of serogroup C and serogroup B cases. The CFR for serogroup Y invasive disease was 10% over the period 1985-2000.

Both serogroup A and W135 IMD are reported uncommonly in Canada. Since the epidemics of the early 1940s the incidence of serogroup A disease has declined dramatically. From 1985 to 2000, a total of 101 cases with invasive serogroup W135 disease were reported (range 1-12 cases per year), with an average incidence of 0.02 per 100,000 population per year (1999 and 2000 data preliminary). The median ages of serogroup A and W135 cases were 18 years and 19 years respectively.

Preparations Licensed for Immunization

Two different types of meningococcal vaccine are available: purified capsular polysaccharide vaccines (Men-Ps) and protein-polysaccharide conjugate vaccines (Men-conjugate). Products licensed in Canada include bivalent MenAC-Ps vaccines containing capsular polysaccharides from serogroups A and C; a quadrivalent MenACYW-Ps vaccine containing capsular polysaccharide from serogroups A, C, Y and W135 meningococci; and two newly licensed monovalent MenC-conjugate vaccines: Menjugate™, Chiron Corp., in which O-acetylated C-polysaccharide is conjugated to the protein CRM_{197} (Cross Reacting Material 197), and NeisVac-C™, Baxter/North American Vaccine, which contains de-O-acetylated C-polysaccharide conjugated to tetanus toxoids. One other MenC-conjugate vaccine not yet licensed in

Canada is Meningitec™, Wyeth-Lederle, which contains *O*-acetylated C-polysaccharide conjugated to the protein CRM_{197}. No vaccine is available against serogroup B meningococci.

Efficacy and Immunogenicity

Purified polysaccharide vaccines

MenAC-polysaccharide vaccines and MenACYW-polysaccharide vaccines have been widely used to control outbreaks and epidemics of serogroup A and C meningococcal disease. MenAC-Ps vaccine efficacy at 2 months after immunization in U.S. military recruits was found to be 87% to 88% and at 12 months after immunization in Italian military recruits was 91%. One year after mass immunization of children aged 2 to 19 years in Spain, efficacy was 94% against serogroup C invasive disease, and in a U.S. case control study in children and adults aged 2 to 29 efficacy was 85%.

Lower efficacy has generally been observed in young children. After 17 months' follow-up in Brazil there was no significant efficacy against IMD in children aged 6 to 36 months, but in a subgroup aged 24 to 36 months efficacy was 67%. MenC-Ps vaccine was found to be non-protective in children < 2 years of age in another study and only 52% effective in 2 to 3 year olds after 17 months of follow-up in yet another one. In Quebec, where 1.7 million doses of polysaccharide vaccine were given during an outbreak in the early 1990s, efficacy was estimated at 79% among children and young adults after 5 years. After 8 years' follow-up in Quebec, protection from serogroup C meningococcal disease was observed in the first 2 years after vaccine administration (vaccine efficacy 65%; 95% confidence interval [CI] 20%-84%) but not in the next 3 years (vaccine efficacy 0%; 95% CI -5% to 65%). Vaccine efficacy was strongly related to age at immunization: 83% (95% CI 39%-96%) for ages 15 to 20 years, 75% (95% CI -17% to 93%) for ages 10 to 14 years, and 41% (95% CI -106% to 79%) for ages 2 to 9 years. There was no evidence of protection in children < 2 years; all eight cases of meningococcal disease in this age group occurred in vaccinees.

These data demonstrate lack of efficacy in those < 2 years, poor efficacy in 2-3 year olds and short duration of efficacy of the serogroup C component of MenAC-Ps and MenACYW-Ps vaccines, particularly in children < 10 years of age.

During a serogroup A epidemic in Africa, the efficacy of polysaccharide vaccines against serogroup A was estimated as 87%. Although protection against serogroup A conferred by MenAC-Ps or MenACYW-Ps vaccine may persist in school-aged children and adults for at least 3 years, the efficacy of the group A vaccine in children aged < 5 years may decrease markedly within this period. In one study, efficacy declined from > 90% to < 10% by 3 years after immunization among children who were aged < 4 years when immunized. Efficacy was 67% at 1 year after immunization among children who were ≥ 4 years.

Vaccines containing serogroups Y and W135 polysaccharides are safe and immunogenic in adults and in children aged > 2 years, but clinical protection has not been studied after immunization with polysaccharides of these serogroups.

Protein-polysaccharide conjugate vaccines

A high level of protection produced by immunization with MenC conjugate vaccine has been predicted from immunogenicity data, even in infants as young as 2 months. There are limited efficacy data available for MenC-conjugate vaccines. Preliminary data from U.K. surveillance after introduction of the MenC-conjugate vaccine throughout childhood have indicated an estimated short-term (follow-up was approximately 9 months) efficacy of 97% in adolescents and 92% in toddlers.

Recommended Usage

The MenC-conjugate vaccine has been licensed for use in infants, children and adults, and NACI recommends that it be used as follows.

Infants

MenC-conjugate vaccine is recommended for routine immunization of infants at ages 2, 4 and 6 months (normally, at least 4 weeks apart) at the same visit as primary immunization with DTaP, IPV and Hib, to prevent serogroup C meningococcal disease. Infants aged 4-12 months who have not previously received the vaccine should be immunized with two doses given at least 1 month apart.

Infants born prematurely should receive the vaccine at the same chronological age as term infants.

Purified polysaccharide vaccine (MenACYW-Ps or MenAC-Ps) is not recommended for routine infant immunization.

Individuals over 1 year of age

A single dose of MenC-conjugate vaccine is recommended for immunization of children aged 1-4 years and for adolescents and young adults to prevent the increased risk of serogroup C meningococcal disease in these age groups. For children ≥ 5 years of age who have not reached adolescence, immunization with a single dose of MenC-conjugate vaccine may also be considered.

Purified polysaccharide vaccine (MenACYW-Ps or MenAC-Ps vaccines) is not recommended for routine childhood immunization.

Contacts of cases

Household and intimate social contacts (kissing, sharing a toothbrush etc.) of sporadic cases of meningococcal disease have a considerably elevated risk of infection, and chemoprophylaxis should therefore be administered to them: rifampin 600 mg every 12 hours for 2 days for adults (10 mg/kg in children > 1 year of age, 5 mg/kg < 1 year); or ciprofloxacin as a single 500 mg oral dose for adults or ceftriaxone

250 mg intramuscularly for adults (50 mg/kg in children). Ceftriaxone is recommended in pregnancy and when compliance with oral antibiotics is unlikely. If antibiotics such as penicillin, which do not reliably eliminate nasopharyngeal carriage, have been used for treatment in hospital, before discharge the index case should also receive antibiotics that clear nasal carriage.

In certain countries where chemoprophylaxis of contacts is routinely administered for sporadic cases, as it is in Canada, 0.3% to 3% of cases of meningococcal disease occur in contacts of the index case. In one study, the median interval between occurrence of the index and secondary case was 7 weeks. Some of these secondary cases can be attributed to failure of chemoprophylaxis (e.g., through failure of administration, poor compliance or the presence of antibiotic resistance). The situation in Canada is unknown.

Vaccination of unimmunized household and intimate social contacts may further reduce the risk of secondary cases beyond the benefit of chemoprophylaxis and is recommended. MenACYW-Ps or MenAC-Ps vaccine should be used for contacts of cases with disease known to be caused by serogroup A meningococci; MenACYW-Ps vaccine should be used for contacts of cases of serogroup Y or W135 disease. For contacts of known serogroup C disease, MenC-conjugate vaccine is preferred, when available, because of the longer duration of protection and induction of immunologic memory. However, MenACYW-Ps or MenAC-Ps will also provide useful protection in older children and adults for the 1-year period of increased risk that may follow an epidemic. These polysaccharide vaccines are ineffective against serogroup C disease for children < 2 years of age, and MenC-conjugate should be used in this situation where possible. No vaccine is currently recommended for contacts of individuals with serogroup B disease or contacts of cases of disease in which the serogroup has not been determined.

High-risk groups

Routine immunization with quadrivalent MenACYW-Ps is recommended for certain groups at increased risk of meningococcal disease. Such individuals include those with functional or anatomic asplenia (vaccines should be given at least 10-14 days before splenectomy) and people with complement, properdin or factor D deficiency. More durable protection against serogroup C meningococcal disease may be achieved by giving MenC-conjugate vaccine to these individuals in addition to MenACYW-Ps vaccine. If the MenC-conjugate vaccine is given first, a period of at least 2 weeks before immunization with MenACYW-Ps vaccine is recommended to allow time for generation of an antibody response. It is possible that a shorter interval may interfere with this response. If the MenACYW-Ps vaccine is given first, an adequate response to MenC-conjugate vaccine has been observed after a delay of 6 months in adults, and this remains the recommended interval until further data are available. Children < 2 years with any of these immunodeficiencies should be immunized with MenC-conjugate vaccine as described in the routine infant schedule above, and should then receive quadrivalent MenACYW-Ps at 2 years of age.

Institutions

Routine immunization with the quadrivalent polysaccharide vaccine, MenACYW-Ps, is recommended for military recruits and may be considered for other groups or institutions where there is an increased risk of disease. New guidance on management of outbreaks in institutions is in preparation.

Although there are no data to suggest an increased risk of meningococcal disease among students in Canada living in residential accommodation, an elevation in risk has been observed in the U.S. among freshmen living in dormitory accommodation and in the U.K. among university students in catered hall accommodation. Clusters of cases of meningococcal disease in students have been reported in a number of countries, and carriage rates increase rapidly among freshmen during the first week of term in the U.K. In this age group in Canada, as in other countries, there is an increase in the rate of meningococcal disease. Immunization against serogroup C meningoccocal infection should be considered for students living in residential or dormitory accommodation. For these students the risk is mainly from serogroup C meningococcal disease, and immunization with a single dose of MenACYW-Ps, MenAC-Ps or MenC-conjugate vaccine is appropriate. MenC-conjugate vaccine may be preferred because of the induction of immunologic memory and the enhanced immunogenicity.

Laboratory and health care workers

Clinical health care workers are only at higher risk of meningococcal disease if they are exposed to respiratory secretions from individuals suffering from meningococcal infection around the time of admission. Significant exposure has been defined as intensive, unprotected contact (mask not worn) with infected patients (e.g., through intubation, resuscitation, or close examination of the oropharynx of patients). By 24 hours after antibiotics have been initiated, meningococci are undetectable in the respiratory secretions of patients, and therefore health care workers are at negligible risk.

For the occasional health care staff who have direct exposure to respiratory secretions the relative risk of meningococcal disease is estimated to be 25 times higher than in the general population. It is recommended that health care workers use barrier precautions to avoid direct contact with respiratory secretions of patients with meningococcal disease during the first 24 hours after commencement of antibiotic therapy, and that those with significant exposure receive antibiotic chemoprophylaxis. Routine immunization of health care workers is not currently recommended, as the risk period for acquisition ends when contact with an untreated patient terminates, and antibiotic chemoprophylaxis should be sufficient in the high-risk situation described.

Laboratory-acquired meningococcal infection is believed to be rare. However, the rate of disease in a recent U.S. survey conducted by the Centers for Disease Control and Prevention (CDC), Atlanta, was higher than expected among microbiology laboratory workers dealing with *N. meningitidis* cultures in the absence of any breaches in laboratory safety practices. In light of this, CDC is currently re-evaluating its recommendations for laboratory workers. Research, industrial and clinical laboratory personnel who are routinely exposed to *N. meningitidis* should be offered immunization with quadrivalent MenACYW-Ps and may be additionally offered MenC-conjugate vaccine to provide enhanced protection against serogroup C meningococcal infection (see Booster Doses and Re-immunization).

Outbreaks of meningococcal disease

Consultation with public health officials and experts in communicable disease is important in the assessment and control of meningococcal disease outbreaks in various settings, and reference to published guidelines (currently being revised) should be made. Most recent outbreaks of meningococcal disease in Canada have involved teenagers and young adults suffering from serogroup C meningococcal disease. Such outbreaks may be controlled by the use of MenACYW-Ps, MenAC-Ps vaccine or MenC-conjugate vaccine. The use of MenC-conjugate vaccine may be preferable because of induction of immunologic memory and prolonged duration of protection. In those previously immunized with a polysaccharide vaccine for whom re-vaccination is considered, MenC-conjugate vaccine is preferred (see Booster Doses and Re-immunization), as further plain polysaccharide immunization may induce immunologic hyporesponsiveness, although the clinical significance of this phenomenon is unknown. In younger children (< 10 years) MenC-conjugate vaccine is recommended for control of outbreaks in view of its superior immunogenicity and efficacy in this age group.

For the control of outbreaks of serogroup A meningococcal disease, MenACYW-Ps or MenAC-Ps vaccine is recommended as a single dose for children > 18 months of age and adults. Children aged 3 to 17 months should receive two doses of vaccine given 3 months apart. For the control of outbreaks associated with serogroup Y or W135 meningococci, one dose of MenACYW-Ps is recommended for people ≥ 2 years.

International travel

Current Canadian guidelines (from the Committee to Advise on Tropical Medicine and Travel) for the prevention of meningococcal disease in travellers should be consulted. In deciding on the need for immunization, there should be particular consideration of the destination to be visited, the nature and duration of exposure, and the age and health of the traveller. Epidemic alerts are published regularly on the following websites:

Travel Medicine Program, Centre for Emergency Preparedness and Response
Health Canada http://www.TravelHealth.gc.ca

U.S. Centers for Disease Control and Prevention (CDC)
http://www.cdc.gov/travel/diseases/menin.htm

World Health Organization (WHO)
http://www.who.int/disease-outbreak-news/disease_indices/men_index.html

Immunization of travellers to areas known to have epidemic meningococcal disease generally aims to prevent serogroup A infection. Epidemics of serogroup A meningococcal disease have been documented every 5 to 10 years in the meningitis belt of sub-Saharan Africa for much of the past century. A similar epidemic pattern has also been described in Asia. Despite the frequency of travel to regions where meningococcal epidemics occur, disease in travellers appears to be very unusual. When vaccine is indicated, a single dose of MenACYW-Ps or MenAC-Ps vaccine should be given to infants $\geq$ 3 months, children, adolescents and adults to prevent serogroup A meningococcal infection.

Large outbreaks of meningococcal disease have affected pilgrims travelling to, and returning from, Mecca, Saudi Arabia, involving serogroup A in 1987, and both serogroup A and W135 in 2000 and 2001. Pilgrims making the annual Hajj pilgrimage to Mecca should receive a single dose of MenACYW-Ps vaccine at least 2 weeks before departure. MenC-conjugate vaccine alone is not appropriate as it does not protect against outbreaks of serogroup W135 or epidemics of serogroup A disease.

Route of Administration and Dosage

MenAC-Ps and MenACYW-Ps vaccines are given as a single 0.5 mL subcutaneous injection to children > 2 years and adults at a separate anatomic site from other co-administered vaccines. For specific protection against serogroup A meningococcal disease this vaccine may be given from 3 months of age.

MenC-conjugate vaccine is given as a single 0.5 mL dose to people > 1 year of age by intramuscular injection. For infants, three doses are given at 2, 4 and 6 months at the same time as the routine primary series, administered at a separate site with a different syringe. Two doses are offered to infants from 4 to 12 months of age who missed the first dose. The minimum interval between doses is normally 4 weeks. The vaccine should preferably be administered in the anterolateral thigh in infants and in the deltoid region in older children and adults.

Booster Doses and Re-immunization

The need for, or effectiveness of, re-immunization with meningococcal polysaccharide vaccine has not been fully established. Repeated immunization may induce immunologic hyporesponsiveness to polysaccharide vaccines, although the clinical significance of this phenomenon is unknown. Re-immunization should be considered, according to the Table, for those continuously or repeatedly exposed to serogroup A disease who have been previously immunized with MenACYW-Ps or MenAC-Ps, particularly for children initially immunized at < 5 years of age. Children or adults with immunodeficiencies resulting in increased risk of meningococcal disease caused by serogroup A, C, Y or W135 meningococci may be re-immunized with MenACYW-Ps according to the Table.

**Recommended Interval Between Repeat Doses of
Meningococcal Polysaccharide Vaccines in Individuals Repeatedly
or Continuously Exposed to Serogroup A Disease**

Age when first immunized	No. of primary doses	Interval since last dose as indication for repeat dose
3-12 months	2 doses: 2-3 months apart	6-12 months
13-23 months	2 doses: 2-3 months apart	1-2 years
2-5 years	1	2-3 years
≥ 6 years	1	≥ 5 years

The new MenC-conjugate vaccine is believed to induce immunologic memory that can be demonstrated for at least 5 years after primary immunization. Re-immunization with MenC-conjugate vaccine is not thought to be necessary at present, although there are insufficient data to predict persistence of immunologic memory (and presumed protection) beyond 5 years. Individuals who have previously received MenACYW-Ps or MenAC-Ps may receive MenC-conjugate vaccine for continued protection against serogroup C meningococcal disease after primary immunization. Since an adequate response to MenC-conjugate vaccine has been observed with a delay of 6 months after immunization with purified polysaccharide vaccine in adults, this remains the recommended interval until further data are available. In other circumstances, when MenC conjugate vaccine has already been administered and protection against serogroup A, Y or W135 meningococci is required, a period of 2 weeks should elapse before immunization with MenACYW-Ps to allow time for generation of an antibody response and avoid possible interference with this response by the polysaccharide vaccine.

Storage and Handling Requirements

All of the available products should be stored at a temperature between 2° C and 8° C and must not be frozen. The vaccines should be reconstituted immediately before use according to the manufacturer's instructions.

Simultaneous Administration with Other Vaccines

Administration of MenC-conjugate vaccine at the same time as, but at a separate injection site from, IPV, DTP, Hib, DTaP, DT, Td and MMR vaccines or OPV does not reduce the immunologic response to any of these other antigens. In a study in Canada, there was no interference noted with Pentacel™ antigens.

There is no information on co-administration of MenC-conjugate vaccine with hepatitis B vaccines.

Adverse Reactions

Purified polysaccharide vaccines

Both MenACYW-Ps and MenAC-Ps vaccines have been used extensively in many countries for mass immunization programs and to immunize military recruits, people who are immunocompromised and travellers. Mild reactions to the vaccines include pain and redness at the injection site in up to 50% and transient fever in 5%, particularly infants. Severe reactions to these vaccines are very unusual but include systemic allergic reactions (urticaria, wheezing, and rash) in ≤ 0.1/100,000 doses, anaphylaxis in < 1 per million doses and occasional neurologic reactions. These vaccines have an established safety record.

No adverse events have been documented during pregnancy or in newborn infants of immunized mothers.

Protein-polysaccharide conjugate vaccines

Safety and adverse event data are available from a number of clinical trials of MenC-conjugate vaccine and MenAC-conjugate vaccine in addition to accumulated data from spontaneous reporting on 12 million doses distributed in the United Kingdom in 1999-2000. Mild reactions were reported as follows: local reactions (redness, tenderness, and swelling at the injection site) in up to 50% of vaccinees, irritability in up to 80% of infants and fever > 38° C in up to 9% when other vaccines were administered. These mild reactions occurred at a lower rate than that produced by other childhood immunizations or other purified polysaccharide vaccines. Headaches and malaise occured in up to 10% of older children and adults. There may be some variation among the three MenC conjugate vaccines in terms of adverse reactions, although one U.K. study found no significant differences in a comparison of the three MenC-conjugate vaccine products in toddlers.

In one Canadian study, MenC-conjugate vaccine (Menjugate™) was administered with Pentacel™ (DTaP/Hib/IPV) in a multi-centre, randomized controlled clinical study involving three centres that compared MenC conjugate vaccine with hepatitis B vaccine (HBV). The frequency of local adverse reactions (tenderness, erythema and induration) among those receiving MenC conjugate vaccine was lower than among those receiving routine infant immunization with Pentacel™, but higher than among those receiving HBV, a vaccine used in a number of provinces for infant immunization. Systemic reactions were experienced at the same rate in those receiving HBV as those receiving MenC-conjugate vaccine.

The frequencies of rare adverse events are based on spontaneous reporting rates from the United Kingdom and have been calculated using the number of reports received as the numerator and the total number of doses distributed as the denominator. Severe reactions were very uncommon and included systemic allergic reactions (lymphadenopathy, anaphylaxis and hypersensitivity reactions, including bronchospasm, facial edema and angioedema) in < 0.01%; neurologic responses (dizziness and convulsions, including febrile convulsions, faints, hypesthesia, paresthesia and hypotonia) in < 0.01%; nausea or vomiting in < 0.01%; rash, urticaria or pruritis in 0.01%; and arthralgia in < 0.01%. No deaths in the United Kingdom have been attributed to this vaccine.

There are no specific studies in humans of MenC-conjugate vaccine during pregnancy or lactation.

Contraindications

Both purified polysaccharide vaccines and the new protein-polysaccharide conjugate vaccine are contraindicated in people with a known hypersensitivity to any component of the vaccine and in those who have shown signs of hypersensitivity after previous administration of the vaccine (see Anaphylaxis section, part I).

Precautions

The new MenC-conjugate vaccine will not protect against meningococcal diseases caused by any of the other types of meningococcal bacteria (A, B, 29e, H, I, K, L, W135, X, Y, or Z, including non-typed). Complete protection against meningococcal serogroup C infection cannot be guaranteed. Conjugate vaccines containing CRM_{197} or tetanus toxoid should not be considered as immunizing agents against diphtheria or tetanus. No changes in the schedule for administering vaccines containing diphtheria or tetanus toxoids are recommended.

MenACYW-Ps and MenAC-Ps vaccines do not provide any cross-protection to meningococci not contained in these vaccines and do not provide complete protection against the vaccine serogroups.

MenC-conjugate has not been studied in pregnancy, and the vaccine should not be used unless there are specific circumstances in which the benefits outweigh the risks.

Other Considerations

The studies described here have clearly demonstrated that MenC-conjugate vaccine can induce immunologic memory for at least 5 years after primary immunization. However, protection is important beyond early childhood even more so than is the case with Hib vaccine. It is currently unknown whether there is a need for a booster dose at some point after infancy to provide protection through adolescence and early adulthood, and this requires close monitoring and further investigation. The ability of MenC-conjugate vaccine to induce herd immunity is unknown.

Based on bactericidal antibody levels at 1 month after immunization it is possible that two doses of MenC-conjugate vaccine in the first 6 months of life may be sufficient. Further data are required on the duration of protective levels of bactericidal antibody following different immunization regimes before this can be recommended.

Although use of MenC-conjugate vaccine probably provides superior protection against serogroup C meningococcal disease than MenC-polysaccharide vaccines, there are no data available on its use in immunodeficient subjects. There are no safety or immunogenicity data available regarding the use of MenC-conjugate vaccine in adults aged > 65 years; no data on the use of the vaccine in outbreak control; and no formal studies of its use in pregnancy or lactation.

The effect of MenC-conjugate vaccine on meningococcal population biology is unknown. It has been suggested that use of a monovalent meningococcal vaccine might induce capsule switching through immunologic pressure, such that hypervirulent serogroup C clones adopt a B, Y or W135 capsule. It may also be the case that use of a monovalent vaccine will have little overall effect on meningococcal disease burden if other meningococci simply replace the niche left by serogroup C meningococci (strain replacement). After the introduction of widespread meningococcal immunization, close epidemiologic and laboratory-based surveillance must be undertaken to monitor changes in meningococcal population biology.

Cost-effectiveness data and information on parental attitudes to immunization are not currently available but would help guide use of meningococcal vaccines in routine immunization in Canada. The merits of MenC-conjugate vaccine relative to other vaccines (e.g., pneumococcal protein polysaccharide conjugate vaccines, adult pertussis vaccine and varicella vaccine) have not been fully studied yet.

New quadrivalent protein-polysaccharide conjugate vaccines (MenACYW-Con) are in development and might provide broad protection against the vaccine serogroups after introduction of an infant immunization program; they could presumably replace monovalent MenC-conjugate vaccines. None of these vaccines offers protection against serogroup B meningococci, a feature that limits the impact that any meningococcal vaccine can have on the disease burden, especially in children.

Selected References

Abramson JS, Spika JS. *Persistence of **Neisseria meningitidis** in the upper respiratory tract after intravenous antibiotic therapy for systemic meningococcal disease*. J Infect Dis 1985;151:370-1.

Almog R, Block C, Gdalevich M et al. *First recorded outbreaks of meningococcal disease in the Israel Defence Force: three clusters due to serogroup C and the emergence of resistance to rifampicin*. Infection 1994;22:69-71.

Anderson EL, Bowers T, Mink CM et al. *Safety and immunogenicity of meningococcal A and C polysaccharide conjugate vaccine in adults*. Infect Immun 1994;62:3391-95.

Birk H. Committee to Advise on Tropical Medicine and Travel (CATMAT*). Statement on meningococcal vaccination for travellers*. CCDR 1999;25:1-12.

Borrow R, Fox AJ, Richmond PC et al. *Induction of immunological memory in UK infants by a meningococcal A/C conjugate vaccine*. Epidemiol Infect 2000;24:427-32.

Borrow R, Southern J, Andrews N et al. *Comparison of antibody kinetics following meningococcal serogroup C conjugate vaccine between healthy adults previously vaccinated with meningococcal A/C polysaccharide vaccine and vaccine-naive controls*. Vaccine 2001;19: 3043-50.

Centers for Disease Control and Prevention. *Serogroup W-135 meningococcal disease among travelers returning from Saudi Arabia—United States, 2000*. MMWR 2000;49:345-6.

Centers for Disease Control and Prevention. *Meningococcal vaccine and college students: recommendations of the Advisory Committee on Immunization Practices (ACIP)*. MMWR 2000;49(RR-7):11-20.

Choo S, Zuckerman J, Goilav C et al. *Immunogenicity and reactogenicity of a group C meningococcal conjugate vaccine compared with a group A+C meningococcal polysaccharide vaccine in adolescents in a randomised observer-blind controlled trial*. Vaccine 2000;18:2686-92.

Cooke RP, Riordan T, Jones DM et al. *Secondary cases of meningococcal infection among close family and household contacts in England and Wales, 1984-7*. BMJ 1989;298:555-8.

Dawson SJ, Fey RE, McNulty CA. *Meningococcal disease in siblings caused by rifampicin sensitive and rifampicin resistant strains*. Commun Dis Public Health 1999;2:215-6.

De Wals P, Hertoghe L, Borlee-Grimee I et al. *Meningococcal disease in Belgium. Secondary attack rate among household, day-care nursery and pre-elementary school contacts*. J Infect 1981;3:53-61.

De Wals P, De Serres G, Niyonsenga T. *Effectiveness of a mass immunization campaign against serogroup C meningococcal disease in Quebec*. JAMA 1002;285:177-81.

English M, MacLennan JM, Bowen-Morris JM et al. *A randomised, double-blind, controlled trial of the immunogenicity and tolerability of a meningococcal group C conjugate vaccine in young British infants*. Vaccine 2000;19:1232-8.

Erickson L, De Wals P. *Complications and sequelae of meningococcal disease in Quebec, Canada, 1990-1994*. Clin Infect Dis 1998;26:1159-64.

Fairley CK, Begg N, Borrow R et al. *Conjugate meningococcal serogroup A and C vaccine: reactogenicity and immunogenicity in United Kingdom infants*. J Infect Dis 1996;174:1360-3.

Gilmore A, Stuart J, Andrews N. *Risk of secondary meningococcal disease in health-care workers*. Lancet 2000;356:1654-5.

Gold R, Lepow ML, Goldschneider I. *Immune response of human infants of polysaccharide vaccines of group A and C **Neisseria meningitidis***. J Infect Dis 1977;136:31-5.

Greenwood BM, Hassan-King M,Whittle HC. *Prevention of secondary cases of meningococcal disease in household contacts by vaccination*. BMJ 1978;1:1317-9.

Hastings L, Stuart J, Andrews N. *A retrospective survey of clusters of meningococcal disease in England and Wales, 1993 to 1995: estimated risks of further cases in household and educational settings*. Commun Dis Rep 1997;7:R195-200.

Health Canada. *Statement on recommended use of meningococcal vaccines*. CCDR 2001;27(ACS-6).

Judson FN, Ehret JM. *Single-dose ceftriaxone to eradicate pharyngeal **Neisseria meningitidis***. Lancet 1984;2:1462-3.

Laboratory-acquired meningococcemia – California and Massachusetts. MMWR 1991;40:46-7, 55.

LCDC. *Guidelines for control of meningococcal disease: Canadian Consensus Conference on Meningococcal Disease*. Can Med Assoc J 1994;150:1825-39.

Leach A, Twumasi PA, Kumah S et al. *Induction of immunologic memory in Gambian children by vaccination in infancy with a group A plus group C meningococcal polysaccharide-protein conjugate vaccine.* J Infect Dis 1997;175:200-4.

MacDonald NE, Halperin SA, Law BJ et al. *Induction of immunologic memory by conjugated vs plain meningococcal C polysaccharide vaccine in toddlers: a randomized controlled trial.* JAMA 1998;280:1685-9.

MacLennan JM, Deeks JJ, Obaro S et al. In: Nassif X (ed), *Meningococcal serogroup C conjugate vaccination in infancy induces persistent immunological memory.* Paris, Nice, France: EDK, 1998.

MacLennan J, Obaro S, Deeks J et al. *Immune response to revaccination with meningococcal A and C polysaccharides in Gambian children following repeated immunisation during early childhood.* Vaccine 1999;17:3086-93.

MacLennan JM, Shackley F, Heath PT et al. *Safety, immunogenicity, and induction of immunologic memory by a serogroup C meningococcal conjugate vaccine in infants: a randomized controlled trial* [see comments]. JAMA 2000;283:2795-801.

MacLennan J, Obaro S, Deeks J et al. *Immunologic memory 5 years after meningococcal A/C conjugate vaccination in infancy.* J Infect Dis 2001;183:97-104.

Meningococcal Disease Surveillance Group. *Meningococcal disease. Secondary attack rate and chemoprophylaxis in the United States, 1974.* JAMA 1976;235:261-5.

Menjugate™ summary of product characteristics, December 2000. UK Marketing Authorization Number PL/13767/0014, 2000.

Neal KR, Nguyen-Van-Tam J, Monk P et al. *Invasive meningococcal disease among university undergraduates: association with universities providing relatively large amounts of catered hall accommodation.* Epidemiol Infect 1999;122:351-7.

Olivares R, Hubert B. *Clusters of meningococcal disease in France (1987-1988).* Eur J Epidemiol 1992;8:737-42.

PHLS Meningococcal Infections Working Group and Public Health Medicine Environmental Group. *Control of meningococcal disease: guidance for consultants in communicable disease control.* Commun Dis Rep 2000;5:R189-95.

Ramsay ME, Andrews N, Kaczmarski EB et al. *Efficacy of meningococcal serogroup C conjugate vaccine in teenagers and toddlers in England.* Lancet 2001;357:195-6.

Richmond PC, Borrow R, Clark S et al. *Meningococcal C conjugate vaccines are immunogenic and prime for memory after a single dose in toddlers.* San Francisco: American Society for Microbiology, 1999.

Richmond P, Borrow R, Miller E et al. *Meningococcal serogroup C conjugate vaccine is immunogenic in infancy and primes for memory.* J Infect Dis 1999;179:1569-72.

Richmond P, Goldblatt D, Fusco PC et al. *Safety and immunogenicity of a new **Neisseria meningitidis** serogroup C-tetanus toxoid conjugate vaccine in healthy adults.* Vaccine 1999;18: 641-6.

Richmond P, Kaczmarski E, Borrow R et al. *Meningococcal C polysaccharide vaccine induces immunologic hyporesponsiveness in adults that is overcome by meningococcal C conjugate vaccine.* J Infect Dis 2000;181:761-4.

Richmond P, Borrow R, Goldblatt D et al. *Ability of 3 different meningococcal C conjugate vaccines to induce immunologic memory after a single dose in UK toddlers.* J Infect Dis 2001;183:160-3.

Samuelsson S, Hansen ET, Osler M et al. *Prevention of secondary cases of meningococcal disease in Denmark.* Epidemiol Infect 2000;124:433-40.

Scholten RJ, Bijlmer HA, Dankert J et al. *Secondary cases of meningococcal disease in The Netherlands, 1989-1990; a reappraisal of chemoprophylaxis.* Ned Tijdschr Geneeskd 1993;137:1505-8.

Stroffolini T, Rosmini F, Curiano CM. *A one year survey of meningococcal disease in Italy.* Eur J Epidemiol 1987;3:399-403.

Twumasi PA Jr, Kumah S, Leach A et al. *A trial of a group A plus group C meningococcal polysaccharide-protein conjugate vaccine in African infants.* J Infect Dis 1995;171:632-8.

Mumps Vaccine

Mumps is an acute infectious disease caused by mumps virus. Subclinical infection is common. Although complications are relatively frequent, permanent sequelae are rare. Before the widespread use of mumps vaccine, mumps was a major cause of viral meningitis. Transient but occasionally permanent deafness may occur, at an estimated rate of 0.5 to 5.0 per 100,000 reported mumps cases. Orchitis occurs in 20% to 30% of post-pubertal male cases and oophoritis in 5% of post-pubertal female cases. Involvement of the reproductive organs is commonly unilateral; therefore, sterility as a result of mumps is rare. Mumps infection during the first trimester of pregnancy may increase the rate of spontaneous abortion.

Since the licensure of vaccine in 1969, the number of reported mumps cases has decreased by > 99%. The number in the past 5 years ranged from 90 (1999) to 402 cases (1995), with an average of 237 per year. Children < 5 years accounted for 17% of cases, and those aged 5 to 14 years accounted for 44%. Outbreaks are rare, but two localized outbreaks have been reported recently. One involved university students in British Columbia in 1997, and the other occurred in Quebec in 1998 among school children from families who had recently emigrated from countries where mumps vaccine was not included in the routine childhood immunization program. Mumps surveillance continues to be necessary to assess the effectiveness of immunization in children as well as adults. With the use of MMR for measles immunization under the currently recommended two-dose schedule, many children now receive two doses of mumps vaccine.

Preparations Licensed for Immunization

Mumps virus vaccine is a live, attenuated virus vaccine and is available in combination with measles and rubella vaccines and in monovalent form. It is prepared from the Jeryl Lynn attenuated virus strain and is grown in chick embryo cell culture.

Efficacy and Immunogenicity

A single dose of the vaccine produces an antibody response in over 95% of susceptible individuals. Antibody levels, though lower than those that follow natural disease, persist for at least 20 years and provide continuing protection. In a Canadian study, however, a significant proportion of the vaccinees were negative for mumps antibodies 5 to 6 years after immunization. There are no data currently available correlating specific antibody titres with susceptibility to mumps, but outbreaks have been reported in highly vaccinated populations. A two-dose measles-mumps-rubella immunization schedule used in Finland resulted in higher mumps-specific antibody levels, higher seropositivity rate and slower decay of antibody levels.

Recommended Usage

Administration of live attenuated mumps vaccine in combination with measles and rubella vaccines (MMR) is recommended for all children $\geq$ 12 months of age. The combined vaccine should be used even in individuals who may have prior immunity to components of the vaccine, and it can be used to immunize susceptible adults against mumps.

Although mumps immunization after exposure may not prevent the disease, it is not harmful. Should the exposure not result in an infection, the vaccine should confer protection against future exposures.

Adverse Reactions

The most frequent reaction (approximately 5% of immunized children) is malaise and fever with or without rash lasting up to 3 days and occurring 7 to 12 days after MMR immunization. One in 3,000 children with fever may have associated febrile convulsions. Parotitis and mild skin rashes may occasionally occur after immunization. Very rarely, viral meningitis without sequelae has been reported.

Precautions and Contraindications

In common with other live vaccines, mumps vaccine should not be given to pregnant women or individuals whose immune mechanism is impaired as a result of disease, injury or treatment. An exception to this, however, is the recommendation that mumps vaccine, in the form of MMR, be given to HIV-infected children who do not have severe immunosuppression.

Mumps vaccine should not be administered less than 2 weeks before an immune globulin injection, or within 3 months after such an injection.

Convincing evidence supports the safety of routine administration of MMR vaccines to all children who have allergy to eggs. Fewer than 2 per 1,000 vaccinated egg-allergic children have been found to be at risk for anaphylactic reaction to MMR (refer to the chapter on Measles Vaccine for further details).

Since mumps vaccine contains trace amounts of neomycin and gelatin, people who have experienced anaphylactic reactions to previously administered neomycin or to a previous dose of mumps-containing vaccine, or who have a documented gelatin allergy should not receive mumps vaccine.

Selected References

Boulianne N, De Serres G, Ratnam S et al. *Measles, mumps and rubella antibodies in children 5-6 years after immunization: effect of vaccine type and age at vaccination.* Vaccine 1995; 13:1611-16.

Buxton J, Craig C, Daly P et al. *An outbreak of mumps among young adults in Vancouver, British Columbia, associated with "rave parties".* Can J Public Health 1999;90:160-63.

Mumps Vaccine

Caplan CE. *Mumps in the era of vaccines*. Can Med Assoc J 1999;160:865-66.

Cheek JE, Baron R. Atlas H et al. *Mumps outbreak in a highly vaccinated school population*. Arch Pediatr Adolesc Med 1995;149:774-78.

Davidkin I, Valle M, Julkunen I. *Persistence of anti-mumps virus antibodies after a two-dose MMR vaccination at nine-year follow-up*. Vaccine 1995;13:1617-22.

Duclos P, Ward BJ. *Measles vaccines: a review of adverse events*. Drug Safety 1998;19:435-54.

Griffin MR, Ray WA, Mortimer EA et al. *Risk of seizures after measles-mumps-rubella immunization*. Pediatrics 1991;88:881-85.

James JM, Burks AW, Roberson PK et al. *Safe administration of the measles vaccine to children allergic to eggs*. N Engl J Med 1995;332:1262-66.

Miller E, Goldacre M, Pugh S et al. *Risk of aseptic meningitis after measles, mumps and rubella vaccine in U.K. children*. Lancet 1993;341:979-82.

Peltola H, Heinonen OP, Valle M et al. *The elimination of indigenous measles, mumps and rubella from Finland by a 12 year two-dose vaccination program*. N Engl J Med 1994;331:1397-1402.

West R, Roberts PM. *Measles, mumps and rubella vaccine current safety issues*. BioDrugs 1999;12(6):423-29.

Pertussis Vaccine

Pertussis (whooping cough) is a highly communicable infection of the respiratory tract caused by *Bordetella pertussis*. The disease can affect individuals of any age; however, severity is greatest among young infants. The goal of pertussis control is to reduce the incidence and severe morbidity of pertussis among young children. Pertussis has been controlled in Canada through immunization, and during the last 50 years its incidence has decreased by > 90% (see Figure), although outbreaks continue to occur.

During the 1980s, pertussis incidence was low but has increased since 1990 in spite of high vaccine coverage. Over the past 10 years, the annual number of reported cases has ranged from 2,400 to 10,000, although these figures likely under-represent the true incidence because of incomplete reporting. The resurgence of pertussis has been partly attributable to the low vaccine efficacy of the previously used whole-cell vaccine, which has been estimated to be in the range of 50% to 60% in children. Hospitalization for pertussis still occurs, with a few deaths (0-4) in some years, usually among unimmunized and under-immunized infants.

Epidemiology

It has long been recognized that protection provided by the whole-cell pertussis vaccine wanes with time. Nevertheless, the use of this vaccine was restricted to children < 7 years of age because the severity of local reactions increased with age. Because of waning immunity, many immunized children became susceptible to pertussis in adolescence or adulthood. Pertussis is a frequent cause of cough illness in adolescents and adults, who constitute a major reservoir of the disease and are an important source of transmission to infants.

Pertussis – Reported Cases, Canada, 1924-2000

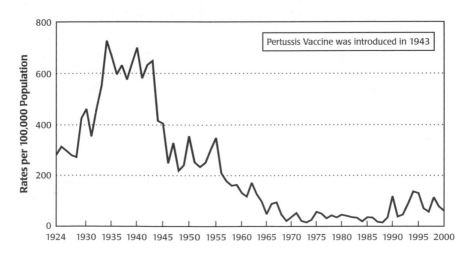

Children < 10 are the most frequently reported cases, but both the number and proportion of older cases have increased, a trend that parallels the increase observed in children. The increase in older groups may be attributable to better recognition, diagnosis and reporting of pertussis in adolescents and adults. Active surveillance for pertussis has found that 1% to 25% of patients with prolonged cough had *Bordetella pertussis* infection. Using a combination of laboratory methods, the Sentinel Health Unit Surveillance System has documented pertussis infection in 9% to 20% of non-improving cough illness of 7 days or more in adolescents and adults.

There has been no large-scale assessment of the proportion of susceptible adolescents and adults, although three Canadian studies have estimated the secondary attack rate (SAR) in household contacts of pertussis cases. A re-analysis of these data only from households where the reported case was also the first case shows that the SAR ranged between 12% and 14% in contacts aged 12 to 17 years, 11% and 18% in adults aged 18 to 29 years and 8% and 33% in those ≥30 years. It can be concluded that between 10% and 25% of adolescents and adults in Canada are susceptible to pertussis and that these individuals play a role in its transmission.

Preparations Licensed for Immunization

Only acellular vaccines made from purified antigens of *B. pertussis* are now available in Canada, and whole-cell preparations are no longer in use. Acellular vaccines have been developed to reduce the frequency and severity of both local and systemic adverse reactions associated with whole-cell pertussis vaccines. All the currently available acellular vaccines contain pertussis toxoid, filamentous hemagglutinin and pertactin. Although recently introduced into North America, acellular pertussis vaccines have been widely used in Japan for over 15 years.

Acellular pertussis vaccines are usually given combined with other agents, including diphtheria and tetanus toxoids (DTaP) with or without inactivated polio vaccine (DTaP-polio) and/or Hib conjugate vaccine (DTaP-Hib, DTaP-polio-Hib). Although not licensed in Canada at this time, combinations with hepatitis B vaccine are in use in other countries.

The dTap adolescent/adult formulation of acellular pertussis vaccine is combined with tetanus and diphtheria toxoids adsorbed on aluminum phosphate. The antigen content of this vaccine (including the pertussis content) is lower than the one found in the vaccines used in preschool children.

Efficacy and Immunogenicity

In 1995-1996, the results of seven studies of the efficacy of eight DTaP vaccines were reported. The studies were not designed to compare the efficacy of the various acellular pertussis vaccines and involved different study designs; therefore, few conclusions can be drawn about the relative merits of the various products. All the acellular vaccines were efficacious, and most were as effective or more effective than the whole-cell DPT vaccines included as controls. All acellular pertussis vaccines licensed in Canada have an estimated efficacy of approximately 85%; a detailed summary of the products and the results of the studies can be found in the 1997 NACI statement on acellular pertussis vaccines.

The duration of protection afforded by acellular pertussis vaccines is not known, but the data seem to indicate that protection does not decline during the first 4 years of follow-up. Long-term follow-up will continue for several of the cohorts that participated in the efficacy studies.

As discussed in the NACI statement in 2000, there are limited data about the efficacy of a single dose of adolescent/adult pertussis vaccine given to previously immunized adolescents or adults in the prevention of pertussis infection, disease and transmission. However, it has been shown that a single dose of this vaccine increased their pertussis antibody levels far in excess of those observed in infants in Sweden who received three doses of acellular pertussis vaccine. As the efficacy demonstrated in the Swedish trial was 85%, it is reasonable to expect that the protection against severe disease in adolescents and adults would be of the same order.

The only study conducted to directly assess vaccine efficacy, by Ward et al., found that a single dose of a tri-component acellular pertussis vaccine gave significant protection. The point estimate of vaccine efficacy for the primary case definition was 78%; however, there were so few cases meeting this case definition that the confidence interval was very wide. De Serres et al. have provided another, indirect, piece of evidence supporting the protective efficacy of a single dose of dTap with data showing the efficacy of a single booster dose of acellular pertussis vaccine in infants or preschool-aged children.

Recommended Usage

Acellular pertussis vaccine is recommended for all children ≥ 2 months of age for whom there are no contraindications. Children who have had natural pertussis should continue to receive pertussis-containing vaccines. Because of concern about the adverse reactions associated with whole-cell pertussis vaccine, it was previously recommended that the pertussis component be removed from subsequent immunizations after a finding of positive culture, because of the immunity conferred by infection. Although further data are needed, the increased safety profile of the acellular pertussis vaccine makes elimination of the pertussis component no longer necessary and thereby simplifies immunization programs. As well, continuation of immunization with acellular pertussis vaccine may confer additional benefit to infants < 6 months of age, who often have a suboptimal antibody response to natural pertussis infection.

In children ≥ 7 years of age who have not had a primary pertussis immunization or for whom the immunization status is unknown (e.g., immigrant children), adolescent/adult dTap should be considered.

Interchangeability

The efficacy of most of the acellular pertussis vaccines has been demonstrated after three doses of the same vaccine; no data are available regarding the interchangeability of acellular pertussis vaccines. Therefore, whenever possible, efforts should be made to complete the first three doses with the same acellular vaccine. Although data are similarly lacking, the acellular vaccines can be considered interchangeable for the fourth and fifth doses, since it may be difficult to ensure supply of the same vaccine during the entire 4-6 year immunization period.

Outbreak control

Acellular pertussis vaccine has been used safely for the control of pertussis outbreaks in defined populations, such as in schools or hospitals, although data supporting its effectiveness are lacking. Ensuring the complete immunization of all children remains the most important preventive measure in maximizing control of pertussis. Updating the immunization of daycare, school and community contacts should be undertaken by public health authorities.

Contacts

Children exposed to a case should have their immunization status reviewed. If immunization is incomplete and in the absence of contraindications, any necessary doses should be given as follows:

- Children who have received fewer than three doses should receive their additional dose(s) as soon as possible, with an interval of 4 weeks between doses.

- Children who have had three doses may receive their fourth dose as early as 6 months after the third dose.

- A booster dose of vaccine, usually as DTaP, should be given to any child ≤ 6 years of age who has had four doses of vaccine, unless the most recent dose was given within the previous 3 years.

If dTap is considered for people ≥ 7 years to achieve outbreak control, this should be undertaken with evaluation of its effectiveness.

The role of chemoprophylaxis in the management of contacts is not discussed here.

Schedule and Dosage

Immunization against pertussis routinely consists of three doses given at 2, 4 and 6 months of age, a fourth dose at 18 months of age and a fifth dose at 4 to 6 years of age. When more rapid protection is preferred, the first three doses may be administered at intervals of 4 weeks and the fourth dose given as soon as 6 months after the third dose. It is important that immunization against pertussis begin and be completed on time to ensure the greatest possible protection to the young infant, in whom the disease can be very serious. The dose to be administered is that recommended by the manufacturer.

For children ≥ 7 years who have not been immunized or immigrants with unknown status, two doses of adolescent/adult dTap with a 4 week interval should be administered and a third dose given at 12 months. Monovalent acellular pertussis vaccine should be administered to children who have been immunized against diphtheria and tetanus but not against pertussis.

Route of Administration

All combined acellular pertussis vaccines are adsorbed vaccines and must be given intramuscularly.

Booster Doses and Re-immunization

Because adverse reactions are more common and the disease is typically less severe in older children, adolescents and adults, immunization with the whole-cell pertussis vaccine is not recommended for people ≥ 7 years of age. However, pertussis in this group is an important source of infection for young infants. For this reason, studies are under way to assess the role of pertussis in adolescents and adults with cough illness, and the safety, immunogenicity and efficacy of acellular pertussis vaccine in these age groups. A single dose of pertussis vaccine in adolescence or adulthood will provide individual protection, but the duration of its effect and whether it prevents transmission to infants is not known. The combined adolescent/adult formulation of dTap should be used to replace the adolescent booster of Td. Until data about the safety of repeated doses are available, only one dose is currently recommended.

Storage Requirements

Pertussis-containing vaccines should be stored at a temperature between 2° and 8° C and should not be frozen. As with all adsorbed vaccines, pertussis-containing vaccines that have been frozen should not be used.

Simultaneous Administration with Other Vaccines

Vaccines that combine antigens against multiple diseases enhance immunization compliance by decreasing the necessary number of injections and visits, and therefore should be encouraged. Acellular pertussis vaccines are available as a pertussis-only vaccine and in combination with diphtheria and tetanus toxoids as well as with inactivated polio vaccine and Hib conjugate vaccine. In general, adverse reactions associated with the combination vaccines are no more frequent than those associated with single constituent vaccines. Antibody responses to combination antigens are complex: the immunogenicity of combination vaccines may be greater, less or the same as that of the individual vaccines, and the effects may differ among products from different manufacturers. As a rule, despite some "immune interference" between antigens, all licensed combination vaccines have demonstrated adequate immunogenicity with each constituent. For this reason, when combination vaccines are available, their use should be encouraged to facilitate compliance. Conversely,

Pertussis Vaccine

however, the need for multiple injections should not delay administration of vaccines that provide advantages of safety, immunogenicity, efficacy or cost.

Vaccines containing acellular pertussis may be administered simultaneously with other inactivated and live vaccines at different sites. Not to do so is a missed opportunity and is likely to result in under-immunization. None of the products should be mixed in the same syringe with any other vaccines unless specifically approved and described in the product monograph.

Adverse Reactions

The rate of reactions to acellular pertussis vaccines is less than that reported with the whole-cell preparations. In clinical trials, the incidence rates of local adverse reactions, including tenderness, erythema, swelling and general reactions of fever, irritability and drowsiness, were significantly lower after immunization with acellular than with whole-cell pertussis vaccines. Less common adverse reactions such as persistent crying and hypotonic-hyporesponsive episodes were also less frequent after administration of acellular pertussis vaccines, and were reported with a frequency similar to that among recipients of vaccines not containing pertussis. Convulsions are unusual and were reported less often after immunization with acellular pertussis vaccines in some of the efficacy studies but not in others. Because of the lower incidence of fever associated with these vaccines, there may be less justification for routine use of prophylactic acetaminophen, as had been recommended with whole-cell pertussis vaccines. Acetaminophen may be considered in children with a high risk of febrile seizures or low pain tolerance.

The size and frequency of local reactions increase with the number of doses administered. These local reactions produce large swelling, but pain is generally limited. The presence of a large, local reaction to a previous dose should not be considered a contraindication to continue the recommended schedule.

Contraindications and Precautions

Pertussis vaccine should not be given to individuals who have had an anaphylactic reaction to a previous dose or to any constituent of the vaccine (see product monographs). Because these events are so rare, it is not known which component of the combined DTP or DTaP (or additional antigens in the combination vaccines) is responsible for allergic reactions. Therefore, no further doses of any of the vaccine components should be given unless an assessment can determine the responsible antigen or other vaccine component. In order to maximize the child's benefit, an assesment should be done rapidly.

Conditions Not Considered Contraindications to Pertussis Vaccine

Certain other events temporally associated with whole-cell pertussis immunization were at one time considered contraindications or precautions to further pertussis immunization. With the use of acellular pertussis vaccine, they are no longer considered contraindications.

- High fever within 48 hours of vaccination, attributed to immunization and not to intercurrent illness, indicates the likelihood of recurrence of fever with subsequent doses. Febrile convulsions may be more likely in a susceptible child who develops high fever. However, there are no long-term sequelae from these convulsions, and pertussis immunization can continue. Acetaminophen prophylaxis reduces the incidence of fever and may reduce febrile convulsions temporally related to pertussis immunization.

- Afebrile convulsions have not been shown to be caused by pertussis vaccine and are not a contraindication to immunization.

- Persistent, inconsolable crying and an unusual high-pitched cry after pertussis vaccination are not associated with any sequelae and are likely to be pain responses at the site of injection in young infants. These reactions do not preclude further pertussis immunization. Acetaminophen prophylaxis may reduce discomfort with subsequent doses.

- Hypotonic-hyporesponsive episodes are not a contraindication to the use of acellular pertussis vaccine. Because these episodes occur after both DTaP and DT, it is difficult to attribute causation to the pertussis components of DTaP; continued immunization with all antigens is recommended.

- Onset of encephalopathy temporally related to pertussis immunization does not indicate that the vaccine was the cause. Encephalopathy itself, from whatever cause, is not a contraindication to pertussis immunization.

- Deferral of pertussis immunization for children with evolving neurologic conditions is no longer necessary because of the availability of acellular pertussis vaccines. Specific data on the use of these vaccines in individuals with neurologic diseases are not available and must await post-marketing surveillance. However, because the incidence of adverse events, including fever and seizures, is no different in recipients of DTaP and DT, it is unnecessary to defer the pertussis component of the vaccine. Moreover, recent advances in the diagnosis and management of neurologic conditions leave little room for natural disease progressions to be misinterpreted as immunization-related events.

Other Considerations

NACI may change its recommendations on the current schedule, so that the five doses are administered before school entry, and on immunization of adolescents/adults. These changes will be based on evidence about the duration of the protection induced by acellular pertussis vaccine.

Selected References

Decker MD, Edwards KM, Steinhoff MC et al. *Comparison of 13 acellular pertussis vaccines: adverse reactions*. Pediatrics 1995;96(l):557-66.

De Serres G, Shadmani R, Boulianne N et al. *Effectiveness of a single dose of acellular pertussis vaccine to prevent pertussis in children primed with pertussis whole cell vaccine*. Vaccine 2001;19:3004-8.

Edwards KM, Meade BD, Decker MD et al. *Comparison of 13 acellular pertussis vaccines: overview and serologic response*. Pediatrics 1995;96(l):548-57.

Edwards KM, Decker MD. *Acellular pertussis vaccines for infants*. N Engl J Med 1996;334:391-92.

Greco D, Salmaso S, Mastrantonio P et al. *A controlled trial of two acellular vaccines and one whole-cell vaccine against pertussis*. N Engl J Med 1996;334:341-48.

Gustafsson L, Hallander HO, Olin P et al. *A controlled trial of a two-component acellular, a five-component acellular, and a whole-cell pertussis vaccine*. N Engl J Med 1996;334:349-55.

Halperin SA, Smith B, Russel M et al. *An adult formulation of a five component acellular pertussis vaccine combined with diphtheria and tetanus toxoids is safe and immunogenic in adolescents and adults*. Pediatr Infect Dis J 2000;19:276-83.

National Advisory Committee on Immunization. *Statement on pertussis vaccine*. CCDR 1997;23(ACS-3):1-16.

National Advisory Committee on Immunization. *Statement on adult/adolescent formulation of combined acellular pertussis, tetanus, and diphtheria vaccine*. CCDR 2000;26(ACS-1):1-8.

Schmitt HJ, von Konig CHW, Neiss A et al. *Efficacy of acellular pertussis vaccine in early childhood after household exposure*. JAMA 1996;275:37-41.

Stehr K, Cherry JD, Heininger U et al. *A comparative efficacy trial in Germany in infants who received either the Lederle-Takeda acellular pertussis component DTP (DtaP) vaccine, the Lederle whole-cell component DTP vaccine, or DT vaccine*. Pediatrics 1998;101:1-11

Trollfors B, Taranger J, Lagergard T et al. *A placebo-controlled trial of a pertussis-toxoid vaccine*. N Engl J Med 1995;333:1045-50.

Ward J, Partridge S, Chang S et al. *Acellular pertussis vaccine efficacy and epidemiology of pertussis in adolescents and adults: NIH multicenter adult pertussis trial (APERT)*. Acellular Pertussis Vaccine Conference, Bethesda, Maryland, November 12-14, 2000.

Pneumococcal Vaccine

Since the publication of the previous edition of the *Canadian Immunization Guide*, the first pneumococcal conjugate vaccine for children < 9 years of age has been licensed in Canada. Information concerning this vaccine and the indications for its use are included here. Additional information can be obtained from the statement by the National Advisory Committee on Immunization (NACI) referenced at the end of the chapter.

Epidemiology

Streptococcus pneumoniae (pneumococcus) is the leading cause of invasive bacterial infections, meningitis, bacterial pneumonia and acute otitis media (AOM) in children. Invasive disease is most common in the very young, the elderly and certain specific groups at high risk, such as individuals with functional or anatomic asplenia and congenital or acquired immune deficiency, including those with AIDS.

In Canada, there are an estimated 65 cases of meningitis, 700 cases of bacteremia, 2,200 cases of pneumonia requiring hospitalization, 9,000 cases of pneumonia not requiring hospitalization, and an average of 15 deaths per year due to *S. pneumoniae* infection in children < 5 years of age.

Preparations Licensed for Immunization

Polysaccharide vaccine

The current polysaccharide pneumococcal vaccine, available since December 1983, contains 25 µg of capsular polysaccharide from each of 23 types of pneumococci: 1, 2, 3, 4, 5, 6B, 7F, 8, 9N, 9V, 10A, 11A, 12F, 14, 15B, 17F, 18C, 19A, 19F, 20, 22F, 23F and 33F (Danish nomenclature). Approximately 90% of cases of pneumococcal bacteremia and meningitis are caused by these 23 types. The six serotypes that most often cause drug-resistant invasive pneumococcal infection are included in this vaccine. An earlier vaccine, which contained 50 µg of each of 14 types, was available between 1978 and 1983. Available vaccines include Pneumovax 23® (Merck Frosst Canada & Co.), Pneumo 23® (Aventis Pasteur) and Pnu-Immune® (Wyeth Ayerst Canada Inc.). They all contain the same serotype polysaccharides.

Conjugate vaccine

The first pneumococcal conjugate vaccine to be licensed in Canada for children < 9 years of age, Prevnar® (Wyeth Ayerst Canada Inc.), is composed of the purified polysaccharides of the capsular antigens of seven *S. pneumoniae* serotypes, individually conjugated to CRM_{197}, a non-toxic mutant of diphtheria toxin. The vaccine is manufactured as a liquid suspension. Each 0.5 mL dose of vaccine is formulated to contain 2 µg of each polysaccharide for serotypes 4, 9V, 14, 18C, 19F and 23F, and 4 µg of serotype 6B per dose (16 µg total polysaccharide); approximately 20 µg of CRM_{197}

carrier protein; and 0.125 mg of aluminum as aluminum phosphate adjuvant. The vaccine contains no thimerosal or other preservatives.

Efficacy and Immunogenicity

Polysaccharide vaccine

In healthy young adults, a single dose of polysaccharide vaccine stimulates an antibody response to each of the component capsular polysaccharides. The immunity conferred is type specific. Efficacy, as measured by serotype-specific protection against invasive bacteremic pneumococcal disease, can surpass 80% among healthy young adults (evidence from randomized controlled trials). It is in the range of 50% to 80% among the elderly and specific patient groups, such as those with diabetes mellitus, anatomic or physiologic asplenia, congestive heart failure or chronic pulmonary disease (evidence from case-control and retrospective cohort studies). Antibody response and clinical protection are decreased in certain groups at particularly high risk of pneumococcal infection. These include patients with renal failure, sickle-cell anemia or impaired immune responsiveness, including HIV infection. The response of children < 2 years of age to polysaccharide vaccine is irregular and unsatisfactory. Following polysaccharide pneumococcal immunization, serotype-specific antibody levels decline after 5 to 10 years and decrease more rapidly in some groups than others. The duration of immunity is not precisely known.

The results of economic analyses indicate that polysaccharide pneumococcal vaccine is cost-effective in the prevention of mortality and morbidity associated with invasive infections among people > 2 years of age at high risk and compares favourably with other standard preventive practices.

Conjugate vaccine

Infants immunized with a three-dose primary series beginning at 2 months of age, with doses separated by 4 to 8 weeks, develop a 3.4 to 20 fold increase in serum antibodies for the vaccine serotypes. Functional antibodies are induced in infants (as measured by opsonophagocytic assay and antibody avidity), together with strong and rapid anamnestic responses upon boosting with either conjugate or polysaccharide vaccines in the 6 to 12 months after the primary series. Serum antibody responses to some conjugate vaccine serotypes are substantial after one to two doses, whereas responses to others require completion of three doses. Approximately 97% of infants achieved protective antibody titres for all serotypes after the primary series (2, 4, 6 months). This correlates with an observed protective efficacy against invasive disease of 89% to 97%.

Satisfactory safety and immunogenicity of conjugate pneumococcal vaccines have been demonstrated in children with sickle cell disease and HIV infection. Protection against development of AOM ranges from 6% against an episode from any cause to a 25% reduction in pneumococcal-associated AOM and a 56% reduction in AOM due to the serotypes included in the vaccine. A 20% reduction in tympanostomy tube placement has also been observed with use of the vaccine.

The long-term efficacy of the conjugate pneumococcal vaccines is not known, but immunologic memory has been demonstrated 18 months after two to three doses in infancy and up to 20 months after one dose in children 2 to 3 years of age. In Canada, 80% of the most common serotypes isolated from the blood or cerebrospinal fluid (CSF) of children, 95% of serotypes isolated with high level penicillin resistance, and 73% of those with intermediate level resistance are included in Prevnar®. **There may be populations or communities, such as Aboriginal children in northern communities, with different distributions of serotypes**.

Recommended Usage

Conjugate pneumococcal vaccine is recommended for routine administration to all children ≤ 23 months of age. Conjugate pneumococcal vaccine is also recommended for children 24 to 59 months of age who are at higher risk for invasive pneumococcal infections. These include children with sickle cell disease and other sickle cell hemoglobinopathies, other types of functional or anatomic asplenia, HIV infection, immunocompromising conditions (e.g., primary immunodeficiencies, malignancies, immunosuppressive therapy, solid organ transplant, long-term systemic corticosteroids, nephrotic syndrome) and chronic medical conditions (e.g., chronic cardiac and pulmonary disease such as bronchopulmonary dysplasia, diabetes mellitus or CSF leak). The conjugate vaccine should be considered for all other children in this age group, especially those who attend child care or Aboriginal children living in isolated communities.

Polysaccharide pneumococcal vaccine is not recommended for children < 2 years of age as it is relatively ineffective and the conjugate vaccine is superior. Children from 2 to 5 years of age may receive polysaccharide vaccine, but the conjugate vaccine is generally preferred because of the age-dependent response. Polysaccharide vaccine may be used both as a booster dose in this age group and to increase the serotype coverage.

Polysaccharide pneumococcal vaccine is recommended for all individuals ≥ 65 years of age. Pneumococcal polysaccharide vaccine may be administered simultaneously with influenza vaccine, at a separate anatomic site. Individuals with unknown immunization histories should receive the vaccine.

Polysaccharide vaccine should be given to all individuals > 5 years of age with asplenia, splenic dysfunction or sickle cell disease if not previously immunized. In addition, those > 5 years of age with the following conditions should receive the polysaccharide vaccine: chronic cardiorespiratory disease (except asthma), cirrhosis, alcoholism, chronic renal disease, nephrotic syndrome, diabetes mellitus, chronic CSF leak, HIV infection and other conditions associated with immunosuppression (Hodgkin's disease, lymphoma, multiple myeloma, induced immunosuppression for organ transplantation). When circumstances permit, the conjugate vaccine may

Pneumococcal Vaccine

be given as the initial dose followed by the polysaccharide vaccine to provide additional serotype coverage and as a booster. Polysaccharide vaccine should be given to smokers, since they are at increased risk.

Immunologic abnormalities may decrease both the antibody response to and protection by either type of vaccine. When possible, vaccine should be given at least 10 to 14 days before splenectomy or initiation of immunosuppression therapy and early in the course of HIV infection. Because of variable vaccine efficacy in certain groups, those at highest risk (and their families) should be counselled regarding the risk of fulminant pneumococcal sepsis, which may occur despite immunization. In these highest risk patients, some authorities recommend continuous antimicrobial prophylaxis.

Schedule and Dosage

The dose of both the polysaccharide and the conjugate vaccine for all age groups is 0.5 mL.

The recommended schedule for infants is four doses of the conjugate vaccine administered at 2, 4, 6 and 12 to 15 months of age. Children ≤ 6 months should receive the first three doses at intervals of approximately 2 months (6 to 8 weeks) apart followed by one dose at 12 to 15 months of age. The first dose should be given no earlier than 6 weeks of age. Infants of very low birth weight (< 1500 grams) should be given their first dose at a chronological age of 6 to 8 weeks, regardless of their calculated gestational age. Children 7 to 11 months old who have not previously been immunized against pneumococcus should receive two doses at least 6 to 8 weeks apart followed by the third dose at 12 to 15 months of age or at least 6 to 8 weeks after the second dose. Children aged 12 to 23 months who were not previously immunized should receive two doses at least 6 to 8 weeks apart. After 24 months of age one dose is sufficient.

Summary Schedule for Pneumococcal Conjugate Vaccine in Previously Unvaccinated Children

Age at first dose	Primary series	Booster*
2-6 months	3 doses, 6-8 weeks apart	1 dose at 12-15 months
7-11 months	2 doses, 6-8 weeks apart	1 dose at 12-15 months
12-23 months	2 doses, 6-8 weeks apart	
24-59 months Healthy children Children with sickle cell disease, asplenia, HIV, chronic illness or immuno-compromising condition	1 dose 2 doses 8 weeks apart	
* Booster given at least 6-8 weeks after final dose of primary series		

When used after administration of the conjugate vaccine, the polysaccharide vaccine should ideally be given no earlier than 8 weeks after the conjugate vaccine. The minimal acceptable time interval is 4 weeks.

Route of Administration

The polysaccharide vaccine may be given by either intramuscular or subcutaneous injection. The conjugate vaccine is given only as an intramuscular injection.

Booster Doses and Re-immunization

Results from serologic and case studies indicate that polysaccharide vaccine-induced immunity decreases over time. Data are not yet available concerning a decline in immunity following the use of conjugate pneumococcal vaccine in infancy. At present, routine re-immunization is not recommended but should be considered for those of any age at highest risk of invasive infection, as detailed below. Experience with re-immunization is still limited, and there are no data on the relative effectiveness of a second dose.

People for whom re-immunization should be considered include those with functional or anatomic asplenia or sickle cell disease; hepatic cirrhosis; chronic renal failure or nephrotic syndrome; HIV infection; and immunosuppression related to disease or therapy. A single re-immunization is recommended after 5 years in those aged > 10 years and after 3 years in those aged ≤ 10 years. Either conjugate vaccine or polysaccharide vaccine may be used for re-immunization. Any need for further subsequent re-immunization remains to be determined.

Serologic Testing

Serologic testing, either pre- or post-immunization, is not recommended.

Storage Requirements

Both the polysaccharide vaccines and the conjugate vaccine should be stored refrigerated at a temperature of 2° C to 8° C (36° F to 46° F) as per the manufacturer's package insert. Freezing must be avoided.

Simultaneous Administration with Other Vaccines

On the basis of expert opinion, it is recommended that, if necessary or convenient, Prevnar® may be safely given with Pentacel™ or Quadracel™, or hepatitis B, measles, mumps and rubella vaccines, at separate sites and with separate syringes at a single visit. The polysaccharide vaccines may be given simultaneously with influenza, Hib conjugate and/or meningococcal vaccines, at a separate location and using a separate syringe.

Pneumococcal Vaccine

Adverse Reactions

Polysaccharide vaccine

Reactions to the polysaccharide vaccine are usually mild. Local soreness and erythema are quite common. Occasionally, slight fever may occur. Studies involving immunocompetent individuals have shown that re-immunization less than 2 years after the initial dose of polysaccharide vaccine increased local and systemic reactions. Local reactions of the Arthus type have been rarely observed but may be severe. When re-immunization is carried out after an interval of 3 years or greater, the rate of adverse reactions is similar to that after a first dose.

Conjugate vaccine

The conjugated pneumococcal vaccines are generally well tolerated when administered at the same time as other childhood vaccines. Fever has been reported more frequently among children receiving their primary immunization series when conjugate pneumococcal vaccine was included. Few serious side effects have been reported. Children are subjected to an additional injection, and redness, swelling and tenderness at the injection site may occur. The severity or frequency of these reactions has not been found to increase with subsequent doses in the primary series or with booster doses.

Contraindications and Precautions

Anaphylactic reaction to polysaccharide pneumococcal vaccine or to conjugate pneumococcal vaccine is a contraindication to re-immunization with that product.

Neither pregnancy nor breast-feeding is a contraindication to either the polysaccharide or the conjugate pneumococcal vaccine.

Other Considerations: Strategies to Improve Vaccine Utilization

Immunization is a safe and effective means of preventing invasive pneumococcal infection among individuals in groups at increased risk of serious illness or death. It offers a partial solution to the emerging problem of disease caused by strains with antibiotic resistance. However, recent surveys show that less than 5% of the population (> 2 years of age) at increased risk have received this vaccine. Several provinces have initiated programs to make the polysaccharide pneumococcal vaccine more readily available to target populations.

Recommended strategies for delivering pneumococcal vaccine to individuals at higher risk of invasive disease include the following:

- Ensuring that all recipients of influenza vaccine are also immunized with pneumococcal vaccine, if appropriate. Providers should have both vaccines available to facilitate their concurrent administration.

- Implementing standing orders for pneumococcal immunization of residents for whom there are indications for use of these vaccines on admission to long-term care facilities.

- Implementing standing orders in hospitals for pneumococcal immunization of patients in high-risk groups to be immunized on discharge or during ambulatory visits.

- Delivering pneumococcal vaccine in adult day care and community centres to people at risk.

- Promoting pneumococcal and influenza immunization programs concurrently to both consumers and providers.

Selected References

American Academy of Pediatrics. *Policy statement: recommendations for the prevention of pneumococcal infections, including the use of pneumococcal conjugate vaccine (Prevnar), pneumococcal polysaccharide vaccine, and antibiotic prophylaxis.* Pediatrics 2000;106:362-66.

American Academy of Pediatrics. *Technical report: prevention of pneumococcal infections, including the use of pneumococcal conjugate and polysaccharide vaccines and antibiotic prophylaxis.* Pediatrics 2000;106:367-76.

Black S, Shinefield H, Fireman B et al. *Efficacy, safety and immunogenicity of heptavalent pneumococcal conjugate vaccine in children.* Pediatr Infect Dis J 2000;19:87-95.

Butler JC, Breiman RF, Campbell JF et al. *Pneumococcal polysaccharide vaccine efficacy: an evaluation of current recommendations.* JAMA 1993; 270:1826-31.

Eskola J, Anttila M. *Pneumococcal conjugate vaccines.* Pediatr Infect Dis J 1999;18:543-51.

Eskola J, Kilpi T, Palmu A et al. *Efficacy of a pneumococcal conjugate vaccine against acute otitis media.* N Engl J Med 2001;344:403-09.

Fedson DS. *Clinical practice and public policy for influenza and pneumococcal vaccination of the elderly.* Clin Geriatr Med 1992;8:183-99.

Fine MJ, Smith MA, Carson CA et al. *Efficacy of pneumococcal vaccination in adults: a meta-analysis of randomized clinical trials.* Arch Intern Med 1994;154:2666-77.

Fine MF, Smith MA, Carson CA et al. *Prognosis and outcome of patients with community-acquired pneumonia. A meta-analysis.* JAMA 1996;275:134-41.

Gable CB, Holzer SS, Engelhart L et al. *Pneumococcal vaccine: efficacy and associated cost savings.* JAMA 1990;264:2910-15.

Marrie TJ, Durant H, Yates L. *Community-acquired pneumonia requiring hospitalization: 5-year prospective study.* Rev Infect Dis 1989;11:586-99.

National Advisory Committee on Immunization (NACI*). Statement on recommended use of pneumococcal conjugate vaccine.* CCDR 2002;28(ACS-2):1-32.

Rodriguez R. *Safety of pneumococcal revaccination.* J Gen Intern Med 1995;10:511-2.

Scheifele D, Halperin S, Pelletier L et al. *Invasive pneumococcal infection in Canadian children 1991-1998: implications for new vaccination strategies.* Clin Infect Dis 2000;31:58-64.

Pneumococcal Vaccine

Shapiro ED, Berg AT, Austrian R et al. *The protective efficacy of polyvalent pneumococcal polysaccharide vaccine.* N Engl J Med 1991;325:1453-60.

Shinefield HR, Black S, Ray P et al. *Safety and immunogenicity of heptavalent pneumococcal CRM197 conjugate vaccine in infants and toddlers.* Pediatr Infect Dis J 1999;18:757-63.

Snow R, Babish JD, McBean AM. *Is there any connection between a second pneumonia shot and hospitalization among Medicare beneficiaries?* Public Health Rep 1995;110:720-25.

Poliomyelitis Vaccine

Poliomyelitis is a disease that may cause irreversible paralysis in a certain proportion of infected individuals. It is a highly infectious disease caused by three types of the enterovirus poliovirus. It is extremely stable and can remain viable in the environment for long periods of time. The last major epidemic in Canada occurred in 1959, when there were 1,887 paralytic cases. Following the introduction of inactivated poliovirus vaccines (IPV) in Canada in 1955 and of trivalent oral poliovirus vaccine (OPV) in 1962, indigenously acquired disease has been eliminated (see Figure).

In 1994, the Pan American Health Organization certified that Canada was polio free. As one of the conditions of certification, Canada established a surveillance system for acute flaccid paralysis (AFP). The IMPACT (Impact Monitoring Program ACTive) system and Canadian Paediatric Surveillance Program, operated by the Canadian Paediatric Society, maintain active surveillance of cases of AFP. The Working Group on Polio Elimination in Canada reviews these and other data collected by Health Canada to ensure that Canada remains polio free.

In 1985, the Pan-American Health Organization adopted a goal of elimination of poliomyelitis from the hemisphere, and this goal was achieved by September 1995. WHO adopted a similar goal of global elimination by the year 2000, subsequently amended to 2005.

Poliomyelitis, Paralytic – Reported Cases, Canada, 1949-2000

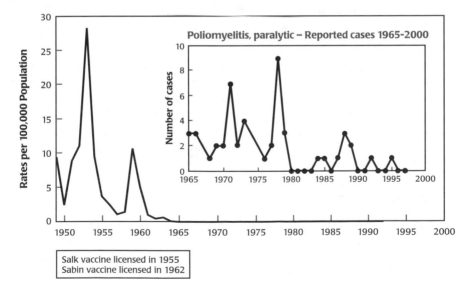

Poliomyelitis, paralytic – Reported cases 1965-2000

Salk vaccine licensed in 1955
Sabin vaccine licensed in 1962

Epidemiology

The last significant outbreak in Canada was in 1978-79, when 11 cases of paralytic disease occurred in unimmunized contacts of imported cases in religious groups in Ontario, Alberta and British Columbia. In 1993, 22 asymptomatic cases of imported wild polio infection were documented in the same religious group in Alberta, and in 1996 a similar case occurred in an asymptomatic child in Ontario. In none of these instances was spread of the virus seen outside the unimmunized groups, presumably because of high levels of immunization in the rest of the population.

Since 1980, 12 paralytic cases have been reported in Canada, 11 of which were determined to be vaccine-associated paralytic poliomyelitis (VAPP). Since 1987, all suspected cases of paralytic poliomyelitis have been reviewed by a subcommittee of NACI or, since 1994, the National Working Group on Polio Eradication. The last reported case caused by a wild poliovirus occurred in 1988 and was found to be due to an imported strain from the Indian subcontinent. Of the other 11 cases, three have been classified as "confirmed" vaccine-associated contact cases, five as "possible" vaccine-associated contact cases, and one as a "confirmed" vaccine- associated recipient case; the two other cases were not reviewed but occurred in known contacts of OPV-vaccinated children. The last reported case of VAPP occurred in 1995.

Preparations Used for Immunization

Both inactivated (IPV) and live oral (OPV) poliovirus vaccines are licensed for use in Canada. However, because in the past decade all cases of polio or suspected polio have been associated with OPV and because importations of wild poliovirus have not led to transmission to anyone in Canada outside of groups that refuse immunization, only IPV is recommended for routine use in Canada. For this reason, OPV is not discussed in detail in this chapter.

Two IPV preparations are licensed, one produced on Vero cells and the other on human diploid (MRC-5) cells. Both are formalin-inactivated products with enhanced potency and are significantly more immunogenic than the original IPV. They each contain the three types of wild poliovirus. Streptomycin, polymyxin B and neomycin may be present as preservatives. Polio vaccine is available as a single agent or in combination with diphtheria and tetanus toxoids and/or acellular pertussis vaccine (DTaP-IPV, Td-IPV).

Efficacy and Immunogenicity

IPV produces immunity to all three types of poliovirus in over 90% of people following two doses of vaccine given at least 6 weeks apart, and in close to 100% following a booster given 6 to 12 months later. The immune response induced in IPV vaccinees reduces the degree and duration of pharyngeal and fecal excretion of poliovirus after OPV challenge, as compared with unvaccinated children. However, IPV produces less mucosal immunity than OPV.

Recommended Usage

Infants and children

To avoid the risk of VAPP, exclusive use of IPV is recommended in Canada. Use of OPV alone or sequential use of IPV followed by OPV provides acceptable levels of protection, but both schedules carry the risk of VAPP in recipients or their contacts and neither offers any protective advantage to the recipient.

Adults

Routine immunization against poliomyelitis for adults living in Canada is not considered necessary. Most adults are already immune and have a negligible risk of exposure to wild polioviruses in the Americas.

Primary immunization with poliomyelitis vaccine is recommended only in those who are unimmunized and are at increased risk of exposure to poliovirus. Such people include the following:

- travellers to areas of countries where poliomyelitis is epidemic or endemic;

- laboratory workers handling specimens that may contain polioviruses;

- health care workers in close contact with individuals who may be excreting wild or vaccine strains of polioviruses;

- unimmunized parents or child care workers who will be caring for children in countries where OPV is used.

Schedule and Dosage

Children

Two doses of IPV are recommended 4 to 8 weeks apart, followed by a booster dose 6 to 12 months later. When given combined with DPT (or DTaP), it is acceptable to give additional doses of IPV 4 to 8 weeks after the second dose and 4 to 6 years after the third dose for convenience of administration. However, two doses of IPV plus a booster dose are considered a complete primary series.

For children who began their polio immunization series in a country where OPV is used, immunization may be completed using IPV; there is no need to re-start the series. Conversely, children who have been started on an immunization series with IPV and who move to an area where OPV is used may receive the necessary doses of OPV to complete their series.

Poliomyelitis Vaccine

Adults

For unimmunized adults at increased risk, primary immunization with IPV is recommended as two doses given at an interval of 4 to 8 weeks with a further dose 6 months to 1 year later. Additional considerations are as follows:

■ *travellers:* travellers who will be departing in < 4 weeks should receive a single dose of IPV and the remaining doses later, at the recommended intervals;

■ *unimmunized parents/child care workers:* in those rare instances in which infants receive OPV, there is a very small risk of OPV-associated paralysis to unimmunized parents or other household contacts. It will generally not be practical for such people to be fully protected with IPV before the infant is immunized; their risk may be reduced if they are given one dose of IPV at the same time as the first dose is given to the infant. Arrangements should be made for the adults to complete their basic course of immunization.

Incompletely immunized adults at increased risk who have previously received less than a full primary course of IPV or OPV should receive the remaining dose(s) of poliovirus vaccine as IPV, regardless of the interval since the last dose.

Route of Administration

IPV is injected subcutaneously according to the dose specified in the manufacturer's package insert. Combination vaccines must be administered intramuscularly because of the presence of adsorbed tetanus and diphtheria toxoids.

Booster Doses and Re-immunization

A need for booster doses of poliovirus vaccine in fully immunized adults has not been demonstrated. For those believed to be at particularly high risk of exposure to polio (e.g., military personnel, workers in refugee camps in endemic areas, travellers to areas where there are epidemics) a single booster dose of IPV (or OPV) might be considered. However, booster doses of vaccine are not usually necessary and are not routinely recommended for travellers.

Outbreak Control

If transmission of paralytic poliomyelitis caused by wild virus occurs in a community, OPV should be administered to all individuals (including infants) who have not been completely immunized or whose immunization status is uncertain. OPV is recommended because it blocks transmission by competing with wild virus in the bowel. As well, the local (gut) immunity produced by OPV is greater than that induced by IPV and is more likely to block asymptomatic infection and transmission. Thus, IPV should not be used for control of outbreaks of poliomyelitis if OPV is available.

Adverse Reactions

The side effects of currently available IPV are normally limited to minor local reactions. As with all vaccines, anaphylaxis has been reported rarely.

OPV may cause paralytic disease in recipients and incompletely immunized contacts at a rate of approximately 1 per 1 million doses distributed. Individuals travelling or living abroad whose children may be exposed to OPV should be made aware of this risk.

Contraindications and Precautions

IPV should not be administered to people who have experienced an anaphylactic reaction to a previous dose of IPV, streptomycin, polymyxin B or neomycin.

IPV can be given without risk to those who are immunodeficient or immunosuppressed or to people who will have household or similarly close contact with such people. Less than optimal protection may be induced in those who are immunocompromised.

IPV is not contraindicated in pregnancy, but its administration should be delayed until after the first trimester, if possible, to minimize any theoretical risk. If risk of exposure is imminent, IPV should be given and is always the vaccine of choice except for outbreak control.

Selected References

American Academy of Pediatrics. *Poliomyelitis prevention: recommendations for use of inactivated poliovirus vaccine and live oral poliovirus vaccine*. Pediatrics 1997;99:300-5.

CDC. *Poliomyelitis prevention in the United States: updated recommendations of the Advisory Committee on Immunization Practices (ACIP)*. MMWR 2000;49(No. RR-5).

Cochi SL, Hull HF, Sutter RW et al. *Commentary: the unfolding story of global poliomyelitis eradication*. J Infect Dis 1997;175(Suppl 1):S1-3.

Duclos P. *Paralytic poliomyelitis eradication: when success and forgetting may mean danger*. Can J Infect Dis 1992;3:142-3.

Hull HF, Birmingham ME, Melgaard B et al. *Progress toward global polio eradication*. J Infect Dis 1997;175(Suppl 1);S4-9.

Kimpen JLL, Ogra PL. *Poliovirus vaccines: a continuing challenge*. Pediatr Clin N Am 1990;37:627-47.

Melnick JL. *Poliomyelitis: eradication in sight*. Epidemiol Infect 1992;108:1-18.

Modlin JF, Halsey NA, Thomas ML et al. *Humoral and mucosal immunity in infants induced by three sequential inactivated poliovirus vaccine-live attenuated oral poliovirus vaccine immunization schedules*. J Infect Dis 1997;175(Suppl 1):S228-34.

Plotkin SA, Orenstein WA. *Vaccines*. 3rd edition. Philadelphia: W.B. Saunders Company, 1999.

Sabin AB. *My last will and testament on rapid elimination and ultimate global eradication of poliomyelitis and measles*. Pediatrics 1992;90:162-9.

Poliomyelitis Vaccine

Strebel PM, Sutter RW, Cochi SL et al. *Epidemiology of poliomyelitis in the United States one decade after the last reported case of indigenous wild-virus associated disease.* Clin Infect Dis 1992;14:568-79.

Vidor E, Meschievitz C, Plotkin S. *Fifteen years of experience with Vero-produced enhanced potency inactivated poliovirus vaccine.* Pediatr Infect Dis J 1997;16:312-22.

Wright PF, Kim-Farley RJ, de Quadros CA et al. *Strategies for the global eradication of poliomyelitis by the year 2000.* N Engl J Med 1991;325:1774-9.

Rabies Vaccine

In September 2000, a young boy died of rabies in Quebec. This was the first case of human rabies in Canada since 1985. The most likely source of the rabies infection in this boy was an unrecognized bat exposure several weeks before the onset of symptoms. Over the past few years the incidence of bat strain rabies across the country has increased, and of the last five human rabies cases in Canada, four followed exposure to bats.

Rabies is a neurotropic viral disease that has two clinical presentations and is almost invariably fatal. After infection, the usual incubation period is 20 to 60 days, although it may vary from several days to years. The more common, agitated (furious) form presents with the classical symptoms of hydrophobia or aerophobia with a rapidly progressing encephalitis and death. The paralytic form of the disease is manifest in progressive flaccid paralysis and has a more protracted course.

Epidemiology

The rabies virus can infect any mammal. In North America, it occurs mainly in certain wild terrestrial carnivore species and is spread by them to domestic livestock and pets. Over the past few years the number of animal rabies cases in Canada has been steadily increasing. There remain regional differences in the prevalence of animal rabies across the country, and the specific species infected in each region vary over time.

Most of the animal rabies reported in Canada is found in Ontario and Manitoba, and the most commonly infected animals across the country are bats, skunks and foxes. Bat rabies is found in all regions except Newfoundland and Labrador, Nunavut and

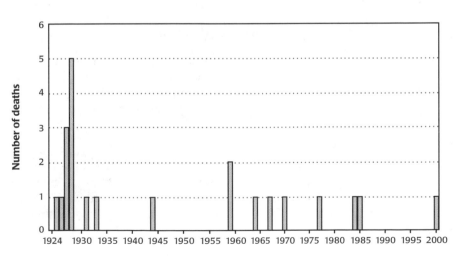

Rabies – Number of Deaths, Canada, 1924-2000

the Northwest Territories and has been the only strain identified in British Columbia, Alberta and Nova Scotia over the past few years. In Saskatchewan, Manitoba and Ontario rabid skunks are the most prevalent, although Ontario has seen increases of rabies in foxes and raccoons since 1999. In Quebec, also, rabies has increased in the fox population. The Northwest Territories and Nunavut report rabies primarily in foxes and dogs. Rabies has been reported sporadically from New Brunswick and Nova Scotia, and recently outbreaks in foxes have been reported in Newfoundland and Labrador. Spread can occur into domestic species of animals, such as horses and cows.

Bat rabies has accounted for 58% of the human rabies cases in the United States since 1980 and appears to be increasing in frequency. The increased incidence is due, in part, to the failure to recognize the small wound inflicted by a biting bat and thus omission of post-exposure prophylaxis. In several cases it is thought that transmission was caused by aerosolized virus across mucous membranes.

Although infections in domestic dogs and cats make up less than 10% of reported animal rabies in Canada, the bites of these species account for the vast majority of suspected rabies exposures in humans and the majority of courses of post-exposure rabies prophylaxis.

Since reporting began in 1925, 22 people have died of rabies in Canada; after 1985 there were no reported cases of human rabies until September 2000. Worldwide, there are estimated to be 30,000 to 50,000 deaths annually. Even though disease may not develop in everyone bitten by a rabid animal, a decision on the management of someone who may have been exposed to rabies virus must be made rapidly and judiciously, since delays in starting post-exposure prophylaxis reduce its effectiveness. Because it is not possible to determine which exposed individuals will develop rabies if untreated and because the infection is almost always fatal, it is essential that everyone exposed to animals with proven or suspected rabies be given post-exposure prophylaxis. Between 1,000 and 1,500 people in Canada receive post-exposure treatment each year.

Preparations Licensed for Immunization

Two rabies vaccines are licensed for active immunization of humans in Canada: Imovax® rabies and Rabies Vaccine Inactivated (Diploid Cell Origin)-Dried. Only Imovax® is currently available (Aventis Pasteur), and this may be used for pre-exposure and post-exposure prophylaxis. Both vaccines are prepared from rabies virus grown in human diploid cell culture, concentrated by ultrafiltration and then inactivated with beta-propiolactone.

Two human rabies immune globulin (RIG) products are licensed in Canada for passive immunization (see page 246). RIG is concentrated by cold ethanol fractionation from the plasma of hyperimmunized donors and undergoes multiple viral clearance procedures during preparation. It is supplied at a standardized concentration of 150 IU per mL.

Pre-exposure Management

Pre-exposure rabies immunization is an elective procedure and should be offered to people at potentially high risk of contact with rabid animals, e.g., certain laboratory workers, veterinarians, animal control and wildlife workers, spelunkers, and hunters and trappers in high-risk areas such as the far north. Travellers to endemic areas where there is not likely to be access to adequate and safe post-exposure measures should consider pre-travel immunization. As well, children who are too young to understand either the need to avoid animals or to report a traumatic contact are considered at greater risk of rabid animal exposure and should be offered pre-exposure immunization when travelling to endemic areas (see page 260).

Post-Exposure Management

Human diploid cell vaccine (HDCV) together with RIG and local treatment are highly effective in preventing rabies in exposed individuals. No post-exposure HDCV failures have occurred in Canada or the United States. The few reported failures elsewhere have been attributed to delay in treatment, lack of appropriate cleansing of wounds, suboptimal methods of immunization or omission of passive immunization. Responses to vaccines received in other countries may be less predictable.

Rabies prophylaxis must be considered in every incident in which potential exposure to rabies virus has occurred, unless rabies is known to be absent from the animal population. In evaluating each case, local public health officials should be consulted. If there has been no exposure, as described below, post-exposure treatment is not indicated.

1. Species of animal

The animals in Canada most often proven rabid are wild terrestrial carnivores (raccoons, foxes and skunks), cattle, bats, and wild dogs and cats. The distribution of animal rabies and the species involved vary considerably across Canada by region and over time, so in cases of possible exposure it is important to consult the local medical officer of health or government veterinarian. Human exposures to livestock are usually confined to salivary contamination with the exception of horses and swine, from which bites have been reported. The risk of infection after exposure to rabid cattle is low. Squirrels, hamsters, guinea-pigs, gerbils, chipmunks, rats, mice or other rodents, rabbits and hares are only rarely found to be infected with rabies and are not known to have caused human rabies in North America; post-exposure prophylaxis should be considered only if the animal's behaviour was highly unusual.

The manifestations of rabies and the incubation periods vary in different species. The length of time virus may be excreted in saliva before the development of symptoms has not been determined for the purpose of defining rabies exposure except in domestic dogs, cats and ferrets. In these animals, rabies virus excretion does not generally precede symptom development beyond 10 days. It remains unclear as to whether asymptomatic carriage of rabies virus in animals in the wild is possible.

2. Type of exposure

Rabies is transmitted when the virus is inoculated into tissues. This occurs most commonly through bites, although when cuts or wounds are contaminated by rabies virus from saliva or infected tissue, transmission is possible. Rarely, transmission has been recorded when virus was inhaled, or infected corneal grafts were transplanted into patients. Thus, two broad categories of exposure are recognized as warranting post-exposure prophylaxis:

Bite: This is defined as any penetration of the skin by teeth. Bites inflicted by most animals are readily apparent. However, bites inflicted by bats to a sleeping person may not be felt, and may leave no visible bite marks. Hence, when people are sleeping unattended in a room where a bat is found or when the possibility of a bite cannot be reasonably excluded — e.g., if a bat is discovered in proximity to an individual who is cognitively impaired — post-exposure prophylaxis should be initiated.

Non-bite: This category includes contamination of scratches, abrasions or cuts of the skin or mucous membranes by saliva or other potentially infectious material, such as the brain tissue of a rabid animal. Petting a rabid animal or handling its blood, urine or feces is not considered to be an exposure nor is being sprayed by a skunk. These incidents do not warrant post-exposure prophylaxis. Post-exposure prophylaxis is warranted and recommended in rare instances of non-bite exposure, such as inhalation of aerosolized virus by spelunkers exploring caves inhabited by infected bats or by laboratory technicians homogenizing tissues infected with rabies virus; however, the efficacy of prophylaxis after such exposures is unknown. Stringent guidelines concerning the suitability of tissue donors have eliminated the probability that rabies virus will be transmitted iatrogenically.

Exposures incurred in the course of caring for humans with rabies could theoretically transmit the infection. No case of rabies acquired in this way has been documented, but post-exposure prophylaxis should be considered for exposed individuals.

3. Investigation of the incident

Each incident of possible exposure requires a full investigation. This should include an assessment of the risk of rabies in the animal species involved and, in a low prevalence area such as Canada, the behaviour of the particular domestic animal involved. An unprovoked attack is more likely to indicate that the animal is rabid. Nevertheless, rabid cats and dogs may become uncharacteristically quiet. Bites inflicted on a person attempting to feed or handle an apparently healthy animal should generally be regarded as provoked.

Domestic pets with up-to-date rabies vaccination are unlikely to become infected with rabies. If vaccinated animals exhibit signs suggestive of rabies they must be carefully evaluated by a veterinarian.

Management of Animals Involved in Biting Incidents

Any animal that has bitten a human or is suspected of being rabid should be reported to the local medical officer of health and to the nearest Canadian Food Inspection Agency veterinarian.[1] These veterinarians are familiar with the regulations concerning rabies and, if necessary, will collect and ship appropriate specimens to a federal laboratory for diagnosis.

Signs of rabies cannot be reliably interpreted in wild animals. These animals, as well as stray or unwanted dogs or cats and other biting animals, should immediately be humanely killed in a way that does as little damage as possible to the head, which should be submitted for laboratory examination. A domestic dog, cat or ferret that is evaluated by a veterinarian and determined to be normal should be kept under secure observation for 10 days even if it has a history of vaccination. If the animal is still clinically well after that time, it can be concluded that it was not shedding rabies virus at the time of the exposure and was therefore non-infectious. If illness suggestive of rabies develops during the holding period, the animal should be killed and the head submitted for examination. Rabies virus is only readily demonstrable in brains of animals that have neurologic symptoms.

If the animal escapes during the 10-day observation period, the need for post-exposure prophylaxis should be carefully re-assessed. Exotic pets (other than ferrets) should be treated as wild animals because the incubation period and period of rabies virus shedding in these animals are unknown. Recent information regarding the pathogenesis of rabies in domestic ferrets has prompted them to be considered in the same category as domestic dogs and cats rather than wild carnivores.

Management of People After Possible Exposure to Rabies

The Table outlines the recommendations for the management of people after possible exposure to rabies. These recommendations are intended as a guide and may need to be modified in accordance with the specific circumstances of the exposure.

Immediate washing and flushing with soap and water and a virucidal agent is imperative and is probably the most effective procedure in the prevention of rabies. Suturing the wound should be avoided if possible. Tetanus prophylaxis and antibacterial drugs should be given as required.

---

[1]   Further information and advice is obtainable from the regional offices of the Canadian Food Inspection Agency in Moncton, N.B. (506) 851-7651; Montreal, Que. (514) 283-8888; Guelph, Ont. (519) 837-9400, 1-800-442-2342 (www.mnr.gov.on.ca/MNR/rabies/cfia.html); Winnipeg, Man. (204) 983-7443; Calgary, Alta. (403) 292-5828; and New Westminister, B.C. (604) 666-8900.

Post-exposure Prophylaxis for People
Not Previously Immunized Against Rabies

Animal species	Condition of animal at time of exposure	Management of exposed person
Dog or cat	Healthy and available for 10 days' observation	1. Local treatment of wound 2. At first sign of rabies in animal, give RIG (local and intramuscular) and start HDCV
	Rabid or suspected to be rabid* Unknown or escaped	1. Local treatment of wound 2. RIG (local and intramuscular) and HDCV
Skunk, bat, fox, coyote, raccoon and other carnivores. Includes bat found in room when a person was sleeping unattended.	Regard as rabid* unless geographic area is known to be rabies free	1. Local treatment of wound 2. RIG (local and intramuscular) and HDCV
Livestock, rodents or lagomorphs (hares and rabbits)	Consider individually. Consult appropriate public health and Food Inspection Agency officials. Bites of squirrels, chipmunks, rats, mice, hamsters, gerbils, other rodents, rabbits and hares may warrant post-exposure rabies prophylaxis if the behaviour of the biting animal was highly unusual.	

RIG = (human) rabies immune globulin, HDCV = human diploid cell vaccine

* If possible, the animal should be humanely killed and the brain tested for rabies as soon as possible; holding for observation is not recommended. Discontinue vaccine if fluorescent antibody test of animal brain is negative.

Schedule and Dosage

Pre-exposure immunization

Three doses of HDCV are required and should be given on days 0, 7 and 21. The vaccine is given as a 1.0 mL dose intramuscularly into the deltoid muscle or the thigh in infants. Although intradermal vaccine has been shown to produce adequate titres, there is no preparation licensed for intradermal use in Canada.

Post-exposure prophylaxis of previously unimmunized individuals

Five doses of 1 mL of HDCV should be given, the first dose (on day 0) as soon as possible after exposure, and additional doses on each of days 3, 7, 14 and 28 after the first dose. Vaccine should be administered intramuscularly into the deltoid muscle (never in the gluteal region) or the anterolateral upper thigh in infants. An appropriate dose of RIG, as described below, should also be given on day 0. Other immunization schedules have also been validated by the WHO.

Post-exposure prophylaxis should be started as soon as possible after exposure and should be offered to exposed individuals regardless of the elapsed interval. If the suspect animal is domestic and is available for quarantine, then immunization may be withheld pending the animal's status after the 10-day observation period. However, if the bite wound is to the head and neck region, prophylaxis should begin immediately and not be delayed until after the 10-day period. When notification of an exposure is delayed, prophylaxis may be started as late as 6 or more months after exposure.

The course of vaccine may be discontinued after consultation with pubic health/ infectious disease experts if the direct fluorescent antibody test of the brain of an animal killed at the time of attack proves to be negative. However, if suspicion of rabies in the animal remains high even in the presence of a negative test, the immunization series should be continued.

The recommended dose of human RIG is 20 IU/kg body weight. This formula is applicable to all age groups, including children. If anatomically feasible, the full dose of RIG should be thoroughly infiltrated into the wound and surrounding area. Any remaining volume should be injected intramuscularly at a site distant from vaccine administration. When more than one wound exists, each should be locally infiltrated with a portion of the RIG. The RIG may be diluted for such purposes. Because of interference with active antibody production, the recommended dose should not be exceeded. Since vaccine-induced antibodies begin to appear within 1 week, there is no value in administering RIG more than 8 days after initiating an approved vaccine course.

Vaccine and immune globulin should be used concurrently for optimum post-exposure prophylaxis against rabies, except in certain previously immunized people, as indicated below. **Under no circumstances should vaccine be administered in the same syringe or at the same site as RIG.**

Post-exposure prophylaxis of previously immunized individuals

Post-exposure prophylaxis for people who have previously received rabies vaccine differs according to which preparation of vaccine was received.

A. Two doses of HDCV, one injected immediately and the other 3 days later, without RIG, are recommended for exposed individuals with the following rabies immunization history:

   (i) Completion of an approved course of pre- or post-exposure prophylaxis with HDCV;

   (ii) Completion of immunization with other types of rabies vaccine or with HDCV according to unapproved schedules so long as neutralizing rabies antibody has been demonstrated in serum.

B. A complete course of HDCV plus RIG is recommended for those who may have received rabies vaccines but do not fulfil the criteria listed in A. A serum sample may be collected before vaccine is given, and if antibody is demonstrated the course may be discontinued, provided at least two doses of HDCV have been administered.

Serologic Testing and Booster Doses

Healthy people immunized with an appropriate regimen will develop rabies antibodies, and therefore routine post-immunization antibody determinations are not recommended. Neutralizing antibodies develop 7 days after immunization and persist for at least 2 years. The Canadian national rabies reference laboratory is the Ontario Provincial Public Health Laboratory, which considers an acceptable antibody response to be a titre of $\geq$ 0.5 IU/mL by the rapid fluorescent-focus inhibition test. Post-immunization antibody titre determination may be advisable for those anticipating frequent exposure or whose immune response may be reduced by illness, medication or advanced age. People with continuing high risk of exposure, such as certain veterinarians, should have their serum tested for rabies antibodies every 2 years; others working with live rabies virus in laboratories or vaccine-production facilities who are at risk of inapparent exposure should be tested every 6 months. Those with inadequate titres should be given a booster dose of HDCV. People previously immunized with other vaccines should be given sufficient doses of HDCV to produce an adequate antibody response.

Delayed systemic allergic reactions (see Adverse Reactions) appear to be less common after booster doses of the vaccine purified by zonal centrifugation (Rabies Vaccine Inactivated [Diploid Cell Origin]-Dried). This vaccine is therefore recommended for people requiring ongoing protection against rabies.

Although protective antibodies are present immediately after passive vaccination with RIG, they have a half-life of 21 days.

Adverse Reactions

HDCV: Local reactions such as pain, erythema, swelling and itching at the injection site may occur in 30% to 74% of recipients; mild systemic reactions such as headache, nausea, abdominal pain, muscle aches and dizziness may occur in about 5% to 40%. Systemic allergic reactions characterized by generalized urticaria and accompanied in some cases by arthralgia, angioedema, fever, nausea and vomiting have been reported. These reactions are uncommon in people receiving primary immunization but have occurred in up to 7% of those receiving a booster dose, with onset after 2 to 21 days. Such reactions have been shown to follow the development of IgE antibodies to beta propiolactone-altered human serum albumin in the vaccine. Vaccines purified by zonal centrifugation appear less likely to be associated with such reactions. Immediate anaphylactic reactions have occurred in 1 in 10,000 people given HDCV. Neurologic complications are rare, but three cases of neurologic illness resembling Guillain-Barré syndrome, which resolved without sequelae within 12 weeks, were reported in the early 1980s.

RIG: Local pain and low-grade fever may follow administration of RIG.

Contraindications

There are no definite contraindications to the use of rabies vaccine after significant exposure to a proven rabid animal.

A history of any previous hypersensitivity reaction to HDCV should be elicited. Hypersensitive individuals should be immunized only under strict medical supervision. Serious allergic or neuroparalytic reactions occurring during the administration of rabies vaccine pose a serious dilemma. The risk of rabies developing must be carefully considered before a decision is made to discontinue immunization. The use of corticosteroids as a possible treatment may inhibit the immune response. The patient's blood should be tested for rabies antibodies and expert opinion should be sought in the management of these individuals.

Corticosteroids and immunosuppressive agents may interfere with the development of active immunity. Therefore, people receiving such therapy should have a rabies antibody determination upon completion of a post-exposure course of rabies vaccine to ensure that an adequate response has developed.

Pregnancy is not a contraindication to post-exposure prophylaxis, but it would be prudent to delay pre-exposure immunization of pregnant women unless there is a substantial risk of exposure.

Selected References

CDC. *Human rabies prevention — United States, 1999: recommendations of the Advisory Committee on Immunization Practices (ACIP).* MMWR 1999;48(RR-1):1-19.

CDC. *Compendium of animal rabies control, 1998.* MMWR 1998;47:RR-9.

Fishbein DB, Dressen DW, Holmes DF et al. *Human diploid cell rabies vaccine purified by zonal centrifugation: a controlled study of antibody response and side effects following primary and booster preexposure immunizations.* Vaccine 1989;7:437-42.

Plotkin SA. *Rabies.* Clin Infect Dis 2000;30:4-12.

Turgeon N, Tucci M, Deshaies D et al. *A case report: human rabies in Montreal, Quebec — October 2000.* CCDR 2000;26(24):209-10.

Varughese P. *Human rabies in Canada — 1924-2000.* CCDR 2000:26(24):210-11.

WHO. *World survey of rabies —1997.* CCDR 2000;26(2):1-4.

Rubella Vaccine

Rubella is a viral disease that results in a transient exanthematous rash, post-auricular or suboccipital lymphadenopathy, arthralgia and low-grade fever. As symptoms are non-specific, it may be mistaken for infection due to parvovirus, adenoviruses or enteroviruses. Adult infection is frequently accompanied by transient polyarthralgia or polyarthritis. Serious complications are rare, and up to 50% of infections are subclinical.

The main goal of immunization is the prevention of rubella infection in pregnancy, which may give rise to congenital rubella syndrome (CRS). This syndrome can result in miscarriage, stillbirth and fetal malformations, including congenital heart disease, cataracts, deafness and mental retardation. The risk of fetal damage following maternal infection is particularly high in the earliest months after conception (85% in the first trimester) with progressive diminution of risk thereafter, and is very uncommon after the 20th week of pregnancy. Infected infants who appear normal at birth may later show eye, ear or brain damage. Congenital infection may become chronic and give rise to such problems as diabetes mellitus and panencephalitis later in life. As well, a small number of congenitally infected infants may shed the virus in the urine and nasopharyngeal secretions for 1 year or more.

Epidemiology

An MMR immunization program for all infants was introduced in Canada in April 1983. Previously, selective immunization of pre-pubertal girls had been practised in some jurisdictions, resulting in susceptible cohorts of males. Large outbreaks, mainly among males, have been reported as a result of selective immunization policies, most recently (1996-97) in Manitoba. In the past decade, several large outbreaks have occurred in North America in clustered, unimmunized populations, including those who refuse immunization for religious reasons.

Fewer than 100 cases of rubella have been reported in each of the past 3 years, and only 1 to 2 cases of CRS. Increasingly, mothers of CRS infants are foreign born and less likely to have been immunized against rubella before immigration to Canada. Studies indicate that immigrant women from countries where rubella vaccine is not routinely used (e.g., the majority of Asian, African and many Caribbean and South and Central American countries as well as Mexico) are particularly susceptible to rubella. Outbreaks in immigrant communities have been documented.

Preparations Licensed for Immunization

The rubella virus vaccine currently licensed in Canada incorporates live attenuated virus strain RA 27/3, prepared in human diploid cell culture. It is available as a monovalent vaccine or in combination with mumps and measles vaccines (MMR) or measles vaccine (MR). The vaccine is lyophilized and should be reconstituted just before administration with the diluent provided.

Efficacy and Immunogenicity

Rubella vaccine stimulates the formation of antibody to rubella virus in over 97% of susceptible individuals. Titres are generally lower than those observed in response to natural rubella infection.

Asymptomatic re-infection, manifest by a rise in antibody, has been observed in vaccinees and may account for the continued endemicity of rubella. Asymptomatic re-infection has also been observed in women with naturally acquired immunity and very low antibody titres. Rarely, transient viremia can occur in people immune by either natural disease or prior immunization, but transmission to the fetus in this circumstance is believed to be rare.

Schedule and Dosage

Immunization schedules and requirements for MMR vaccine vary by province/territory and can be obtained from the local public health department.

The dose of rubella vaccine, given either alone or combined with measles vaccine or measles and mumps vaccines, is 0.5 mL given as subcutaneous injection.

Infants and children

One dose of live rubella vaccine is recommended routinely for all children on or as soon as practical after their first birthday in combination with measles and mumps vaccines. Rubella vaccine should not be administered prior to 12 months of age.

In all provinces and territories, a second dose of rubella vaccine is given at the time of the second dose of measles vaccine, administered at 18 months of age or at school entry and at least 1 month after the first dose. Although a second dose of rubella vaccine is not believed to be necessary for achieving elimination of CRS, it is not harmful and may benefit those who do not respond to primary immunization (1% to 3% of people).

Adolescents and adults

Rubella vaccine should be given to all female adolescents and women of childbearing age unless they have proof of immunity, which is either a record of prior immunization or laboratory evidence of detectable antibody. At the first visit, rubella immunization status should be assessed. If there is no documentation of prior immunization, one dose of rubella vaccine should be given, preferably as MMR vaccine, since a high proportion of women susceptible to rubella are likely also susceptible to measles.

A clinical history of rubella without laboratory confirmation is not a reliable indicator of immunity.

Every effort should be made to immunize foreign-born adolescents and women from countries where rubella vaccine is in limited use (see Epidemiology section) as soon as possible after entry to Canada or, for women who are pregnant upon presentation, immediately post-partum.

Since up to one-third of cases of CRS occur in second and subsequent pregnancies, it is essential that all women found to be susceptible during pregnancy receive rubella vaccine (preferably given as MR or MMR vaccine) in the immediate post-partum period and as soon as practical after delivery. Every effort should be made to immunize before hospital discharge. Canadian, U.S. and U.K. studies show that a large proportion of rubella-susceptible women are not immunized post-partum. Hospital standing order policies have been shown to be effective in increasing post-partum immunization rates.

In educational institutions, such as schools, colleges and universities, particular emphasis should be placed on immunization of susceptible female staff and female students of childbearing age because of their relatively high risk of exposure.

In health care settings, the rubella immune status of female employees of childbearing age should be carefully reviewed, and those without documented immunity should be immunized. In addition, vaccine should be given to susceptible people of either sex who may expose pregnant women to rubella.

Booster Doses and Re-immunization

Antibody levels developed in response to earlier rubella vaccines decline over time, but this decline may not have great significance since any detectable antibody generally protects against viremic infection. The duration of protection is not yet known, but studies indicate that the duration of both cellular and humoral immunity exceeds 20 years. Booster doses are not considered necessary but are not harmful and may provide a marginal protective benefit in the population.

Serologic Testing

Pre-immunization: A documented history of immunization is presumptive evidence of immunity. Serologic screening in a person without documented immunization is neither necessary nor recommended, and may result in a missed opportunity to immunize.

Post-immunization: Serologic testing after immunization is unnecessary. Women of childbearing age without a prior record of immunization who are tested and found to be non-immune serologically should be offered one dose of rubella-containing vaccine. Those with a prior record of immunization who are serologically non-immune may be offered immunization, but such tests are likely to be falsely negative. It is not necessary to repeat immunization even if subsequent serologic tests are also negative, because such individuals usually have other evidence of rubella immunity.

Prenatally: Serologic testing for rubella antibody should be a routine procedure during prenatal care for those without written serologic evidence of immunity or prior immunization. Prenatal testing in Ontario and Quebec indicates rates of serosusceptibility of about 7% and 7% to 11% respectively.

Storage Requirements

Rubella-containing vaccines should be stored in the refrigerator at a temperature of 2° C to 8° C. Once reconstituted, the vaccine should be administered promptly.

Simultaneous Administration with Other Vaccines

Rubella-containing vaccines may be administered at the same time but at a separate injection site as DPT-containing vaccines routinely given at 18 months and school entry, as well as adult tetanus-diphtheria vaccine. When administered at the same time as live virus vaccines other than measles and mumps, rubella-containing vaccine(s) should be given at a separate injection site or, if possible, separated by a 4-week interval.

Adverse Reactions

Rash and lymphadenopathy occur occasionally. Acute transient arthritis or arthralgia may occur 1 to 3 weeks after immunization, usually persists for 1 to 3 weeks, and rarely recurs. These reactions are uncommon in children, but the frequency and severity increase with age, and they are more common in post-pubertal females, among whom arthralgia develops in 25% and arthritis-like signs and symptoms in 10% after immunization with RA 27/3. Recently published studies indicate no evidence of increased risk of new onset chronic arthropathies or neurologic conditions in women receiving RA 27/3 rubella vaccine. Paresthesia or pain in the extremities lasting 1 week to 3 months has been reported rarely. However, both the frequency and severity of adverse reactions are less than those associated with natural disease. Serious adverse reactions are rare. There is a growing body of literature to suggest a genetic predisposition to joint manifestations following rubella immunization. However, these manifestations are more serious after natural infection, and immunization against rubella among such people is indicated.

Contraindications

Administration of live rubella vaccine during pregnancy should be avoided because of the theoretical risk of CRS in the fetus.

Rubella vaccine should not be administered to people known to be hypersensitive to the vaccine components, such as antibiotics, used in its preparation; such reactions include anaphylactic hypersensitivity to neomycin. Convincing evidence supports the safety of routine administration of MMR vaccines to all children who have allergy to eggs. Fewer than 2 per 1,000 immunized egg-allergic children have been found to be at risk of anaphylactic reaction to MMR vaccine (see the chapter on Measles Vaccine for further details).

Rubella Vaccine

Precautions

Women of childbearing age should be advised to avoid pregnancy for 1 month after immunization. This recommendation is based on the duration of viremia after natural infection and evidence of vaccine safety.

Rubella vaccine is occasionally administered to women who were unknowingly pregnant at the time or who became pregnant shortly after immunization. Reassurance can be given that no fetal damage has been observed in the babies of over 700 susceptible women who received vaccine during their pregnancy and carried to term. The theoretical risk of teratogenicity, if any, is very small. Therefore, receipt of rubella vaccine in pregnancy, or conception within 1 month after receipt, should not be a reason to consider termination of pregnancy.

Breast-feeding is not a contraindication to rubella immunization. Although vaccine virus has been detected in breast milk and transmission can occur, no illness has been reported in the infants.

As with other live vaccines, rubella vaccine should not be administered to people whose immune mechanism is impaired as a result of disease or therapy, except under special circumstances (see section on Immunization in Immunocompromised Hosts). These vaccines would generally be administered to provide protection against measles. The immune response in such individuals may be impaired. Rubella-containing vaccines may be administered to HIV-infected people who are not severely immunosuppressed and among whom use of the vaccine has not been associated with serious adverse reactions.

Other Considerations

Small quantities of vaccine strain virus may be detected in the nasopharynx of some vaccinees 7 to 28 days after immunization, but the risk of transmission to contacts seems to be very low. After many years of vaccine use, only a few cases of possible transmission have been documented; in only one instance was the contact known to be previously immune by serologic testing. Therefore, it is safe to administer vaccine to those who are in contact with susceptible, pregnant women and with immunocompromised people.

Anti-Rho(D) immune globulin may interfere with response to rubella vaccine. Rubella-susceptible women who receive anti-Rho(D) immune globulin post-partum should either be given rubella vaccine at the same time and tested 3 months later for rubella immunity, or should be immunized with rubella vaccine 3 months post-partum, with follow-up ensured.

Vaccine must not be administered less than 2 weeks before an immune globulin injection. When immune globulin has been administered, rubella immunization should be delayed for 3 months; it should be delayed for 5 months if given as MMR vaccine (see Chapter on Passive Immunizing Agents). It has been shown that previous or simultaneous blood transfusion does not generally interfere with the antibody response to rubella immunization. In such cases, however, it is recommended that a serologic test be done 6 to 8 weeks after immunization to test the individual's immune status. If the individual is seronegative, a second dose of vaccine should be administered.

Passive immunization

The effectiveness of immune globulin for post-exposure prophylaxis of rubella is unknown and as such is not recommended.

Management of outbreaks

During outbreaks, people at risk who have not been immunized or do not have serologic proof of immunity should be given vaccine promptly without prior serologic testing. A history of rubella illness is not a reliable indicator of immunity.

Even though rubella immunization has not been shown to be protective when given after exposure, it is not harmful. It will protect the individual in future if the current exposure does not result in infection.

Surveillance

All suspected and confirmed cases of rubella and CRS must be reported to the appropriate local or provincial/territorial public health authority. In addition to this passive surveillance, CRS is monitored through the Canadian Paediatric Surveillance Program.

Laboratory confirmation is carried out by serodiagnostic laboratory methods or culture. The specific diagnosis is particularly important in suspect cases who are contacts of pregnant women and in suspect cases of CRS, as well as during outbreaks. A significant, rising antibody titre from acute and convalescent serum samples is confirmatory, the first sample being taken within the first 7 days after illness and the second 10 days after the first. Rapid confirmation may be obtained by testing for rubella-specific IgM antibody in a serum sample taken between 3 days and 1 month after rash onset. There may be false-negative results if the serum sample is taken too early or too late after the clinical illness, and false positives occur frequently, since the test has low positive predictive value outside the outbreak setting.

Congenital infection may be confirmed by isolation of the virus in neonatal urine or nasopharyngeal secretions, detection of IgM antibody to rubella virus in blood, or the persistence of antibody to rubella virus beyond the age of 3 months. Consultation with the regional public health laboratory will indicate the availability and applicability of various diagnostic methods for rubella.

Rubella Vaccine

Selected References

Balfour HH, Groth KE, Edelman CK et al. *Rubella viraemia and antibody responses after rubella vaccination and reimmunization.* Lancet 1981;1:1078-80.

Bottiger M, Morsgren M. *Twenty years' experience of rubella vaccination in Sweden: 10 years of selective vaccination (of 12-year-old girls and of women postpartum) and 13 years of a general two-dose vaccination.* Vaccine 1997;15(14):1538-44.

Enders G, Nickerl-Pacher U, Miller E et al. *Outcome of periconceptional maternal rubella.* Lancet 1988;1:1445-47.

Gyorkos TW, Tannenbaum TN, Abrahamowicz M et al. *Evaluation of rubella screening in pregnant women.* Can Med Assoc J 1998;159(9):1091-97.

Kimerlin DW. *Rubella immunization.* Pediatr Ann 1997;26(6):366-70.

Libman MD, Behr MA, Martel N et al. *Rubella susceptibility predicts measles susceptibility: implications for postpartum immunization.* Clin Infect Dis 2000;31(6):1501-3.

Macdonald A, Petaski K. *Outbreak of rubella originating among high-school students — Selkirk, Manitoba.* CCDR 1997;23(13):97-101.

Mitchell LA, Tingle AJ, Grace M et al. *Rubella virus vaccine associated arthropathy in postpartum immunized women: influenza of preimmunization serologic status on development of joint manifestations.* J Rheumatol. 2000;27(2):418-23.

Mitchell LA, Tingle AJ, Decarie D et al. *Identification of rubella virus T-cell epitopes recognized in anamnestic response to RA27/3 vaccine; associations with boost in neutralizing antibody titer.* Vaccine 1999;17(19):2356-65.

Mitchell LA, Tingle AJ, MacWilliam L et al. *HLA-DR class II associations with rubella vaccine-induced joint manifestations.* J Infect Dis 1998;177(1):5-12.

Parkman PD. *Making vaccination policy: the experience with rubella.* Clin Infect Dis 1999;28(suppl 2):S140-6.

Ray P, Black S, Shinefield H et al. Vaccine Safety Datalink Team. *Risk of chronic arthropathy among women after rubella vaccination.* JAMA 1997;278(7):551-56.

Stevenson J, Murdoch G, Riley A et al. *Implementation and evaluation of a measles/rubella vaccination campaign in a campus university in the UK following an outbreak of rubella.* Epidemiol Infect 1998;121(1):157-64.

Tingle AJ, Mitchell LA, Grace M et al. *Randomised double-blind placebo controlled study on adverse effects of rubella immunisation in seronegative women.* Lancet 1997;349(9061):1277-81.

Tookey PA, Peckham CS. *Surveillance of congenital rubella in Great Britain, 1971-96.* BMJ 1999;318:769-70.

Tookey PA, Jones G, Miller BH et al. *Rubella vaccination in pregnancy.* CDR (Lond Engl Rev) 1991;1(8):R86-8.

Valiquete L, Saintonge F, Carsley J et al. *Survey of postpartum rubella vaccination, Montreal, Laval, and Montérégie, Quebec, 1992.* CCDR 1996;22(5):38-40.

Weibel RE, Benor DE. *National Vaccine Injury Compensation Program, US Public Health Service, Rockville, Maryland 20857, USA.* Arthritis Rheum 1996;29(9):1529-34; published erratum in Arthritis Rheum 1996;29(11):1930.

Smallpox Vaccine

The last known case of naturally occurring smallpox occurred in Somalia in 1977, and 3 years later the World Heath Organization published the Declaration of the Global Eradication of Smallpox. Immunization programs were terminated shortly afterwards. Eradication of this dreaded disease was one of the most significant advances in public health in the 20th century.

For research purposes, remaining virus stocks are kept in two WHO reference laboratories in the United States and Russia. There are concerns that other countries may have access to the virus, particularly in the light of recent terrorist events. Health Canada requested NACI to make recommendations regarding immunization, and a detailed statement was subsequently published in *Canada Communicable Disease Report* (15 January, 2002, volume 28, ACS-1).

There is currently no evidence to support routine smallpox immunization of the general Canadian population. The threat of dissemination of smallpox virus as a biological weapon is unknown, but is believed to be very small. Groups at greatest potential risk include laboratory workers who may handle the virus and first responders to a suspected case or outbreak, such as ambulance attendants, hospital emergency room staff and other health care workers.

WHO considers the occurrence of a single case of smallpox anywhere in the world as a global emergency. WHO's Executive Board has recently endorsed a commitment by all countries to provide mutual assistance in the event of a case.

The Canadian Smallpox Contingency Plan is currently being updated by the Centre for Emergency Preparedness and Response, Health Canada, in consultation with the provinces and territories. The plan will include recommendations for action to be taken if a case of smallpox occurs in Canada or elsewhere.

Tetanus Toxoid

Tetanus is an acute and often fatal disease caused by an extremely potent neurotoxin produced by *Clostridium tetani*. The organism is ubiquitous in soil, but has also been detected in the intestines of animals and humans. Wounds that are contaminated with dirt, feces or saliva and that are associated with tissue injury and necrosis are most frequently associated with tetanus. Cases associated with injection drug use, animal bites and lacerations have been reported as well as rare cases occurring after bowel surgery. In North America, approximately 23% of cases occur in people who do not report any antecedent injury.

Tetanus is rare in Canada. In the 1990s, the number of cases reported annually ranged from 1 to 7, with an average of 5 (see Figure). The last death was recorded in 1995. The immunization status of most of the cases was not known. People > 50 years of age accounted for about half, and most were males. Birth in a foreign country was indicated for 11%.

Tetanus immunization programs are highly effective, provide long-lasting protection and are recommended for the whole population. However, serosurveys suggest that a substantial proportion of Canadians have nonprotective tetanus antitoxin levels. Factors associated with lack of immunity to tetanus include increasing age (particularly among women, few of whom received immunization as part of military service), birth outside Canada and absence of immunization records. Continued attention should be given to improving tetanus immunization in these groups.

Tetanus – Number of Cases and Deaths, 1924-2000

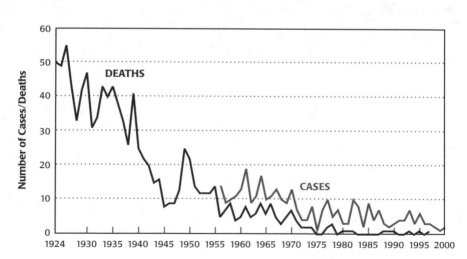

Preparations Licensed for Immunization

Tetanus toxoid is prepared by detoxification of tetanus toxin with formalin. The toxoid is combined with aluminum salts, generally aluminum phosphate, in an adsorbed form. Tetanus toxoid is available alone or in various combinations with diphtheria toxoid, pertussis, inactivated poliomyelitis and *Haemophilus influenzae* vaccines. All preparations contain comparable amounts of tetanus toxoid. The preparations contain either thimerosal or 2-phenoxyethanol with or without formaldehyde, as preservatives. Preparations that also contain inactivated polio vaccine may contain trace amounts of polymyxin B and neomycin from the cell growth medium.

Efficacy and Immunogenicity

Tests for measuring the immune response to tetanus toxoid include the serum toxin neutralization bioassay performed in mice and serologic tests, which include enzyme immunoassays (EIA). Because the bioassay is expensive and time-consuming, the EIA is more widely used. Protective EIA antibody levels have been variously defined as greater than 0.10-0.15 IU/mL in serosurveys; controversy exists regarding the accepted cut-off level. Correlation of serologic test results with the toxin bioassay is useful, as the latter assesses actual neutralization *in vivo*.

Protective antitoxin levels occur in virtually all healthy infants and children who receive primary immunization. The immune response in premature infants is comparable to that of term infants of the same chronologic age. A double-blind, randomized controlled trial in rural South America demonstrated that two or three doses of tetanus toxoid administered to previously unvaccinated women of childbearing age protected their infants. Efficacy in standard pre-exposure and post-wound booster immunization regimens among adults has not been assessed in randomized trials, but was demonstrated by observational studies during World War II.

Most children who are perinatally infected with HIV develop adequate antitoxin antibody responses following immunization with vaccines containing tetanus toxoid. The antibody response to boosters given to adults with HIV or other humoral immune deficiencies is suboptimal. Tetanus immunity is lost in approximately half of patients undergoing chemotherapy for lymphoma or leukemia. Patients undergoing bone marrow or stem cell transplantation should be re-immunized with two doses, 12 and 24 months after the procedure.

Very rare cases of tetanus have been reported despite full immunization and the presence of toxin-neutralizing antibody. These cases may present with a clinical spectrum ranging from mild or localized to severe disease. Explanatory theories include the "overwhelming" of host defences by large quantities of toxin, selective suppression of the immune response or antigenic differences between toxin and toxoid.

Recommended Usage

It is recommended that all Canadians receive a primary immunizing course of tetanus toxoid in childhood, followed by routine booster doses every 10 years. Adults who have not previously received a primary tetanus toxoid series require three doses as part of an adult primary immunization regimen (see Schedule and Dosage).

Active immunization against tetanus should be undertaken for patients who have recovered from this disease, because infection does not confer protective immunity.

Schedule and Dosage

The dose of the various forms of tetanus toxoid licensed in Canada is 0.5 mL. For children < 7 years of age, tetanus toxoid is most commonly used in combination with diphtheria toxoid, acellular pertussis, inactivated polio and *H. influenzae* type b antigens. For individuals ≥ 7 years of age, use of an adult-type preparation is recommended e.g. Td, Td-Polio or dTap.

For children < 7 years of age, the primary immunizing series of adsorbed tetanus toxoid in Canada consists of a dose at 2, 4 and 6 months of age, plus a fourth dose at 18 months. If the fourth primary dose was given before the fourth birthday, a booster dose is also given at 4 to 6 years of age (school entry). Immunization schedules for children not vaccinated in early infancy are shown in Tables 2 and 3 in Part 2: A. Recommended Immunization Schedules for Infants and Children. In adults requiring a primary immunization series, the first two doses of toxoid (preferably given as Td) should be given 4 to 8 weeks apart and the third 6 to 12 months later.

Route of Administration

Tetanus toxoid is administered intramuscularly.

Booster Doses and Re-immunization

To maintain immunity to tetanus after completion of primary immunization, booster doses administered as Td are recommended at 10-year intervals. More frequent boosters may lead to severe local and systemic reactions. Some experts have suggested that booster doses may be given less frequently, because tetanus cases are uncommon in people who received a primary immunization series but have not received subsequent boosters every 10 years. On the basis of this observation, it has been suggested that immunization status should be reviewed at least once during adult life, e.g., at 50 years of age, and a dose of Td given to everyone who has not had one within the previous 10 years. However NACI's continued recommendation for tetanus boosters every 10 years is based on concern regarding the decline of antibody levels with age and potential failure of single booster doses to produce protective levels in older individuals.

For individuals planning to travel to developing countries where safe tetanus toxoid administration may not be available if required, it may be prudent to offer an early tetanus booster prior to travel if more than 5 years have elapsed since the last dose.

Storage Requirements

Toxoid preparations should be stored in the refrigerator, at a temperature between 2° C and 8° C. They should not be frozen, and any that have been frozen should not be used.

Post-exposure Prevention of Tetanus in the Context of Wound Management

The Table below summarizes the recommended use of immunizing agents in wound management. It is important to ascertain the number of doses of toxoid previously given and the interval since the last dose. When a tetanus booster dose is required, the combined preparation of tetanus and diphtheria toxoid formulated for adults (Td) is preferred. Appropriate cleansing and debridement of wounds is imperative, and use of antibiotics may be considered.

Some individuals with humoral immune deficiency, including those with HIV infection, may not respond adequately to tetanus toxoid. Therefore, tetanus immune globulin (TIG) should be used in addition to tetanus toxoid if a wound occurs that is not clean, regardless of the time elapsed since the last booster.

Guide to Tetanus Prophylaxis in Wound Management

History of tetanus immunization	Clean, minor wounds		All other wounds	
	Td*	TIG†	Td	TIG
Uncertain or < 3 doses of an immunization series**	Yes	No	Yes	Yes
≥ 3 doses received in an immunization series**	No‡	No	No§	No¶

Note: Table format changed from previous edition, but recommendations remain unchanged.

* Adult-type tetanus and diphtheria toxoids. If the patient is < 7 years old, a tetanus toxoid-containing vaccine is given as part of the routine childhood immunization.

† Tetanus immune globulin, given at a separate site from Td

** The immunization series for tetanus is described in the text (Schedule and Dosage)

‡ Yes, if > 10 years since last booster.

§ Yes, if > 5 years since last booster. More frequent boosters not required and can be associated with increased adverse events. The bivalent toxoid, Td, is not considered to be significantly more reactogenic than T alone and is recommended for use in this circumstance. The patient should be informed that Td has been given.

¶ Yes, if individuals are known to have a significant humoral immune deficiency state (e.g., HIV, agammaglobulinemia), since immune response to tetanus toxoid may be suboptimal.

Simultaneous Administration with Other Vaccines

Tetanus toxoid preparations may be given concurrently with other vaccines in circumstances in which this would be advantageous.

Adverse Reactions

Adverse reactions to primary immunization with tetanus toxoid are rare, especially in children. Their incidence in adults increases with age. Following booster doses, local erythema and swelling are not uncommon. Severe local reactions occur rarely and may be associated with high levels of circulating antitoxin resulting from over-immunization. Lymphadenopathy may occasionally occur. Fever has been infrequently reported and usually occurs in cases showing a marked local reaction. Systemic reactions, such as generalized urticaria, anaphylaxis, serum sickness and brachial plexus neuropathy, have rarely been reported. Attribution of adverse reactions to tetanus toxoid may be confounded if other antigens are present in the preparation.

Trismus associated with tetanus toxoid immunization has rarely been reported. Outcomes have been favourable. The pathogenesis is unexplained.

Contraindications and Precautions

It is recommended that tetanus toxoid not be given routinely to a patient who has received a booster dose in the preceding 5 years.

Tetanus toxoid should not be given if a severe systemic reaction, including severe hypersensitivity or a neurologic event, followed a previous dose.

People who experience a major local reaction or high fever following a dose of tetanus toxoid should not be given another dose for at least 10 years. In those who have experienced severe local reactions or fever after tetanus toxoid, plain toxoid may be considered for subsequent booster doses, since it is reported to cause fewer reactions than adsorbed toxoid. When a contraindication to tetanus toxoid exists and a patient sustains a major or unclean wound, tetanus immune globulin should be given.

Before a combined vaccine is given, it is most important to ensure that there are no contraindications to the administration of any of the components.

There is no evidence that tetanus toxoid is teratogenic, but it is prudent to wait until the second trimester of pregnancy to administer a routinely required dose, to minimize concern about the theoretic possibility of a relation with any observed birth defect. In the event of a tetanus-prone wound during pregnancy the recommendations in the table should be followed. Neonatal tetanus may occur in infants born to unimmunized mothers under unhygienic conditions.

Selected References

Bardenheier B, Prevots DR, Khetsuriani N et al. *Tetanus surveillance – United States, 1995-1997.* MMWR 1998;47(SS-2):1-13.

Fiorillo L, Robinson JL. *Localized tetanus in a child.* Ann Emerg Med 1999;33:460-63.

Katz K, Walmsley S. *Postoperative tetanus: a case report.* Can Med Assoc J 2000;163(5):571-73.

Mayand C, Loupi E, Charara O et al. *Trismus et vaccination antitétanique.* Arch Pediatr 1999;6(7):752-54.

Shimoni Z, Dobrousin A, Cohen J et al. *Tetanus in an immunised patient.* BMJ 1999;319:1049.

Wassilak SGF, Orenstein WA, Sutter RW. *Tetanus toxoid.* In: Plotkin SA, Orenstein WA, eds. *Vaccines.* 3rd edition. Philadelphia: W.B. Saunders 1999:441-74.

Yuan L, Lau W, Thipphawong J et al. *Diphtheria and tetanus immunity among blood donors in Toronto.* Can Med Assoc J 1997;156:985-90.

Tetanus Toxoid

Typhoid Vaccine

Typhoid fever is caused by *Salmonella typhi*, which differs from most other *Salmonella* species in that it infects only humans and frequently causes severe systemic illness. The organism is generally transmitted via food contaminated with the feces or urine of people with the disease or those who are *S. typhi* carriers. The fatality rate is approximately 16% for untreated cases and 1% for those given appropriate antibiotic therapy. Between 2% and 5% of typhoid cases become chronic carriers, sometimes shedding bacteria in stool for years. The risk of severe illness is increased in people with depressed immunity (e.g., due to HIV) or decreased gastric acid levels.

Epidemiology

In endemic areas (such as Africa, Asia, Central and South America), typhoid fever has long been considered a disease with the greatest impact in individuals 5 to 19 years of age. Age-specific incidence rates vary from one country to another, however, and significant illness and deaths have been reported in children < 5 in some settings. Reports of typhoid fever in children < 2 years of age are quite unusual. Several factors may contribute to this apparently lower risk in very young children, including age-specific changes in the immune response, atypical or milder disease in this population and under-reporting. Whatever the cause(s), the observation is important in light of our incomplete knowledge of vaccine immunogenicity and efficacy in this age group.

The incidence of typhoid fever is very low in the industrialized world. An average of 70 cases have been reported annually in Canada over the past 5 years. The low incidence rates in industrialized countries is attributable to overall good living conditions, in particular the high quality of drinking water and the treatment of sewage. The rates were achieved without vaccines, and vaccination has no ongoing role in their maintenance.

The greatest risk of typhoid infection for Canadians occurs while they are travelling in countries or regions of countries where sanitation is likely to be poor. However, not all travellers in these countries or regions are at markedly increased risk. Indeed, the risk of suffering from typhoid fever in many settings in developing countries is minimal (e.g., business-class hotels, conference centres and resort hotels). The greatest risk appears to be associated with exposures to food and water in uncontrolled settings (e.g., market stalls, street vendors, home restaurants and family settings). Even relatively short visits with friends and family can put Canadian travellers (the so-called VFR or "visiting friends and relatives" group) at substantial risk of typhoid in some areas.

Regardless of the setting, typhoid immunization is not a substitute for careful selection and handling of food and water. The available vaccines provide only 50% to 60% protection and do not prevent disease in those who ingest a large number of organisms. However, immunization may reasonably be expected to reduce the risk of typhoid fever among otherwise healthy travellers in areas where this disease is either endemic or epidemic.

Preparations Licensed for Immunization

Two typhoid vaccines are currently available for protection against typhoid fever.

Parenteral, capsular polysaccharide vaccine

This vaccine is an injectable solution of Vi (virulence) antigen prepared from the capsular polysaccharide (ViCPS) of *S. typhi* strain TY2. The vaccine is produced by Aventis Pasteur and distributed in Canada under the name of Typhim Vi™. Each 0.5 mL dose of vaccine contains 25 μg of purified polysaccharide.

Oral, live attenuated vaccine

Ty21a is an attenuated strain of *S. typhi* that was produced by chemical mutagenesis. This bacterium has lost some virulence factors and replicates for only a limited period of time in human hosts. The vaccine is produced by Swiss Serum and Vaccine Institute and is supplied either as enteric-coated capsules (four doses containing lyophilized bacteria) or as foil sachets (three doses of lyophilized bacteria). Although both formulations are available at this time, it is likely that the capsular form will be eclipsed by the simpler, sachet form in the coming years. Both formulations contain buffer to enhance passage of the attenuated bacteria through the gastric acid barrier. The components included in these vaccines are listed in the Table.

Components of the Oral, Live Attenuated Vaccine against Typhoid Fever

Formulation	Capsule	Sachet (reconstituted)
Viable *S. typhi* Ty21a	2-10 x 10⁹ cfu*	2-10 x 10⁹ cfu*
Non-viable *S. typhi* Ty21a	5-60 x 10⁹ cfu*	5-60 x 10⁹ cfu*
Amino acid mixture	0.8-2.1 g	0.8-15 mg
Ascorbic acid	0.6-1.6 mg	0.6-10 mg
Aspartame	†	20-30 mg
Lactose	135.8-166.6 mg	1.68-2.31 g
Magnesium stearate	3.4-4.2 mg	†
Sodium bicarbonate	†	2.4-2.9 gm
Sucrose	16.7 – 41.7 mg	15-250 mg
* Colony-forming units		
† Not present in this formulation		

Efficacy and Immunogenicity

Parenteral, capsular polysaccharide vaccine

The parenteral vaccine stimulates a specific antibody response (i.e., ≥ fourfold rise in antibody titre) in about 93% of healthy adults. Controlled trials have demonstrated that the serologic response to vaccine is correlated with protective efficacy. Two randomized, double-blind, controlled field trials of ViCPS in disease-endemic areas have demonstrated protective efficacy rates of 55% (95% confidence interval [CI] 30%-71%). The efficacy of immunization with ViCPS has not been systematically studied in people from industrialized countries who travel to disease-endemic regions or in children < 5 years of age. ViCPS has not been tested among children < 1 year of age. Its protective efficacy in people previously immunized with earlier parenteral formulations or the oral vaccine is unknown. Although antibody titres fall with time after vaccination, immunity following Typhim Vi™ is thought to last for 2 to 3 years.

In some regions of the world, virulent but Vi-negative strains of *S. typhi* have been reported. Typhim Vi™ would not be expected to protect against these rare isolates. Novel conjugated Vi vaccines that have enhanced efficacy in adults and children may soon be available.

Oral, live attenuated vaccine

The Ty21a vaccines stimulate a cell-mediated immune response as well as inducing both secretory and humoral antibody. Healthy subjects do not shed vaccine-strain organisms in their stool. As a result, secondary transmission to contacts does not occur. Despite the limited capacity of the vaccine-strain organism to replicate, individuals who are significantly immunocompromised should not receive oral vaccine.

In studies delivering at least three doses of the capsular form of the vaccine in typhoid endemic regions, a protective efficacy of 51% (95% CI 35%-63%) can be expected. Although less information is available about the liquid formulation in field trials, the available data suggest that this vaccine is at least as effective as the capsular form. The oral vaccines appear to be less effective for disease prevention in children 5 to 9 years of age (17%-19%) than older children (54%-72% among 10 to 19 year olds). Protective antibodies after the administration of three doses of vaccine are detectable for 3 to 4 years and may persist for longer periods in some individuals.

There are no data on the efficacy or duration of protection in travellers from industrialized countries or in children < 5 years of age (capsular formulation) or < 3 years of age (liquid formulation). Neither are there reports regarding the protective efficacy of the oral formulations in people previously immunized with parenteral vaccines. The activity of the Ty21a vaccines against the rare Vi-negative isolates is unknown.

Recommended Usage

Routine typhoid immunization is not recommended in Canada. However, selective immunization should be considered in the following groups:

- Travellers who will have prolonged (> 4 weeks) exposure to potentially contaminated food and water, especially those travelling to or working in small cities, villages or rural areas in countries with a high incidence of disease. Individuals billeted with or visiting families in such areas may be at particularly high risk. Immunization is not routinely recommended for business travel or short-term (< 4 weeks) holidays in resort hotels in such countries.

- Travellers with reduced or absent gastric acid secretion.

- People with ongoing household or intimate exposure to an *S. typhi* carrier.

- Laboratory workers who frequently handle cultures of *S. typhi*. Technicians working in routine microbiology laboratories do not need to receive this vaccine.

Typhoid immunization is not routinely recommended for workers in sewage plants, for controlling common-source outbreaks, for people attending rural summer or work camps or for people in nonendemic areas experiencing natural disasters such as floods. It is not recommended for the control or containment of typhoid outbreaks in Canada. Typhoid vaccine does not confer complete protection against disease, and immunity may be overwhelmed by a large inoculum of *S. typhi*. Therefore, it is necessary to warn travellers that immunization is only an additional preventive measure against typhoid fever in high-risk situations and that care in the selection of food and water remains of primary importance.

Route of Administration and Storage

Parenteral, Vi capsular polysaccharide vaccine

Adults and children > 2 years of age should receive a single dose of 0.5 mL (25 μg) intramuscularly. The optimum interval for booster doses has not been established, but the manufacturer recommends booster doses every 3 years if continued or renewed exposure is expected. There are no data on the use of this vaccine as a booster for people who have received other vaccines previously. However, a single dose of the vaccine at the appropriate interval should re-establish protection.

Oral typhoid vaccine (Ty21a) – capsular formulation

For adults and children > 5 years of age, one enteric-coated capsule (Vivotif™, Berna Vaccine) should be taken on alternate days to a total of four capsules. Each capsule should be taken on an empty stomach with a liquid no warmer than 37° C. The capsules should be kept refrigerated (at a temperature of 2° C to 8° C) until used. Although refrigeration is recommended, this formulation is stable for up to 7 days at 20° C to 25° C. All four capsules must be taken for optimal protection.

Typhoid Vaccine

Oral typhoid vaccine (Ty21a) – liquid formulation

The liquid preparation (Vivotif L™, Berna Vaccine) is licensed for adults and children > 3 years of age. Each package contains three foil sachets with lyophilized vaccine in one half and buffer in the other half. The contents of both halves of one sachet must be mixed with liquid no warmer than 37° C, and the diluted vaccine-buffer mix should be taken on an empty stomach. This procedure is repeated on alternate days for a total of three doses. The sachets should be kept refrigerated (at a temperature of 2° C to 8° C) until used. Although refrigeration is recommended, this formulation is stable for at least 48 hours at 20° C to 25° C in the sachets. The vaccine is less stable once reconstituted, and should be drunk immediately upon reconstitution (within 1 hour). All three doses must be taken for optimal protection.

Booster Doses

Relatively few data are available to guide recommendations for either the frequency or timing of booster doses in Canadians residing abroad and in travellers. Nonetheless, periodic booster doses in those at continued risk may reasonably be expected to increase antibody titres and protection (e.g., every 2-3 years for the parenteral formulation and every 3-4 years for the oral formulations). Although there are no data regarding the interchangeability of typhoid vaccines, it is presumed that boosting can be performed with any of the available formulations regardless of the vaccine used initially.

Simultaneous Administration with Other Vaccines

Although all possible combinations have not been specifically studied, there is no known interaction between the ViCPS vaccine and a number of other relevant travel vaccines such as hepatitis A vaccine, yellow fever vaccine and hepatitis B vaccine. The liquid form of the oral typhoid vaccine can be given simultaneously with oral cholera vaccine, and such a combined formulation is now available (Colertif Berna). Administration of the capsular form of the oral vaccine should be separated from administration of the oral cholera vaccine by at least 8 hours. Other combination formulations targeting travellers (e.g., hepatitis A vaccine with typhoid Vi) will likely become available in the near future.

Comments Applicable to Both Oral Formulations

Antibiotics with activity against *S. typhi* or other Salmonellae (e.g., broad-spectrum penicillins or cephalosporins, fluoroquinolones, trimethoprim-sulfamethoxazole) may interfere with replication of the vaccine-strain bacterium. For people receiving therapy with such antibiotics, immunization should be deferred until at least 48 hours after the antibiotic course has been completed. Antimalarial drugs may also limit replication of the vaccine-strain bacterium (e.g., proguanil, mefloquine) or interfere with antigen presentation (e.g., chloroquine). Ideally, typhoid immunization should be completed before anti-malarial prophylaxis is initiated. If immunization must occur while one or another of these anti-malarials is being taken, at least 8 hours should separate the administration of oral vaccine and the antimalarial.

Minor variations in dosing schedule are not expected to affect the efficacy of either of the oral typhoid formulations. However, if it is deemed necessary to repeat the series because of long intervals between doses (> 4 days), the administration of an additional full course of vaccine would not be harmful. Although compliance can be an issue with these products, since they are self administered, recent evidence suggests that most travellers take the vaccines competently if properly instructed.

Adverse Reactions

The parenteral ViCPS vaccine is far less reactogenic than the previous parenteral (whole bacterium) product. A recent meta-analysis suggests that local reactions (e.g., pain, redness, swelling) can be expected in approximately 4% of vaccinees (95% CI 1.3%-10%), whereas only about 1% report systemic effects such as fever (95% CI 0.1%-12.3%). Virtually all of the available data regarding adverse events following immunization with the Vi polysaccharide vaccine have been acquired in studies of children and young adults (age < 25 years).

The reported adverse events following oral immunization are also relatively rare and mild. Local reactions, such as vomiting (2.1%: 95% CI 0.6%-7.8%) and diarrhea (5.1%: 95% CI 1.7%-14.5%), seldom prevent completion of the course of immunization. Low grade fever can be expected in approximately 2% of vaccinees (95% CI 0.7%-5.3%). Recent case reports raise the possibility that the Ty21a vaccines may, very rarely, predispose vaccinees to reactive arthritis.

Contraindications and Precautions

The only contraindication to administration of the parenteral ViCPS vaccine is a history of a severe local or systemic reaction to a previous dose of this vaccine. Similarly, the oral live typhoid vaccine is contraindicated in subjects with hypersensitivity to any component of the vaccine or the enteric-coated capsule. The oral vaccines should not be given to anyone with an acute gastrointestinal condition or inflammatory bowel disease.

Pediatric use

The ViCPS vaccine can be used in children > 2 years of age. The capsular form of the oral vaccine can be used in children > 5 years of age (if they can be induced to swallow the rather large capsules). The liquid formulation of the oral vaccine can be used in children > 3 years of age. As noted above, there is some controversy regarding the frequency and severity of typhoid fever in children < 5 years of age.

Immunization in pregnant women and nursing mothers

Although the highly purified ViCPS vaccine would not be expected to have any adverse effects, its safety in pregnancy has not been directly studied. Therefore, the

Typhoid Vaccine

benefits of vaccine must be carefully weighed against any potential adverse effects before it is given to pregnant women. Oral typhoid vaccines should not be given to pregnant women. Although there are no data, it is reasonable to assume that either vaccine could be used safely in nursing mothers.

Immunization in immunocompromised hosts

The oral vaccines should not be given to immunocompromised or immunosuppressed people, including those with known HIV infection. Safe storage should be emphasized in households with small children and immunocompromised individuals. Note that these concerns for immunocompromised hosts are purely theoretical, and no case of disseminated infection with the attenuated bacterium has been reported. The limited capacity of the attenuated strain to replicate in the human host is independent of the host's immune status.

Summary of Recommendations

- Both inactivated and oral typhoid vaccines can provide some degree of protection against typhoid fever in children and young adults in typhoid endemic regions.

- These vaccines are also likely to be useful in Canadians returning for family visits in their countries of origin and in Canadian travellers who spend prolonged periods of time in endemic areas.

- Both inactivated and oral typhoid vaccines are likely to provide at least some degree of protection against typhoid fever in subjects who travel from non-endemic regions to endemic regions.

- Individuals with decreased gastric acid barriers (e.g., achlorhydria, medications that reduce gastric acidity, antacid abuse) who travel to typhoid endemic regions should be offered either parenteral or oral immunization.

- Immunocompromised subjects and pregnant women for whom typhoid immunization is advisable should receive the parenteral vaccine.

- Typhoid immunization may also reasonably be considered in a control program to limit a typhoid fever epidemic (e.g., in closed communities, refugee settings).

- Booster doses of a typhoid vaccine for Canadians residing abroad and frequent travellers should be considered every 2 to 3 years for the parenteral formulation and every 3 to 4 years for the oral formulations.

- Typhoid vaccines can be considered to be interchangeable for booster doses.

- Typhoid immunization is not recommended for the large majority of business travellers and short-term holiday travellers.

- Typhoid immunization in non-travelling Canadians is ONLY recommended for individuals regularly working with this organism in clinical or research laboratories and in family members and close contacts of a chronic carrier of *S typhi*.

- Typhoid immunization may also provide some degree of protection in children as young as 2 (inactivated vaccine) or 3 (liquid formulation oral vaccine) years of age when these children will be staying with families abroad or will be travelling for prolonged periods of time in endemic areas.

Selected References

Acharya IL, Lowe CU, Thapa R et al. *Prevention of typhoid fever in Nepal with the Vi capsular polysaccharide of **Salmonella typhi**.* N Engl J Med 1987;317:1101-04.

Barnett ED, Chen R. *Children and international travel: immunizations.* Pediatr Infect Dis J 1995;14:988-89.

CDC. *Typhoid immunization recommendations of the Advisory Committee on Immunization Practices (ACPI).* MMWR 1994;43:RR-14.

Committee to Advise on Tropical Medicine and Travel (CATMAT). *Statement on overseas travelers and typhoid.* CCDR 1994;20:61-2.

Cryz SJ Jr. *Post-marketing experience with live oral Ty21a vaccine.* Lancet 1993;341:49-50.

Cryz SJ Jr. *Patient compliance in the use of Vivitif Berna™ vaccine, typhoid vaccine, live oral Ty21a.* J Travel Med 1998;5:14-17.

Engels EA, Falagas ME, Lau J et al. *Typhoid fever vaccines: a meta-analysis of studies on efficacy and toxicity.* BMJ 1998;316:110-16.

Engels EA, Lau J. *Vaccines for preventing typhoid fever.* Cochrane Database Syst Rev 2000;2:CD001261.

Horowitz H, Carbonaro CA. *Inhibition of the **Salmonella typhi** oral vaccine strain, TY21a, by mefloquine and chloroquine.* J Infect Dis 1992;166:1462-64.

Ivanoff B, Levine MM, Lambert PH. *Vaccination against typhoid fever: present status.* Bull WHO 1994;72:957-71.

Keitel WA, Bond NL, Zahradnik JMB et al. *Clinical and serological responses following primary and booster immunization with **Salmonella typhi** Vi capsular polysaccharide vaccines.* Vaccine 1994;12:155-59.

Klugman KP, Gilbertson IT, Koornhof HJ et al. *Protective activity of Vi capsular polysaccharide vaccine against typhoid fever.* Lancet 1987;2:1165-69.

Levine MM, Ferrecio C, Black RE et al. *Comparison of enteric coated capsules and liquid formulation of Ty21a typhoid vaccine in randomized controlled field trial.* Lancet 1990;2:891-94.

Levine MM, Ferrecio C, Black RE et al. *Large scale field trial of Ty21a live oral typhoid vaccine in enteric-coated capsule formulation.* Lancet 1987;1:1049-52.

Levine MM, Taylor DN, Ferrecio C. *Typhoid vaccine comes of age.* Pediatr Infect Dis J 1989;8:374-81.

Levine MM, Ferrecciio C, Abrego P et al. *Duration of efficacy of Ty21a, attenuated Salmonella typhi live oral vaccine.* Vaccine 1999;17:S22-27.

Lin FY, Ho VA, Khiem HB et al. *The efficacy of a **Salmonella typhi** Vi conjugate vaccine in two-to-five year old children.* N Engl J Med 2001;344:1322-3.

Mahle WT, Levine MM. ***Salmonella typhi** infection in children younger than 5 years of age.* Pediatr Infect Dis J 1993;12:627-31.

Sinha A, Sazawal S, Kumar R et al. *Typhoid fever in children aged less than 5 years*. Lancet 1999;354:734-37.

Taylor DN, Levine MM, Kuppens L et al. *Why are typhoid vaccines not recommended for epidemic typhoid fever?* J Infect Dis 1999;180:2089-90.

Varicella Vaccine

Varicella-zoster virus (VZV) is a DNA virus of the herpesvirus family. As with other herpesviruses, VZV causes a primary illness (varicella or chickenpox), establishes latency in the sensory nerve ganglia and may be reactivated later as herpes zoster (shingles). VZV is spread by direct contact with the virus shed from skin lesions or in oral secretions as well as by the airborne route. The incubation period is from 10 to 21 days, usually in the range of 14 to 16 days. Infectiousness begins 1 to 2 days before onset of the rash and lasts until the last lesion has crusted. Attack rates among susceptible contacts in household settings are high.

Epidemiology

Varicella is largely a disease of childhood, developing in 50% of children by the age of 5 years and 90% by the age of 12 years. The Figure shows the estimated age-related prevalence of varicella immunity due to natural disease based on Newfoundland serosurvey data and caregiver surveys in Manitoba and Quebec. The lifetime risk of developing varicella is 95% and of having at least one reactivation to herpes zoster is 15% to 20%; disseminated zoster occurs in about 2% of cases. Post-herpetic neuralgia lasting longer than 6 months is more frequent at older ages and occurs in 35% of those aged ≥ 50 years. People from the tropics are less likely to acquire immunity in childhood and they have higher rates of susceptibility as adults, especially if they come from rural areas.

Decrease in Susceptibility to Varicella with Age as Determined by Seroprevalence Data in Newfoundland (1992-1997) and School-based Caregiver Surveys in Manitoba (1996-1997) and Quebec (1995-1997)

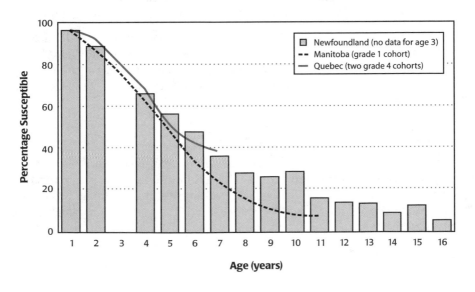

Varicella is often considered to be a fairly benign disease in otherwise healthy children aged up to 12 years. However, not only does this group account for approximately 90% of all varicella cases, but also for 80% to 85% of varicella-associated physician visits, 85% to 90% of hospitalizations, nearly 50% of fatal cases and the majority of annual costs, most of which are related to productivity losses by caregivers.

Complications include secondary bacterial skin and soft tissue infections, otitis media, bacteremia, osteomyelitis, septic arthritis, endocarditis, necrotizing fasciitis, toxic shock-like syndrome, mild hepatitis and thrombocytopenia. Studies in Canada and the U.S. have estimated that varicella increases the risk of severe infection with invasive group A beta hemolytic streptococcus in previously healthy children by a factor of 40- to 60-fold. Rare neurologic complications include cerebellar ataxia and encephalitis. Complications are more likely to occur when chickenpox is acquired in adolescence or adulthood, or in immunocompromised hosts, with higher rates of pneumonia, encephalitis and death. Case fatality rates among adults are 10 to 30 times higher than among children. In the U.S., adults account for 5% of cases but 55% of the 100 chickenpox deaths each year. In Canada, 71% of the 59 reported chickenpox deaths from 1987 to 1997 occurred in those > 15 years of age.

Congenital varicella syndrome following maternal infection during pregnancy is very rare when infection occurs in the first or second trimester, and exact estimates of risk are not available. After 20 weeks, the risk is considered exceedingly small and based on a few case reports. The syndrome may be mild or severe. Manifestations may include low birth weight, cicatricial skin scarring, ophthalmic abnormalities, limb hypoplasia and cortical atrophy as well as a variety of other anomalies. Almost one-third of affected infants die by early in the second year of life. Maternal varicella occurring in the 5 days before to 2 days after birth is associated with severe neonatal varicella in 17% to 30% of infants and with high case fatality for the newborn.

The total medical and societal costs of varicella in Canada were estimated from a multicentre study to be $122.4 million yearly, or $353.00 per individual case. Eighty-one percent of this amount went towards personal expenses and productivity costs, 9% towards the cost of ambulatory medical care and 10% towards hospital-based medical care.

Preparations Licensed for Immunization

Three varicella vaccines are licensed in Canada. These are Varivax®, Varivax II® (Merck Frosst Canada & Company) and Varilrix® (GlaxoSmithKline). Each is a preparation of lyophilized, live, attenuated varicella virus designated the Oka strain, which was developed in Japan in the early 1970s. Only Varivax II® is marketed in Canada at the time of publication.

Efficacy and Immunogenicity

Clinical studies of healthy children have shown detectable varicella antibodies in over 99% from 1 to 4 years after receipt of one dose and in over 96% up to 7 to 10 years after immunization, a level comparable with that of children with a history of natural infection. Over 97% of healthy adolescents and adults who received two doses 4 to 8 weeks apart demonstrated detectable antibody up to 3 years later. In pre-licensure placebo-controlled trials of the vaccine in healthy children aged 1 to 14 years, the observed protective efficacy was 100% in the first year and 96% in the second year after immunization. No placebo-controlled trials have been done in adolescents and adults.

In actual use, it is estimated that the vaccine will offer 70% to 90% protection against varicella of any severity and 95% protection against severe varicella for at least 7 to 10 years after immunization, the observation period reported to date. Varicella in vaccine recipients is associated with a significantly reduced number of lesions (fewer than 50, as compared with several hundred among unvaccinated people) and no or little fever. Illness in those who experience vaccine failure does not appear to increase in severity with time since immunization. People who are immunocompromised because of disease or treatment may not achieve as high a level of protection with immunization as healthy people.

Recommended Usage

Varicella vaccine is recommended for people ≥ 12 months of age who are susceptible to varicella infection. Because most adults in Canada have had varicella, they need not routinely receive this vaccine. Specific groups of adults for whom the vaccine should be considered are listed below; the listing order is not intended to reflect priority.

Healthy children, adolescents, and adults

1. Children between 12 and 18 months of age as a part of routine immunization, preferably at the same time as MMR is given (note: if varicella vaccine is given at the same visit as MMR, it should be given with a separate needle and syringe at a separate site; if not given at the same visit, MMR should be given first, and there should be at least 28 days between the administration of the two vaccines).

2. Susceptible older children and adolescents

3. Susceptible women of childbearing age (note: this vaccine should not be given during pregnancy; for post-exposure management in pregnancy, see chapter on Passive Immunizing Agents, Part 4).

4. Susceptible health care workers

5. Susceptible household contacts of immunocompromised people

6. Susceptible adults who may be exposed occupationally to varicella (e.g., teachers of young children, day care workers)

7. Other susceptible adults, especially new immigrants from tropical climates who are more likely to be susceptible

Susceptible people at high risk of severe varicella or its complications because of underlying disease

1. Children and adolescents given chronic salicylic acid therapy

2. People with cystic fibrosis

3. Immunocompromised individuals – special considerations:

   - Varicella vaccine should not be given to people with blood dyscrasia, leukemia (except acute lymphoblastic leukemia), lymphomas of any type, other malignant neoplasms affecting the bone marrow or lymphatic system, or people with other defects in cell-mediated immunity or receiving treatment associated with T-cell abnormalities (e.g., intensive chemotherapy, high dose steroids, cyclosporine, azathioprine, methotrexate, tacrolimus).
   - An infectious disease expert should be consulted before immunization of people with congenital transient hypogammaglobulinemia, HIV-infected individuals with normal immune status, and solid organ transplant recipients (vaccine should be given a minimum of 4 to 6 weeks before transplantation). Some HIV infected children should be considered for immunization if they are asymptomatic or mildly symptomatic, in CDC class N1 or A1 with age-specific CD4+ T-lymphocyte percentages of $\geq 25\%$. Such eligible children should receive two doses of varicella vaccine with a 3-month interval between doses. They should be encouraged to return for assessment if they experience a post-vaccination varicella-like rash.
   - There is no additional or undue risk in immunizing the following subjects:
     - if they are not taking immunosuppressive medications, patients with nephrotic syndrome or those undergoing hemodialysis and peritoneal dialysis;
     - patients taking low dose steroid therapy, e.g., less than 2 mg prednisone/kg daily and to a maximum of 20 mg/day for more than 2 weeks;
     - patients taking inhaled or topical steroids.

Post-exposure and outbreak use

Varicella vaccine has been shown to be effective in preventing or reducing the severity of varicella if given to a susceptible individual within 3 days, and possibly up to 5 days, after exposure to varicella. Such use has not been associated with increased rates of adverse events. Use of varicella vaccine beyond 5 days after exposure has not been shown to be effective. Post-exposure use should be considered in settings where it may be desirable to prevent secondary cases or to control an outbreak, such as hospitals and child care facilities. Post-exposure immunization has particular value in preventing illness in susceptible individuals who may be at higher risk of complications (e.g., adults or selected immunocompromised people for whom vaccine is recommended). Serologic testing for susceptibility need not be carried out before immunization in an outbreak situation, unless specific circumstances warrant it.

Other considerations

The vaccine is not currently indicated for people with a previous history of varicella to prevent herpes zoster, although clinical trials are under way to address this indication.

Schedule and Dosage

Children aged 12 months to 12 years: A single dose given after the 1st birthday.

Adolescents aged ≥ 13 years and adults: Two doses given at least 4 weeks (28 days) apart. There is no need to re-start the schedule if administration of the second dose has been delayed.

The dose is 0.5 mL, containing at least 1350 plaque-forming units (PFU) of VZV for Varivax II® and not less than 1995 PFU for Varilrix®.

Route of Administration

The lyophilized varicella vaccine should be reconstituted with the diluent provided for this purpose immediately before administration and given subcutaneously.

Booster Doses and Re-immunization

The need for booster doses at this time is unknown. Follow-up evaluation of children immunized during pre-licensure clinical trials in the U.S. reveals protection for at least 11 years, and studies in Japan indicate protection for at least 20 years. Follow-up of clinical trial subjects is under way to determine the need for additional doses. It is unknown whether protection may be less durable when the incidence of natural varicella declines as a result of vaccine use and allows fewer opportunities for "natural boosting". As with measles and rubella vaccines (other live virus vaccines), protection may persist throughout life in people who have a primary response to immunization.

Serologic Testing

There are several commercially available test methods to confirm immunity to VZV. The most widely available are enzyme-linked immunoassay (ELISA) and latex agglutination, using varicella glycoproteins as antigens. As a history of varicella is highly reliable, serologic testing before immunization is most cost-effective in adolescents and adults without a history of varicella, in whom two doses of the vaccine would be indicated.

Varicella Vaccine

Before immunization

A reliable history of varicella disease is adequate evidence of immunity, and there is little value in administering the vaccine to such people. A history of varicella disease should therefore be obtained before immunization.

For those aged ≥ 13 years with an unknown history of prior varicella infection, serologic testing before immunization may be helpful in determining the need for immunization. In routine adolescent immunization programs, it may be more efficient to offer vaccine to those without a history of chickenpox than to screen prior to immunizing.

After immunization

Post-immunization serologic testing for immunity is not recommended because of the high level of immunity conferred by the vaccine. As well, currently available commercial laboratory tests are not sufficiently sensitive to detect vaccine-induced antibodies, unlike the highly sensitive but commercially unavailable gpELISA, which was used in clinical trials for testing immunogenicity.

Before childbirth

Women of childbearing age should be asked about a prior history of varicella disease. Those without a history should be offered serologic testing for evidence of immunity, as most will be immune and will have had subclinical varicella. Susceptible women should be offered the vaccine, in the standard two-dose series. Pregnant women without a history of varicella disease should be offered prenatal screening and, if they are susceptible, post-partum immunization. Immunization during pregnancy is not recommended (see Contraindications).

Storage Requirements

Varivax II® has the same composition as Varivax® (the first licensed varicella vaccine in Canada) but has a higher initial potency level at the time of lot release. This higher potency improves the product stability. Recommendations for storage of both Varivax® and Varivax II® include freezer storage at −15° C, but Varivax II® may be transferred to and stored in the refrigerator at +2° to +8° C for up to 90 continuous days. In contrast, Varivax® may be stored in the refrigerator for only 72 hours.

Immediately after production, Varivax II® has a shelf life of 18 months, and this expiry date is printed on the package. When transferring it from the freezer to the refrigerator, the user must calculate the new 90 day shelf life using a "date wheel" supplied by the manufacturer, and must write the new expiry date on the vial. As an alternative, NACI recommends that a period of exactly 3 months from the date of removal from the freezer may be used as the new expiry date. Once the vaccine has been placed in the refrigerator it should not be returned to the freezer.

Varilrix® may be stored at +2° C to +8° C.

The diluent provided for reconstitution of both products should be stored separately, either in the refrigerator or at room temperature, but should not be placed in the freezer.

After reconstitution Varivax II® must be administered within 30 minutes, and Varilrix® must be administered within 90 minutes.

Simultaneous Administration with Other Vaccines

Varicella vaccine may be administered at the same time as but at a separate injection site from MMR vaccines routinely given at 12 months, DPT-containing vaccines given at 18 months and school entry, or adult tetanus-diphtheria vaccine given in adolescence and adulthood. When not given at the same time as other live virus vaccines, administration of the vaccines should be separated by a 4-week interval.

Varicella vaccine should not be given concurrently with immune globulin (IG), including varicella zoster immune globulin (VZIG). For administration of varicella vaccine after IG, blood or plasma transfusions, follow the guidelines for measles-containing vaccine in the section on Recent Administration of Human Immune Globulin Products (Part 1).

Adverse Events

Varicella vaccine is very safe. Reactions are generally mild and include injection site reactions among 20% of recipients. A small number of vaccinees (about 5.5% after the first injection and 0.9% after the second injection) will develop a non-injection site rash manifest as a small number of varicella-like papules or vesicles. A low-grade fever has been documented among 15%. Lesions usually appear within 5 to 26 days after immunization. Most varicelliform rashes that occur within the first 2 weeks after immunization are due to wild-type virus. In the health care setting, people with a post-vaccine rash at the injection site may continue to work if the rash is covered. Those with a varicella-like rash not confined to the injection site should be excluded from work in high-risk patient care areas until lesions are dry and crusted, unless lesions can be covered. Serious adverse events have occurred rarely following immunization and, in most cases, data are insufficient to determine a causal association.

Post-marketing surveillance in the U.S. through the CDC's Vaccine Adverse Event Reporting System and through analysis and follow-up of reports received by the manufacturer has demonstrated vaccine safety after licensure.

Contraindications

People with a prior history of anaphylaxis to the vaccine or a component (including gelatin or neomycin) of the vaccine should not receive further doses. A history of contact dermatitis to neomycin is not a contraindication. The vaccine does not contain egg proteins, thimerosal or aluminum. It is not routinely recommended for people who are immunosuppressed because of disease or therapy, with the exceptions outlined under Recommended Usage. Pregnant women should not be immunized with varicella vaccine because the effects on fetal development are unknown. Women should postpone pregnancy for 1 month after immunization with the two-dose series. To assist in evaluation of outcomes of immunization during or before pregnancy, incidents of inadvertent immunization during pregnancy or of pregnancy occurring within 3 months after immunization should be reported to Merck Frosst Canada Inc., Medical Services (tel: 1 800 684 6686).

Breast-feeding is not a contraindication to varicella immunization of the mother or child. Varicella vaccine may be given to people in households with a newborn.

Precautions

Between 1995 and 2000, U.S. data indicate that after 14 million doses of vaccine had been distributed, only three cases were identified of well-documented, vaccine-associated virus transmission to recipient contacts; all recipients had experienced a mild rash with a few lesions.

Other Considerations

Adverse events have not been reported in association with the use of salicylates after varicella immunization. Because of the association of varicella and Reye syndrome in children given salicylate therapy, the manufacturer recommends avoidance of salicylate use for 6 weeks after varicella immunization. Despite this, children with rheumatoid arthritis or other conditions requiring chronic salicylate therapy are at higher risk of Reye syndrome following wild varicella and should be considered for immunization, with close subsequent monitoring. Physicians need to weigh the theoretical risks associated with varicella vaccine against the known risks of wild varicella in children taking long-term salicylates.

Passive immunization

For recommendations on the use of VZIG, please refer to the appropriate section in Specific Immune Globulins (Part 4, Passive Immunizing Agents). For recommendations on the use of passive immunizing agents before or after varicella immunization, refer to Recent Administration of Human Immune Globulin Products (Part 1) and follow the guidelines stated for measles-containing vaccines. There are no data about the interference by passively acquired antibodies with the immune response to varicella vaccine. Because it is a live vaccine, the immune response may be blunted if the vaccine is given after transfusion of blood (except washed red blood cells) or plasma, or administration of immune globulin or VZIG.

Surveillance

The best Canadian data on varicella incidence and age-specific rates originate from serosurveys. Varicella is not consistently reportable in all jurisdictions, and case-by-case reporting has not been implemented because of continuing high rates of disease. Surveillance of hospitalized cases is being conducted through the Immunization Monitoring Program Active (IMPACT) system to provide baseline data prior to widespread introduction of immunization programs.

Selected References

Arbeter AM, Starr SE, Plotkin SA. *Varicella vaccine studies in healthy children and adults.* Pediatrics 1986;78(suppl):748-56.

Asano Y, Nakayama H, Yazaki T et al. *Protection against varicella in family contacts by immediate inoculation with varicella vaccine.* Pediatrics 1977;59:3-7.

Davies HD, McGeer A, Schwartz B et al. and the Ontario Group A Streptococcal Study Group. *Invasive group A streptococcal infections in Ontario, Canada.* N Engl J Med 1996;335:547-54.

De Nicola LK, Hanshaw JB. *Congenital and neonatal varicella.* J Pediatr 1979;94:175-6.

Enders G. *Varicella-zoster virus infection in pregnancy.* Prog Med Virol 1984;29:166.

Kjersem H, Jepsen S. *Varicella among immigrants from the tropics, a health problem.* Scand J Soc Med 1990;18(3):171-4.

Kuter BJ, Weibel RE, Guess HA et al. *Oka/Merck varicella vaccine in healthy children: final report of a 2-year efficacy study and 7-year follow-up studies.* Vaccine 1991;9:643-47.

Law B, Scheifele D, MacDonald N et al. *The Immunization Monitoring Program-active (IMPACT) prospective surveillance of varicella zoster infections among hospitalized Canadian children: 1991-1996.* CCDR 2000;26(15):125-31.

Law BJ, Fitzsimon C, Ford-Jones L et al. *Cost of chickenpox in Canada: Part 1. Cost of uncomplicated cases.* Pediatrics 1999;104:1-6.

Law BJ, Fitzsimon C, Ford-Jones L et al. *Cost of chickenpox in Canada: Part 2. Cost of complicated cases and total economic impact.* Pediatrics 1999;104:7-14.

Levin MJ, Gershon AA, Weinberg A et al. and the AIDS Clinical Trials Group 265 Team. *Immunization of HIV-infected children with varicella vaccine.* J Pediatr 2001;139:305-10.

Mandal BK, Mukherjee PP, Murphy C et al. *Adult susceptibility to varicella in the tropics is a rural phenomenon due to the lack of previous exposure.* J Infect Dis 1998;178 Suppl 1:S52-4.

National Advisory Committee on Immunization. *Statement on recommended use of varicella virus vaccine.* CCDR 1999;25(ACS-1):1-16.

National Advisory Committee on Immunization. *NACI update to statement on varicella vaccine.* CCDR 2002;28(ACS-3):1-8.

Proceedings of the National Varicella Consensus Conference. CCDR 1999;25S5.

Salzman MB, Garcia C. *Postexposure varicella vaccination in siblings of children with active varicella.* Pediatr Infect Dis J 1998;17(3):256-7.

Sharrar RG, LaRussa P, Galea SA et al. *The postmarketing safety profile of varicella vaccine.* Vaccine 2001(19):916-23.

Shields KE, Galil K, Seward J et al. *Varicella vaccine exposure during pregnancy: data from the first 5 years of the pregnancy registry.* Obstet Gynecol 2001;98:14-9.

Shinefield HR, Black SB, Staehle BO et al. *Safety, tolerability and immunogenicity of concomitant injections in separate locations of M-M-R®II, VARIVAX® and TETRAMUNE® in healthy children vs. concomitant injections of M-M-R®II and TETRAMUNE® followed six weeks later by VARIVAX®.* Pediatr Infect Dis J 1998;17:980-5.

Smith KJ, Roberts MS. *Cost effectiveness of vaccination strategies in adults without a history of chickenpox.* Am J Med 2000;108(9):723-9.

Vazquez M, LaRussa PS, Gershon AA et al. *The effectiveness of the varicella vaccine in clinical practice.* N Engl J Med 2001;344(13):955-60.

Vessey SJR, Chan CY, Kuter BJ et al. *Childhood vaccination against varicella: persistence of antibody, duration of protection, and vaccine efficacy.* J Pediatr 2001;139:297-304.

Weibel RE, Neff BJ, Kuter BJ et al. *Live attenuated varicella virus vaccine. Efficacy trial in healthy children.* N Engl J Med 1984;310:1409-15.

Wise RP, Salive ME, Braun MM et al. *Postlicensure safety surveillance for varicella vaccine.* JAMA 2000;284(10):1271-9.

Yellow Fever Vaccine

Yellow fever (YF) is a zoonotic hemorrhagic fever caused by an arbovirus spread by *Aedes aegypti* mosquitoes. YF evolves though a spectrum of three periods of illness, from a nonspecific febrile illness with headache, malaise, weakness, nausea and vomiting, through a brief period of remission, to a hemorrhagic fever with gastrointestinal tract bleeding and hematemesis, jaundice, hemorrhage, cardiovascular instability, albuminuria, oliguria and myocarditis. There is a 50% case fatality rate.

YF is a quarantinable disease subject to international health regulations. It must be reported to the WHO within 24 hours through Health Canada's Division of Quarantine, Travel and Migration Health. The Division must be contacted immediately in the event of a suspected YF case (telephone 613-954-3236). After hours, contact the medical officer on call, at 613-545-7661.

Epidemiology

Yellow fever is endemic in the tropical areas of equatorial subSaharan Africa and tropical South America between latitudes 15 degrees north and 10 degrees south (see maps 1 and 2). It does not occur in Asia, although the vector *Aedes aegypti* is present. Many countries have endemic *Aedes* mosquitoes but do not have the virus. They are able, by means of the international health regulations, to request proof of YF immunization as a requirement of entry.

Worldwide, 90% of YF cases occur in Africa and 10% in the Americas. The disease manifests itself in two epidemiologic forms, the urban and the sylvatic or jungle, both forms caused by the same virus. Urban outbreaks occur as a result of transmission by *Aedes aegypti*, which is widely distributed throughout the tropics. Urban disease is a particular problem in Africa and a potential problem in South America. Jungle YF is a disease of monkeys in the forests of South America and Africa; the virus that causes it is transmitted by forest *Aedes* mosquitoes to humans, such as forestry or oil company employees.

A recent resurgence of YF in certain countries prompted the WHO to include YF vaccine routinely within the Expanded Program on Immunization.

Disease control includes protection from the day-biting *Aedes* mosquitoes, elimination of *A. aegypti* from urban areas, and immunization of those at risk of exposure. Unimmunized Canadians can acquire YF when travelling abroad but cannot transmit the disease on their return to Canada, since the recognized mosquito vectors are not present in this country.

Since 1996 there have been reports of YF occurring in American and European travellers visiting YF endemic areas of Africa and South America. Notably, none of these tourists had received YF vaccine. There have been no cases of YF reported to Health Canada since surveillance began in 1924.

– Map 1 –

Yellow Fever Endemic Zones in Africa

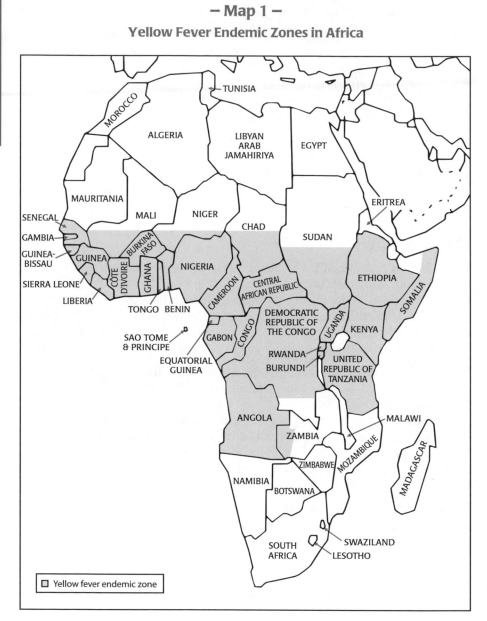

Yellow fever endemic zone

Source: WHO. *International travel and health: vaccination requirements and health advice.* Geneva: WHO, 2001.

– Map 2 –

Yellow Fever Endemic Zones in the Americas

Source: WHO. *International travel and health: vaccination requirements and health advice.* Geneva: WHO, 2001.

Preparations Licensed For Immunization

A live YF vaccine (YF-VAX®), produced by Aventis Pasteur, is licensed in Canada. It is prepared in chick embryos from the attenuated 17D strain, is lyophilized and contains sorbitol and gelatin as stabilizers. There is no preservative in the vaccine or the accompanying diluent.

Efficacy and Immunogenicity

Immunity develops 10 days after primary immunization and persists for more than 10 years.

Recommended Usage

The vaccine is recommended for all travellers ≥ 9 months of age passing through or living in countries in Africa, Central America and South America where YF infection is officially reported or YF immunization is required. It is also recommended for travel outside of urban areas of countries that do not officially report YF but lie in the YF endemic zones (see Maps 1 and 2). Immunization is also recommended for laboratory personnel who work with YF virus.

Infants 4 to 9 months of age, pregnant women, immunocompromised people and those over the age of 65 years should be considered for immunization only if they are travelling to high-risk areas, travel cannot be postponed and a high level of prevention against mosquito exposure is not feasible. Infants < 4 months of age should not be given YF vaccine.

Immunization is required by law upon entry to certain countries irrespective of the traveller's country of origin, and in other countries when travellers have passed through endemic areas. In some cases, immunization against YF is recommended, even though not required by law, e.g., if the disease has been reported in the country of destination. In some Asian and other tropical countries where YF does not exist but the transmitting mosquito is present, immunization is required for arrivals from an endemic country to prevent importation of the disease. Current information on the countries for which an International Certificate of Vaccination is required can be obtained from local health departments or from Health Canada's Travel Medicine Program through the Internet (http://www.travelhealth.gc.ca).

Only Yellow Fever Vaccination Centre clinics approved by Health Canada carry out immunization, which is then recorded on an appropriately validated International Certificate of Vaccination. A list of Centres can be obtained from the Travel Medicine Program at Health Canada (613-957-8739). The period of validity of the International Certificate of Vaccination for YF is 10 years, beginning 10 days after primary immunization and immediately after re-immunization.

Travellers requiring the Certificate but in whom the YF vaccine is contraindicated (see Contraindications and Precautions) should be provided an exemption from a designated Yellow Fever Vaccination Centre after completion of an individual risk assessment.

Health care providers should note that travellers without a valid International Certificate of Vaccination may be denied entry into a country requiring such documentation or reasons for exemption. It is also possible that they may be offered immunization at the point of entry (e.g., airport), where immunization practices fall below Canadian standards.

Route of Administration

Subcutaneous injection.

Booster Doses

Re-immunization is recommended every 10 years, if required. Re-immunization boosts antibody titre, although evidence from several studies suggests that immunity persists for at least 30 to 35 years and probably for life.

Serologic Testing

Not required or recommended.

Storage Requirements

The lyophilized preparation should be stored in a freezer at the temperature specified by the manufacturer until it is reconstituted by the addition of the diluent (sterile, physiologic saline) supplied. The diluent should not be allowed to freeze. Any unused reconstituted vaccine must be discarded 1 hour after reconstitution.

Simultaneous Administration with Other Vaccines

Concurrent administration of other live vaccines, including live oral cholera and live oral typhoid vaccines, does not inhibit the serologic response to YF vaccine. If live vaccines are not given concurrently, they should be spaced at least 4 weeks apart. Inactivated vaccines may be given concurrently or at any interval after YF vaccine. An exception is the inactivated parenteral cholera vaccine (no longer used in Canada), which should be given separately from YF vaccine by 3 or more weeks to avoid interference with antibody responses.

The administration of immune globulin and YF vaccine either simultaneously or within a short span of time does not alter the immunologic response, because immune globulin is unlikely to contain antibody to YF virus.

Although chloroquine inhibits replication of YF virus *in vitro*, it does not adversely affect antibody responses to the vaccine in humans receiving chloroquine for antimalarial prophylaxis.

Adverse Reactions

Overall, the vaccine has proved to be very safe and effective. Local reactions have been reported after administration, and 2% to 5% of vaccinees have mild headache, myalgia, low-grade fever or other minor symptoms 5 to 10 days after immunization. Less than 0.2% of vaccinees curtail regular activities. Immediate hypersensitivity reactions, characterized by rash, urticaria and/or asthma, are uncommon (estimated incidence of 1/130,000 to 1/250,000) and occur principally in people with a history of egg or other allergies. Recently, gelatin stabilizers have been implicated as a cause of allergic reactions in other vaccines.

In the U.S. there have been two cases of encephalitis temporally associated with immunization (out of 34 million doses distributed). In one of these cases, which was fatal, the 17D virus was isolated from the brain.

Worldwide from 1996 to 2001, there have been seven cases of sepsis-like syndrome temporally associated with 17D YF vaccine administration, an adverse event not previously reported. Of those seven, four were U.S. citizens (aged 63, 67, 76 and 79 years) and one an Australian citizen (aged 53 years), all of whom became ill 3 to 4 days after receiving 17D 204 vaccine. Two Brazilian citizens (aged 5 and 22 years) became ill 3 to 4 days after receiving 17DD vaccine (note that this is a different vaccine from the one used in Canada, the U.S. or Australia). All these individuals experienced severe illness requiring intensive medical care; their sepsis-like syndrome included fever, hypotension, renal failure, elevated hepatocellular enzymes, hyperbilirubinemia, lymphocytopenia and thrombocytopenia. Six of them (85.7%) died. An estimate of the reported incidence of sepsis-like syndrome in the U.S. was 2.5/1,000,000 and in Brazil was 1/11,500,000. At the time of these adverse events there was no formal adverse event reporting system in Brazil. In four of the cases vaccine strain virus was isolated from tissues other than blood, including cerebrospinal fluid, heart, brain, liver, kidney or spleen.

The conclusion reached after expert consultation was that the live attenuated YF vaccine must be considered as a possible cause of the sepsis-like syndrome in these cases. Studies are in progress to better define the cause and risk factors for these rare adverse events temporally associated with two subtypes of the 17D YF vaccine.

In Canada, vaccine-associated adverse events are reported by health care providers through a passive voluntary system. Health Canada reviewed all adverse events reported after use of YF vaccine in Canada between 1987 and 2000. There were 159 reports of adverse events, either alone (67 cases) or in combination with other vaccines (92 cases). Of these, 61.8% occurred in females, and 65.6% were between the ages of 20 and 49 years (mean 37.3 years). The most frequent adverse events reported were local reaction or pain in the arm and shoulder (54.3%), systemic symptoms such as allergic reaction (32.1%), and fever (27%). In most cases the adverse events were mild and self-limiting, although 43 (27%) of the patients had consulted their doctor and 12 (7.6%) were hospitalized.

Outcome data were unavailable in 51 (32.1%) of these reports. Of those with outcome data, 102/108 (94.4%) had fully recovered and 6/108 (5.6%) had residual damage at the time of reporting. Most of the cases were healthy, although 26 (16.4%) noted a history of allergies. A recent review in the U.S. of adverse events passively reported to the Vaccine Adverse Event Reporting System between 1990 and 1998 suggested that people aged ≥ 65 years may be more at risk of systemic adverse events after YF immunization than younger people.

Contraindications and Precautions

Allergy to any vaccine component or previous anaphylactic reaction to the YF vaccine is a contraindication to immunization. Because YF vaccine is prepared from chick embryos, it should not be given to individuals with known anaphylactic hypersensitivity to hens' eggs, manifested as urticaria, swelling of the mouth and throat, difficulty breathing or hypotension. If immunization of an individual with a questionable history of egg hypersensitivity is considered essential because of a high risk of exposure, an intradermal test dose (as per the package insert) may be administered under close medical supervision. As well, a graded challenge can be considered, as outlined on page 13 of the *Guide*.

Infants < 4 months of age should not be given YF vaccine because of the risk of encephalitis.

Pediatric use

Infants < 4 months of age are more susceptible to serious adverse reactions (encephalitis) to YF vaccine than older children. The risk of this complication appears to be age related. Whenever possible, immunization should be delayed until 9 months of age. For children 4 to 9 months old, immunization should be avoided unless there is a significant risk of exposure to an ongoing epidemic of YF.

Use in pregnant women and nursing mothers

Animal reproductive studies have not been conducted with YF vaccine. The use of the vaccine in pregnant women should be avoided unless clearly indicated by the risk of acquiring natural infection. Historically, many pregnant women have received YF vaccine without significant adverse events. One small study demonstrated that the vaccine virus can infect the developing fetus, but the potential risk of adverse events associated with congenital infection is unknown. Inadvertent immunization of women in pregnancy is not an indication for therapeutic abortion.

YF virus is not excreted in breast milk following immunization, and there is no contraindication to immunizing breast-feeding mothers with YF vaccine.

Use in immunocompromised hosts

Infection with the vaccine virus poses a theoretical risk to patients with immunosuppression due to HIV infection/AIDS, leukemia, lymphoma or generalized malignancy, or to those whose immunologic responses are suppressed by corticosteroids, alkylating drugs, antimetabolites or radiation. Therefore, the vaccine should be used with caution in immunosuppressed individuals. An individual risk assessment should be carried out, weighing the true risk of disease and the degree to which the person is immunocompromised before proceeding with immunization.

When a certificate of YF vaccination is required but this vaccine is contraindicated, the traveller should be provided an exemption from a designated Yellow Fever Vaccination Centre. For more information on the use of live virus vaccines in immunocompromised travellers, please refer to Part 6 of the *Guide*.

On the basis of the recent reports of adverse events in older travellers, already discussed, immunization in those over the age of 65 should be carried out only after an individual risk assessment.

Summary of Recommendations

- YF vaccine is recommended for travellers ≥ 9 months of age passing through or living in countries in Africa, Central America and South America where the infection is officially reported or YF immunization is required. It is also recommended for travel outside of urban areas of countries that do not officially report YF but lie in the YF endemic zones (see Maps 1 and 2).

- Immunization is also recommended for laboratory personnel who work with YF virus.

- YF vaccine should not be administered to children < 4 months of age because of the risk of encephalitis.

- YF vaccine should not routinely be administered to children aged 4 to 9 months, to travellers > 65 years of age, or to those who are immunocompromised. An individual risk assessment is required before the vaccine is given to these individuals.

- Travellers requiring an International Certificate of Vaccination in whom the YF vaccine is contraindicated should be provided with an exemption from a designated Yellow Fever Vaccination Centre.

Selected References

Barnett ED, Chen R. *Children and international travel: immunizations*. Pediatr Infect Dis J 1995;14:982-92.

CDC. *Fever, jaundice and multiple organ system failure associated with 17D-derived yellow fever vaccination, 1996-2000*. MMWR 2001;50(30):643-5.

CDC. *Fatal yellow fever in a traveler returning from Venezuela, 1999*. MMWR 2000;49(14):303-5.

Choudri Y, Walop W. *Review of adverse events reported following use of yellow fever vaccine – Canada, 1987-2000*. CCDR 2002;28:9-15.

Coursaget P, Fritzell B, Blondeau C et al. *Simultaneous injection of plasma derived or recombinant hepatitis B vaccines with yellow fever and killed polio vaccines.* Vaccine 1995;13:109-11.

Döller C. *Vaccination of adults against travel-related infections, diseases, and new developments in vaccines.* Infection 1993;21:7-23.

Kollavitsch H, Que JU, Wiedermann X et al. *Safety and immunogenicity of live oral cholera and typhoid vaccines administered alone or in combination with antimalaria drugs, oral polio vaccine and yellow fever vaccines.* J Infect Dis 1997;175:871-75.

McFarland JM, Baddour LM, Nelson JE et al. *Imported yellow fever in a United States citizen.* Clin Infect Dis 1997; 25:1143-47.

Monthan TP. *Yellow fever.* In: Plotkin SA, Orenstein WA, eds. *Vaccine.* 3rd edition. Philadelphia, Pennsylvania: WB Saunders, 1999:815-879.

Teichmann D, Grobusch MP, Wesselmann H et al. *A haemorrhagic fever from Côte d'Ivoire.* Lancet 1999;354(9190):1608.

Tsai TF, Paul R, Lynberg MC et al. *Congenital yellow fever virus infection after immunization in pregnancy.* J Infect Dis 1993;163:15220-23.

WHO. *International travel and health: vaccination requirements and health advice.* Geneva: World Health Organization, 2000.

– Part 4 –
Passive Immunizing Agents

Protection against certain infections or a reduction in the severity of the illness they cause can be achieved by administration of preformed antibodies derived from humans or animals. The preparations available are of two types: standard immune globulin (IG) of human origin, sometimes referred to as "immune serum globulin" or "gamma globulin"; and special preparations of either human or animal sera containing high titres of specific antibodies to a particular microorganism or its toxin, such as tetanus immune globulin. Products of human origin are preferred over those of animal origin because of the high incidence of adverse reactions to animal sera and the longer lasting protection conferred by human globulins.

Passive immunization should be considered when vaccines for active immunization are not available or are contraindicated, or in certain instances when vaccines have not been used before exposure to the infective agent, as may be the case when an unimmunized patient sustains a wound that may be contaminated with tetanus bacilli. In the latter situation, passive immunization is used in combination with toxoid to ensure both immediate (conferred by passive immunization) and long-term protection. Passive immunization may also have a role in the management of immunosuppressed people unable to respond to a vaccine. The beneficial effects provided by passive immunizing agents are of relatively short duration, and protection may be incomplete.

In these guidelines, emphasis is on the prophylactic use of immune sera, and only brief reference is made to their use as therapeutic agents in established infections.

As with all immunizing agents, including these blood-derived products, the risks and benefits need to be explained before administration, and the lot number should be recorded.

Immune Globulin (Human)

Immune globulin (IG) is a sterile, concentrated solution containing between 100 g/L and 180 g/L (10% to 18%) of protein and the preservative thimerosal. It is obtained from pooled human plasma and contains mainly IgG with small amounts of IgA and IgM. The potency of each lot of final product of immune globulin is tested against international standards or reference preparations for at least two different antibodies, one viral and one bacterial. IG is stable for prolonged periods when stored at 2° C to 8° C. Maximum plasma levels are reached about 2 days after intramuscular injection, and the half-life in the recipient's circulation is 21 to 27 days.

Intravenous immune globulin (IGIV) is a preparation that contains 50 g/L (5%) of protein with maltose, sucrose or glycine as a stabilizing agent. It is used for continuous passive immunization for patients with selected congenital or acquired immuno-globulin deficiency states and certain diseases. **Detailed discussion of IGIV is beyond the scope of this document**. Consult appropriate sources and the manufacturer's package instructions.

Recommended Usage

Prophylactic use of IG has been shown to be effective in a limited number of clinical situations. Commonly recommended doses are used for the following conditions (the dose may vary by manufacturer, and recommendations in the package inserts should be followed).

1. Measles

IG can be given to prevent or modify measles in susceptible people within 6 days after exposure. To prevent disease, it should be given as soon as possible after exposure, preferably within 3 days. The recommended dose is 0.25 mL/kg of body weight with a maximum dose of 15 mL. The dose of IG for exposed individuals who have underlying malignant disease or who are otherwise immunologically deficient is 0.5 mL/kg or 15 mL maximum.

IG should be considered for susceptible contacts of measles, particularly all children < 1 year of age and immunologically compromised individuals for whom measles vaccine is contraindicated. Susceptible immunocompetent people who present within 4 to 6 days after exposure, i.e., too late for vaccine, can also be considered for IG. When clinical measles does not develop in a person given IG, measles vaccine should be given 5 months later, provided the individual is ≥1 year of age and there are no contraindications to the vaccine.

IG should not be used in an attempt to control measles outbreaks.

2. Hepatitis A

Hepatitis A vaccine is the preferred agent for pre-exposure prophylaxis against hepatitis A. IG will provide protection against hepatitis A when administered intra-muscularly before exposure or during the incubation period. Its relative effectiveness depends upon both the timing of administration and the dose given. IG may be indicated if the vaccine is unavailable or unaffordable, as well as for infants < 1 year of age, immunocompromised people who may not respond to the vaccine and people for whom the vaccine is contraindicated (see page 93, Hepatitis A chapter).

The recommended dose of IG varies according to the duration of required protection. It also varies with the manufacturer, so the package insert should be consulted prior to administration. In general, for protection lasting < 3 months, the dose is 0.02 mL/kg; for > 3 months, 0.06 mL/kg should be administered; for > 5 months, 0.06 mL/kg should be repeated every 5 months. For post-exposure prophylaxis, the dose of IG is usually 0.02 mL/kg. IG prophylaxis should be given as soon as possible after exposure, since it is of very little value administered more than 2 weeks afterwards.

3. Rubella

IG given soon after exposure to rubella may modify or suppress symptoms but is not certain to prevent infection, including congenital infection. Therefore, the routine use of IG in susceptible women exposed to rubella early in pregnancy is not recommended.

If used, a dose of 0.55 mL/kg should be given intramuscularly within 48 hours of contact. Serum rubella antibody measurements before and for several months after IG administration can determine whether infection occurred.

4. Hepatitis C

IG is not efficacious in preventing or treating hepatitis C and should not be used.

Safety of Immunoglobulin Preparations

Human IG preparations are among the safest blood-derived products available. Plasma found positive for hepatitis B surface antigen, HIV antibody or hepatitis C is excluded from donor pools. As is the case for other blood or organ donations, individuals with known risks for other blood-borne pathogens are excluded from donating plasma for IG preparation. The method of preparation includes one or more steps that exclude or inactivate hepatitis B and C viruses, and HIV. There are no known reports of transmission of hepatitis B, hepatitis C, HIV or other infectious agents after the intramuscular injection of IG. There have been rare reports of transmission of hepatitis B or hepatitis C following the use of certain intravenous IG preparations that did not undergo the currently required inactivation steps during the manufacturing process.

Adverse Reactions

Reactions at the site of injection include tenderness, erythema and stiffness of local muscles, which may persist for several hours. Mild fever or malaise may occasionally occur. Less common side effects include flushing, headache, chills and nausea. Anaphylactic reactions may occur rarely with repeat administration.

Contraindications

IG should not be given to people with known isolated IgA deficiency or with a known allergy to the preservative thimerosal, a mercury derivative. Pregnancy is not a contraindication to the use of IG or other immune globulins.

Precautions

Currently available preparations, with the exception of IGIV, must not be given intravenously because of the risk of rare anaphylactic reactions.

Large volumes for intramuscular injection should be divided and injected at two or more sites.

People with severe thrombocytopenia or coagulation disorders that contraindicate intramuscular injections should not be given intramuscular IG unless the expected benefits outweigh the risks.

IG administration may interfere transiently with the subsequent immune response to measles, mumps and rubella vaccines. See Table 7, page 34, for specific recommendations regarding the interval between the administration of IG and these vaccines.

There are no data to indicate that immune globulin administration interferes with the response to inactivated vaccines, toxoids or the following live vaccines: yellow fever, or the oral preparations of typhoid, cholera or polio.

Specific Immune Globulins

Specific immune globulins are derived from the pooled sera of people with antibody to the specific infectious agents. Antisera from animals, usually horses that are hyperimmunized against a specific organism, are used when human products are not available. Because of the relatively high risk of serum sickness following the use of animal products, human immune globulin should be used whenever possible. *Before antisera of animal origin is injected, testing for hypersensitivity to the preparation should be carried out in accordance with the manufacturer's recommendation.* Many of the following products are not readily available and, in some instances, their use may require special access applications. In those situations, local and provincial public health departments should be contacted to facilitate their acquisition.

1. Botulism antitoxin (equine)

Trivalent (type A, B and E) and monovalent (type E) antitoxin preparations, both containing phenol as a preservative, are available on an emergency basis (consult with local public health authorities). These products are used therapeutically in people with established or suspected botulism as well as prophylactically in asymptomatic people strongly suspected of having eaten food contaminated with botulism toxin. Type E botulism is most likely to be associated with the consumption of uncooked fish or fish products, or the flesh of marine mammals, including whales and seals. The monovalent type E antitoxin should be used only if such foodstuffs are considered the most likely vehicle of disease or if laboratory tests have established that the toxin involved is type E.

In populations at risk for repeated exposures to botulism toxin because of particular food habits, the repeated use of prophylactic antitoxin can lead to an increased incidence of severe reactions. Caution should therefore be exercised in the use of botulism antitoxin in such circumstances, even if preliminary sensitivity tests are negative.

2. Diphtheria antitoxin (equine)

This preparation, which also contains phenol as a preservative, is available on an emergency basis (consult with local public health authorities) for treatment of the disease. Antitoxin should be administered before bacteriologic confirmation when there is clinical suspicion of diphtheria. The method of testing for sensitivity to equine serum, as well as the dose and route of administration, are indicated in the manufacturer's package insert. Intramuscular administration usually suffices, but intravenous administration may be necessary in some cases. If sensitivity tests are positive, desensitization must be undertaken according to the manufacturer's recommendations.

Diphtheria antitoxin is not recommended for prophylaxis in close, unimmunized contacts of diphtheria cases, given the substantial risk of allergic reaction to horse serum and no evidence of additional benefit of antitoxin for contacts who have received antimicrobial prophylaxis.

3. Hepatitis B immune globulin (HBIG)

HBIG is prepared from pooled human plasma from selected donors with a high level of antibody to hepatitis B surface antigen. HBIG provides immediate and effective short-term passive immunity. HBIG administered concurrently with vaccine, but at a different site, does not interfere with the antibody response to the vaccine. The indications for use are percutaneous or mucosal exposure to blood containing hepatitis B virus, sexual contact with an acute case of hepatitis B, and birth of an infant to a mother with acute or chronic hepatitis B infection. All infants born to infected mothers should be given an intramuscular dose of 0.5 mL HBIG immediately after birth in addition to the first of the three-dose course of the hepatitis B vaccine. It is important that HBIG be given within the first few hours of birth, since its efficacy decreases sharply after 48 hours. The dose of HBIG for older children and adults is 0.06 mL/kg given intramuscularly. In general, it should be administered to susceptible individuals within 48 hours of exposure. The exception to this is prophylaxis of sexual contacts of an infected individual, when HBIG may be given up to 2 weeks after the last known contact. See Table 2 and pages 5-6 for further details concerning prevention of hepatitis B.

4. Rabies immune globulin (RIG)

Passive immunization with this product is undertaken as part of post-exposure prophylaxis against rabies (see page 193). Rabies immune globulin (RIG) provides rapid protection that persists for only a short period of time (half-life about 21 days). Vaccine and RIG can be administered concurrently but **under no circumstances should vaccine be administered in the same syringe or at the same site as RIG.** A dose of up to 20 IU/kg of RIG should be administered once, as soon as possible after exposure. If anatomically feasible, the full dose of RIG should be thoroughly infiltrated into the wound and surrounding area. Any remaining volume should be injected intramuscularly at a site distant from vaccine administration. When more than one wound exists, each should be locally infiltrated with a portion of the RIG. Because of interference with active antibody production, the recommended dose should not be exceeded. Since vaccine-induced antibodies begin to appear within 1 week, if the vaccine has been administered without the administration of RIG, there is no value in giving RIG more than 8 days after the vaccine course was initiated.

5. Respiratory syncytial virus immune globulin intravenous (human) (RSV-IGIV)

RSV-IGIV is an intravenous IG derived from pools of human plasma with high concentrations of protective antibodies that neutralize RSV. RSV-IGIV was approved in August 1997 for prevention of RSV infection among children aged < 2 years old with bronchopulmonary dysplasia (BPD) or a history of premature birth (≤ 35 weeks' gestation). Rates of re-admission for RSV infection among premature infants have ranged from 2% to 22% during the first year of life and require further study. RSV-IGIV in a placebo-controlled trial was shown to decrease the RSV-related hospitalization rate by 41%, the RSV-related length of stay by 53% and the duration of oxygen therapy by 60%.

Adverse events are the same as for all IG products given by intravenous infusion. Fluid overload may be precipitated by infusion of infants with pulmonary disease, especially those with BPD. Appropriate precautions, as outlined in the product monograph, must be taken.

Children with cyanotic congenital heart disease treated with RSV-IGIV were observed to have a greater frequency of severe or life-threatening adverse events than similar children who received no infusions during the study period. Until the relation between the infusions and subsequent adverse events is better understood, it is recommended that children with cyanotic congenital heart disease not be given RSV-IGIV. It is unknown whether RSV-IGIV can prevent significant RSV disease among immunocompromised hosts.

RSV-IGIV has no proven benefit in the treatment of established RSV infection.

It is anticipated that RSV-IGIV prophylaxis may be most beneficial for the following children:

■ Infants and children < 2 years of age with BPD who are currently receiving or have received oxygen therapy within 6 months before the onset of the RSV season.

■ Infants who were born at 32 weeks of gestation or less, including those without BPD:

 ▪ infants born at 28 weeks of gestation or less may benefit from prophylaxis up to 12 months of age;
 ▪ infants born at 29-32 weeks of gestation may benefit from prophylaxis up to 6 months of age.

The recommended dose is 750 mg/kg given every 4 weeks, starting before and continuing through the local RSV season. In Canada, the annual RSV outbreak usually begins in November or December and extends through April or May. Regional variations occur. It is best to consult local experts to determine the usefulness of RSV-IGIV on an individual patient basis. A more detailed discussion can be found in the statement published by the Canadian Paediatric Society (see Selected References).

Local and practical issues in delivery, the costs involved, and the data showing that prevention is not complete after administration of RSV-IGIV all preclude a universal recommendation being made at this time. Thus each centre has to consider a number of factors before embarking upon an RSV-IGIV prophylaxis program. The use of RSV-IGIV may not prove to be very feasible or practical in many centres when these factors or circumstances are taken into account.

6. Tetanus immune globulin (TIG)

The use of TIG in the management of wounds is discussed in the section on Tetanus Toxoid (see pages 208-213). When used in the treatment of tetanus, TIG should be administered intramuscularly in an effort to neutralize tetanus toxin in body fluids. It has no effect on toxin already fixed to nerve tissue. The optimal therapeutic dose has not been established.

7. Varicella-zoster immune globulin (VZIG)

VZIG is prepared from pooled plasma of people with high antibody titres to varicella-zoster virus (VZV). VZIG is available through the Canadian Blood Services and HÉMA-QUÉBEC distribution centres.

Passive immunization with VZIG is indicated after exposure to chickenpox or zoster in susceptible individuals whose risk of serious morbidity or mortality from chickenpox is substantially increased. Varicella vaccine may also be considered as an acceptable alternative to VZIG (see pages 223-232)

People with chickenpox are most contagious from 1 to 2 days before and for a few days after onset of the rash. The contagious period may extend to 5 days after onset and in immunocompromised patients until crusting of lesions. Skin lesions of zoster or shingles are infectious only until the eruption has crusted and dried. The following contact situations are considered significant exposures to VZV:

- continuous household contact (living in the same dwelling);

- playing indoors for more than 1 hour with a contagious case;

- sharing the same hospital room with a contagious patient;

- prolonged face-to-face contact of a worker or staff member with an individual with chickenpox.

The determinants of susceptibility to varicella are as follows:

- People with a history of chickenpox are usually considered immune.

- All recipients of heterologous bone marrow transplants should be considered susceptible in the early post-transplantation period regardless of a history of varicella or positive serologic test results.

- People with a negative or uncertain history of chickenpox should be tested serologically to establish susceptibility, since as many as 70% to 95% of such individuals have immunity to varicella. Prospective serologic testing to determine susceptibility may eliminate the need for emergency post-exposure tests. Prospective testing should be considered for health care workers without a history of chickenpox, and for individuals with congenital or acquired immunodeficiency due to disease or therapy, including those undergoing solid-organ heterograft transplantation and those with hematologic or reticuloendothelial malignant disease. VZIG may give detectable levels of antibody causing false-positive tests of varicella immunity for up to 2 months after administration.

VZIG is recommended for the following susceptible people, providing significant exposure has occurred:

Infants and children

1. Immunocompromised patients, such as those with congenital or acquired immunodeficiency due to disease or treatment, including some patients receiving corticosteroid therapy (see pages 20-30). Patients receiving regular monthly infusions of 100 to 400 mg/kg of IGIV and whose most recent dose was within 3 weeks before exposure do not require VZIG.

2. Newborn infants of mothers who develop varicella during the 5 days before or 48 hours after delivery.

3. Hospitalized premature infants exposed during the first weeks of life. Exposed infants of < 28 weeks' gestational age should receive VZIG regardless of maternal immune status. Exposed infants of 29 to 37 weeks' gestational age should receive VZIG if the mother was not immune.

Adults

1. Pregnant women. Because the risk of complications of chickenpox in pregnant women may be greater than in other adults, VZIG should be given to exposed, susceptible pregnant women. There is no evidence that VZIG will prevent or alter disease in the fetus.

2. Immunocompromised adults. See previous section on immunocompromised infants and children and pages 20-30.

3. Healthy adults. The value of VZIG in healthy adults is unclear. Chickenpox can be more severe in healthy adults than children, but the risk of pneumonia is now considered less than was formerly believed. In addition, VZIG may prolong the incubation period to 28 days, which has implications for health care workers. Finally, acyclovir therapy initiated within 24 hours after onset of the rash is

effective in accelerating skin lesion healing and is thus a therapeutic alternative to prophylactic VZIG in this population.

The recommended dose of VZIG is 125 units (1 vial) per 10 kg body weight to a maximum of 625 units, administered intramuscularly. The optimal dose for adults is uncertain.

VZIG is of benefit if administered within 96 hours after the exposure. Protection is believed to last for 3 to 4 weeks. Subsequent exposures more than 3 weeks after a dose of VZIG may require additional doses.

Selected References

Buckley RH, Schiff RI. *The use of intravenous immune globulin in immunodeficiency diseases.* N Engl J Med 1991;325:110-17.

Canadian Paediatric Society Committee on Immunization and Infectious Diseases. *Respiratory syncytial virus — immune globulin intravenous (RSV-IVIG).* Paediatr Child Health 1998;3:11-4.

Gershon AA. *Chickenpox, measles and mumps.* In: Remington JS, Klein JO, eds. *Infectious diseases of the fetus and newborn infant.* 3rd ed. Philadelphia: WB Saunders, 1990:395-445.

McIntosh D, Isaacs D. *Varicella zoster virus infection in pregnancy.* Arch Dis Child 1993;68:1-2.

Miller E, Cradock-Watson JE, Ridehalgh MKS. *Outcome in newborn babies given anti-varicella-zoster immunoglobulin after perinatal maternal infection with varicella-zoster virus.* Lancet 1989;2:371-73.

Patou G, Midgley P, Meurisse EV et al. *Immunoglobulin prophylaxis for infants exposed to varicella in a neonatal unit.* J Infection 1990;20:207-13.

PREVENT Study Group. *Reduction of respiratory syncytial virus hospitalization among premature infants and infants with bronchopulmonary dysplasia using respiratory syncytial virus immune globulin prophylaxis.* Pediatrics 1997;99:93-9.

Siber GR, Snydennan DR. *Use of immune globulins in the prevention and treatment of infections.* In: Remington JS, Swartz MN, eds. *Current clinical topics in infectious diseases.* Vol. 12. Boston: Blackwell Scientific, 1992:208-56.

Siber GR, Werner BC, Halsey NA et al. *Interference of immune globulin with measles and rubella immunization.* J Pediatr 1993;122,2:204-1 1.

– Part 5 –
Immunization of Health Care Workers and Others Providing Personal Care

Hospital employees, students in health care disciplines, laboratory workers and other health care personnel are at risk of exposure to communicable diseases because of their contact with patients or material from patients with infections, both diagnosed and undiagnosed. Maintenance of immunity against vaccine-preventable diseases is an integral part of an occupational health program of health care facilities and personal care organizations. Optimal usage of immunizing agents in hospitals and for other health care staff will not only safeguard the health of staff members but may also, in some instances, prevent them from infecting patients. In certain circumstances, family members should also be considered as health care workers, since they provide a significant and growing amount of care and because in-home transmission of infectious disease does occur.

The immunization status of each worker should be assessed at the time of initial employment. A full vaccination history should be elicited and efforts made to obtain documentation of the doses received and dates of administration. People who cannot provide acceptable information or evidence of adequate immunity should be offered immunization at the earliest opportunity. Records of all immunizations and serologic tests should be kept by both employer and employee and a recall system for boosters instituted.

Immunization policies at individual institutions will vary, and decisions about which vaccines to be included should take account of the size and nature of the institution, the exposure risks for the health care worker and the nature of employment. It is important to include, as an educational objective in employee in-service, increased acceptance of vaccinations as well as increased awareness of illnesses or symptoms that require evaluation.

Vaccines Recommended for All Health Care Workers

Diphtheria and tetanus toxoid

Immunization against diphtheria and tetanus is recommended for all adults in Canada. The opportunity should be taken on entry into health care employment to ensure that the appropriate series and booster doses have been given. Booster doses of Td are recommended every 10 years for optimal protection.

Measles vaccine

Newly employed health care workers born after 1970 who will have patient contact should have proof of two live measles vaccinations, documentation of physician-diagnosed measles or laboratory evidence of immunity. For those workers who have already received one dose of measles vaccine, a second dose is recommended, generally as MMR vaccine. People born before 1970 have probably been infected naturally and may usually be considered immune. It is not necessary to initiate a serologic testing program to detect susceptible health care workers.

Polio vaccine

Primary immunization with inactivated poliomyelitis vaccine (IPV) is indicated for all health care workers who may be exposed to poliovirus and who have not had a primary course of poliovirus vaccine (OPV or IPV). OPV is not recommended for health care workers because they may shed the virus and inadvertently expose immunocompromised patients to live virus. People who have not been given a full primary course should have the series completed with IPV regardless of the interval since the previous dose. Booster doses of IPV are not required for health care workers in Canada.

Rubella vaccine

In health care settings, the rubella immune status of female employees of childbearing age should be carefully reviewed, and those without documented immunity should be immunized with MMR unless there are contraindications. In addition, vaccine should be given to susceptible people of either sex who may, through frequent face-to-face contact, expose pregnant women to rubella. Women should be advised to avoid pregnancy for 1 month after immunization.

Hepatitis B vaccine

Hepatitis B is the most important infectious occupational disease for health care workers. The risk of being infected is a consequence of the prevalence of virus carriers in the population receiving care, the frequency of exposure to blood and other body fluids and the contagiousness of hepatitis B virus. Hepatitis B vaccine is recommended for health care workers and others who may be exposed to blood or blood products, or who may be at increased risk of sharps injury, bites or penetrating injuries (for example, clients and staff of institutions for the developmentally challenged). Health care workers who have been exposed, either percutaneously or through the mucous membranes, to a source that is known or is likely to be positive for hepatitis B surface antigen should be assessed for the need for hepatitis B vaccine and immune globulin, according to the recommendations outlined in the chapter on hepatitis B (see pages 102-116).

Influenza vaccine

Annual influenza immunization is recommended for all health care personnel who have contact with individuals in high-risk groups. Such personnel include physicians, nurses and others in both hospital and outpatient settings; employees of chronic care facilities who have contact with residents; and providers of home care, visiting nurses or volunteers, and household members of people at high risk. Influenza immunization of health care workers has been shown to reduce the mortality and morbidity of patients under their care in long-term settings and to reduce worker absenteeism during the influenza season.

Acetaminophen (650 mg taken 4, 8 and 12 hours after influenza immunization) has been shown to significantly reduce the incidence of side effects such as sore arm and nausea, and may reassure those for whom concern about side effects is an impediment to immunization. Vaccination should be available in the workplace.

Other vaccines

Indications for the use of other licensed vaccines are generally the same for health care workers as for the general population. However, additional vaccines may be indicated for certain workers believed to be at particularly high risk of exposure, such as laboratory workers in specialized reference or research facilities. For example, typhoid immunization should be considered for laboratory staff who frequently handle cultures of *Salmonella typhi.*

Vaccines for Specific Risk Situations

Hepatitis A

Prevention of hepatitis A transmission within a hospital should be based on the use of good hygienic practices and patient care techniques, especially proper hand washing and management of potentially infected materials.

There may be limited indications for hepatitis A vaccine, e.g. for those who are not immune and who have had unusually close contact with patients with hepatitis A, such as direct oral exposure to a patient's secretions or excretions soon after the onset of illness. However, immune globulin should be given if contacts are immunocompromised or if they are children < 1 year of age.

BCG vaccine

Comprehensive application of infection control practices remains the primary strategy to protect health care workers from infection with *M. tuberculosis*. However, outbreaks of multidrug-resistant tuberculosis in health care settings have led to a reconsideration of BCG immunization for health care workers in some situations. BCG immunization may be considered for health care workers (including medical laboratory workers) who are at considerable risk of exposure to tubercle bacilli, especially drug-resistant bacilli, when protective measures against infection are known to be ineffective or not feasible.

Selected References

Advisory Committee on Immunization Practices (ACIP) and the Hospital Infection Control Practices Advisory Committee. *Immunization of health-care workers*. Atlanta, Georgia: US Department of Health and Human Services, Public Health Service, Centers for Disease Control and Prevention, October 8, 1996.

Aoki Fy, Yassi A, Cheang M et al. *Effects of acetaminophen on adverse effects of influenza vaccination in health care workers*. Can Med Assoc J 1993;149:1425-30.

Brewer TF, Colditz GA. *BCG vaccination for the prevention of tuberculosis in healthcare workers*. Clin Infect Dis 1995;20:136-42.

Clever LH, LeGuyader Y. *Infectious risks for health care workers*. Annu Rev Public Health 1995;16:141-64.

Diekema DJ, Doebbeling BN. *Employee health and infection control*. Infect Control Hosp Epidemiol 1995;16:192-301.

Doebbeling BN, Ning Li MB et al. *An outbreak of hepatitis A among health care workers: risk factors for transmission*. Am J Public Health 1993;83:1679-84.

Furesz J, Scheifele DW, Palkonyay L. *Safety and effectiveness of the new activated hepatitis A virus vaccine*. Can Med Assoc J 1995;152:343-48.

Gardner P, Schaffner W. *Immunization of adults*. N Engl J Med 1993;328:1252-58.

Krause PJ, Gross PA, Barrett TL et al. *Quality standards for assurance of measles immunity among health care workers*. Infect Control Hosp Epidemiol 1994;15:193-99.

Murata PJ, Young LC. *Physicians' attitudes and behaviors regarding hepatitis B immunization*. J Fam Pract 1993;36:163-68.

Oakley K, Gooch C, Cockcroft A. *Review of management of incidents involving exposure to blood in a London teaching hospital, 1989-91*. BMJ 1992;304:949-51.

Potter J, Stott DJ, Roberts MA et al. *Influenza vaccination of health care workers in long-term care hospitals reduces the mortality of elderly patients*. J Infect Dis 1997;175:1-6.

Schwarz S, McCaw B, Fukushima P. *Prevalence of measles susceptibility in hospital staff: evidence to support expanding the recommendations of the Immunization Practices Advisory Committee*. Arch Intern Med 1992;152:1481-83.

Sepkowitz KA. *Occupationally acquired infections in health care workers. Part I*. Ann Intern Med 1996;125(10):826-34.

Sepkowitz KA. *Occupationally acquired infections in health care workers Part II*. Ann Intern Med 1997;126(7):588.

– Part 6 –
Immunization of Travellers

A detailed discussion of immunization and other preventive measures recommended for travellers to other countries is beyond the scope of this *Guide*. Current information on immunization requirements and recommendations should be obtained from travel health clinics or public health agencies.

Readers are referred to the Travel Medicine Program section on Health Canada's web site (http://www.travelhealth.gc.ca). This Program provides extensive information, including statements on travel medicine and tropical medicine from CATMAT (Committee to Advise on Tropical Medicine and Travel). CATMAT statements are updated every 4 years or when new information becomes available.

Readers are also referred to *Health Information for International Travel* (U.S. Centers for Disease Control and Prevention, www.cdc.gov/travel), and *International Travel and Health: Vaccination Requirements and Health Advice* (World Health Organization, www.who.int/ith).

There is no single schedule for the administration of immunizing agents to travellers. Each schedule must be personalized according to the individual traveller's immunization history, the countries to be visited, the type and duration of travel, and the amount of time available before departure.

With some notable exceptions, most immunizing agents can be given simultaneously at different sites. Concerns about individual vaccines and their potential compatibility with other vaccines or antimicrobials (including antimalarials) are dealt with in the specific vaccine chapters of the *Guide*.

A health care provider or travel medicine clinic should be consulted 2 to 3 months in advance of travel in order to allow sufficient time for optimal immunization schedules to be completed. A listing of travel clinics across Canada can be found in the Travel Medicine Program section of Health Canada's web site (http://www.travelhealth.gc.ca).

It must be emphasized that the most frequent health problems faced by international travellers are not preventable by immunizing agents. As well, immunization is not a substitute for careful selection and handling of food and water.

Travel is a good opportunity for the health care provider to review the immunization status of infants, children, adolescents and adults. Unimmunized or incompletely immunized travellers should be offered vaccination as recommended in the specific vaccine chapters in this *Guide*.

Immunizations related to travel can be divided into three general categories: those that are considered **routine** (part of the primary series of immunizations), those **required** by international law, and those **recommended** for maintenance of health while travelling. The immunization recommendations for travel will vary according to the traveller's age, existing medical conditions, the nature of travel (whether the traveller is staying in urban hotels or visiting remote rural areas), the legal requirements for entry into countries being visited and the duration of travel.

Routine Immunizations

The following section specifically discusses the indication for "extra" or booster doses of routine immunizations or a change in the routine immunization schedule as it applies to travellers.

Tetanus and diphtheria

Adult travellers should be revaccinated against tetanus and diphtheria every 10 years for optimal protection. For individuals planning to travel to developing countries where safe tetanus vaccine administration may not be available if required, it may be prudent to offer an early tetanus booster prior to travel if more than 5 years have elapsed since the previous dose.

Poliomyelitis

The risk of polio for travellers has substantially decreased as we move towards global polio eradication. A single booster dose of IPV in adulthood is recommended for international travellers who plan to visit regions of the world where poliovirus continues to circulate in either epidemic or endemic fashion. The need for subsequent boosters of poliovirus vaccine has not been established.

Measles, mumps, rubella – adults

Measles, mumps and rubella are endemic in many countries. Protection against measles is especially important for people planning foreign travel, including adolescents and adults who have not had measles disease and have not been adequately immunized. Two doses of measles-containing vaccine (preferably MMR) are recommended for all unimmunized adult travellers who were born after 1970 and who are en route to a measles endemic area, unless there is serologic proof of immunity or physician documentation of prior measles. Similarly, protection against rubella is especially important for women of childbearing age who are not immune to the disease.

Measles – infants and children

Measles vaccine should be given at an earlier age than usual for children travelling to countries where measles is endemic. Measles-containing vaccine (preferably MMR) may be given as early as 6 months of age, but then the routine series of two doses must still be re-started after the child is 12 months old.

Hepatitis B – adults

Travel is a good opportunity to offer hepatitis B immunization to adults who have not been previously vaccinated. It should be recommended particularly to travellers residing in areas with high levels of endemic hepatitis B or working in health care facilities, and those likely to have contact with blood or to have sexual contact with residents of such areas.

Hepatitis B – infants and children

The age at which infants, children and adolescents are offered hepatitis B vaccine varies from jurisdiction to jurisdiction in Canada. Since hepatitis B carrier rates are much higher in developing countries, every effort should be made to arrange full hepatitis B immunization for children of any age who will live in an area where hepatitis B is endemic.

Required Immunizations

The following may be a requirement of international law, or proof of immunization may be considered a visa requirement.

Yellow fever

Yellow fever is the only vaccine required as a condition of entry under the World Health Organization's International Health Regulations. A valid International Certificate of Vaccination, issued within the previous 10 years, is mandatory for entry into certain countries in Africa and South America. Other countries have requirements for proof of immunization from travellers who have passed through yellow fever endemic zones (see maps 1 and 2 on pages 234-235).

The period of validity of the International Vaccination Certificate for yellow fever is 10 years, beginning 10 days after primary vaccination and immediately after re-vaccination.

Only Health Canada-designated Yellow Fever Vaccination Centre clinics can provide the International Certificate of Vaccination in Canada. A list of these centres can be obtained from Health Canada's Travel Medicine Program web site (http://www.travelhealth.gc.ca).

The decision to immunize against yellow fever will depend on the itinerary of the individual traveller and the specific requirements of the country to be visited (including stopovers). As well as being necessary for entry into certain countries, immunization against yellow fever is recommended for all travellers who are passing through or living in countries in Africa and South America where yellow fever infection is officially reported. It is also recommended for travel outside of urban areas in countries that do not officially report yellow fever but lie in the yellow fever endemic zones (see maps 1 and 2).

Meningococcal disease

As a condition of entry, Saudi Arabia requires proof of meningococcal immunization for pilgrims to Mecca during the Hajj.

For other indications for this vaccine see the meningococcal disease section under Recommended Immunizations.

Cholera

Cholera vaccine has not been required for border crossing under International Health Regulations since 1973. Some travellers to parts of Africa have reported being asked to provide a certificate of immunization against cholera. This "requirement" is not usually the policy of the national government but, rather, of local authorities. Given the related risks of immunization in some countries, certain travel clinics provide a cholera "exemption certificate", which is used to help travellers avoid being given cholera vaccine while abroad.

Recommended Immunizations

On the basis of a risk assessment of the itinerary, the style of travel and the traveller's underlying health, the following vaccines should be considered in consultation with a health care provider.

Hepatitis A

Hepatitis A is the most common vaccine-preventable disease in travellers. Protection against hepatitis A is highly recommended for all travellers to developing countries, especially to rural areas or places with inadequate sanitary facilities in countries where the disease is endemic. Protective antibodies are detectable within 2 weeks of administration. Given the long incubation period of hepatitis A (2 to 7 weeks), the vaccine can be administered up to the day of departure and still protect travellers.

The advent of active immunizing agents has made the use of immune globulin virtually obsolete for the purposes of travel prophylaxis. The only exceptions would be people for whom hepatitis A immunization is contraindicated or may not be effective (e.g., immunocompromised travellers and infants < 1 year of age). Immune globulin provides protection for only 3 to 5 months and should be given immediately before departure.

Typhoid

Typhoid vaccine is recommended for travellers who will have prolonged exposure (> 4 weeks) to potentially contaminated food and water, especially those travelling to smaller cities and villages or rural areas off the usual tourist itineraries in countries with a high incidence of disease. Individuals billeted with or visiting families in such areas may be at particularly high risk. Immunization is not routinely recommended for business travel or short-term (< 4 weeks) holidays in resort hotels in such countries. Currently, parenteral and live oral vaccines are available.

Meningococcal disease – adults

Meningococcal polysaccharide vaccine is recommended for travellers planning a prolonged stay in areas with a high incidence of meningococcal disease. Short-term travellers (< 3 weeks) on business or holiday (including safaris) who will have little contact with local populations are at minimal risk and therefore immunization is not routinely recommended. When doubt about the nature of exposure exists, it may be prudent to offer immunization.

However, in special circumstances, immunization should be considered for short-term travellers if (a) there will be close contact with the local population in endemic areas, (b) there will be travel to epidemic areas or (c) the traveller will be providing health care to others.

As noted previously, proof of polysaccharide meningococcal immunization may be required by certain countries e.g., Saudi Arabia, for pilgrims to Mecca during the Hajj. Outbreaks of meningococcal disease have affected these pilgrims in the past, involving serogroup A in 1987, and both serogroups A and W135 in 2000 and 2001.

Meningococcal conjugate C vaccine was licensed in Canada in 2001. This vaccine only protects against serogroup C and therefore is not appropriate for protection of travellers, as it does not protect against outbreaks of serogroup W135 or epidemics of serogroup A disease.

Meningococcal disease – infants and children

Because of the relative inability of very young children to respond to polysaccharide vaccine, infants aged 2 to 12 months should be immunized with at least two doses of meningococcal C conjugate vaccine 1 month apart, if they have not previously received it. However, bivalent meningococcal polysaccharide AC vaccine or quadrivalent ACYW135 may be considered for children as young as 3 months who are travelling to regions where broader protection is needed (see Meningococcal Vaccine chapter).

Japanese encephalitis

Japanese encephalitis is the leading cause of viral encephalitis in Asia, but the disease is rare in travellers. Its incidence has been decreasing in China, Korea and Japan but increasing in Bangladesh, India, Nepal, Pakistan, northern Thailand and Vietnam. It occurs in epidemics in late summer and early fall in temperate areas and sporadically throughout the year in tropical areas of Asia. Immunization should generally be considered for those who will spend 1 month or more in endemic or epidemic areas during the transmission season, especially if travel will include rural areas. In special circumstances, immunization should be considered for some people spending < 1 month in endemic areas, e.g. travellers to areas where there is an epidemic, travellers making repeated short trips, or people with extensive outdoor rural exposure.

Cholera

In specific, limited circumstances (e.g., health professionals working in endemic areas or aid workers), the oral live cholera vaccine may be considered. A detailed, individual risk assessment should be made in order to determine which travellers may benefit from immunization.

Rabies

Pre-exposure immunization should be considered for travellers intending to live or work in areas where rabies is enzootic and where rabies control programs for domestic animals are inadequate, or where adequate and safe post-exposure facilities are not available. Children, particularly those who are too young to understand the need to avoid animals or to report bites, should also be considered for pre-exposure immunization.

Since pre-exposure immunization may not provide complete protection, administration of two booster doses is imperative as soon as possible after exposure to a rabid animal. In this situation, rabies immune globulin is not necessary.

Influenza

People at high risk of influenza complications embarking on foreign travel to destinations where influenza is likely to be circulating should be immunized with the most current available vaccine. In the tropics, influenza can occur throughout the year. In the southern hemisphere, peak activity occurs from April through September and in the northern hemisphere from November through March. Influenza transmission is enhanced in the crowded conditions associated with air travel, cruise ships and tour groups.

BCG

Immunization with BCG may be considered for travellers planning extended stays in areas of high tuberculosis prevalence, particularly where a program of serial skin testing and appropriate chemoprophylaxis may not be feasible or where primary isoniazid resistance of *Mycobacterium tuberculosis* is high. Travellers are advised to consult a specialist in travel medicine or infectious diseases when considering a decision for or against BCG immunization.

Travellers Who are Immunodeficient or Infected with HIV

In general, live vaccines should be avoided in individuals who are immunodeficient. These vaccines include yellow fever, oral typhoid, oral cholera, varicella, MMR (measles, mumps, rubella) and BCG.

For more detailed information, see the chapter in this *Guide* for recommendations on the use of vaccines in immunodeficient people.

Travellers Who Are Pregnant

In general, live vaccines should be avoided in pregnancy, whereas inactivated (killed) vaccines are considered safe. In practice, the benefits of inactivated vaccines for pregnant travellers usually outweigh the risks.

For more detailed information, see the individual vaccine chapters in this *Guide* for recommendations and contraindications of vaccines in pregnancy.

Malaria Prophylaxis

There is no licensed vaccine against malaria yet.

Four components of malaria protection should be discussed with travellers: a) the risk of acquiring malaria, b) personal protective measures to prevent mosquito bites, c) chemoprophylactic drugs (where appropriate), and d) the need to seek early diagnosis and treatment for a febrile illness. Information concerning malaria, drug-resistant strains of *Plasmodium*, and recommended drugs for prophylaxis and other preventive measures is regularly updated by CATMAT and published in the *Canada Communicable Disease Report*. Information is also available from local health departments, travel clinics, the Centre for Infectious Disease Prevention and Control, Health Canada, and the Travel Medicine Program section on Health Canada's web site (http://www.travelhealth.gc.ca).

All travellers should be informed that malaria should be suspected if fever occurs during or after travel. Medical attention should be sought as soon as possible, and the traveller should request that a blood film be examined for malarial parasites.

Selected References

Centers for Disease Control and Prevention. *Health information for international travel 1999-2000*. DHHS, Atlanta, GA, 2000.

WHO. *International travel and health: vaccination requirements and health advice*. Geneva: World Health Organization, 2001.

– Appendix I –
Definitions Used For
Reportable Adverse Events

Consult the facsimile of the reporting form included in this Guide for definitions. The following notes are clarifications and amplifications, where necessary, of the definitions or notations on the reporting form.

Adenopathy

Report severe or unusual enlargement or drainage of the lymphatic nodes.

Allergic Reaction

Indicate whether therapy with antihistamines was found clinically necessary and/or useful.

Anaphylaxis

Should be distinguished from vaso-vagal episodes. If unsure whether it was true anaphylaxis (epinephrine given rapidly), describe the episode as completely as possible while noting the uncertainty. True anaphylaxis is rare.

Anesthesia/Paresthesia

Describe patient symptoms and course of illness in detail.

Arthralgia/Arthritis

Note any pre-existing history of arthritis, as well as any diagnostic testing done, and persistence of symptoms if follow-up information available.

Convulsion/Seizure

Episodes shortly after vaccination are more likely secondary to the act of vaccinating (i.e., features of a vaso-vagal episode). Note if this is the suspected etiology. Otherwise, carefully note the presence or absence of fever, as well as any antipyretic use.

Encephalopathy

Describe symptom onset and clinical course.

Fever

Report temperatures 39° C or above (rectal equivalent) or believed high with accompanying systemic symptoms.

Guillain-Barré Syndrome

Indicate if the patient had any other recent illnesses (GBS may have an antecedent viral etiology).

Hypotonic-Hyporesponsive Episode

This condition is non-specific. Follow definition carefully but report any possible cases. Tends to be related to pertussis-containing vaccines.

Infected Abscess

If antibiotics have been prescribed for a possible cellulitis, and signs and symptoms appear to have responded to the treatment, code this definition.

Meningitis and/or Encephalitis

Describe symptom onset and clinical course.

Paralysis

Differentiate from weakness or immobility due to pain (which may be seen in children).

Parotitis

Swelling and/or tenderness of the parotid glands.

Rashes

No need to code those that are part of an allergic reaction, but descriptions of all rashes should be made.

Screaming Episode/Persistent Crying

The key is the persistence and abnormal character (for that infant). Should be differentiated from a dramatic pain response if possible.

Severe Pain and/or Severe Swelling

Lasting for at least 4 days, or requiring hospitalization.

Severe Vomiting and/or Diarrhea

Note the possibility of any co-existing illness that may be responsible.

Sterile Abscess/Nodule

Since small nodules are common, report those that are significant; usually this means that they persist for > 1 month and are > 2.5 cm in diameter.

Thrombocytopenia

Please indicate laboratory values and/or basis for the diagnosis.

Other Severe or Unusual Events

Describe any other reaction that is significant enough to warrant reporting. Please include reason for reporting (of medical/epidemiologic interest, dramatic, not listed in product information, unexpected, patient very concerned, etc.). Indicate a specific diagnosis in addition to clinical description.

– Appendix II –

Health Canada / Santé Canada

REPORT OF A VACCINE-ASSOCIATED ADVERSE EVENT
Protected when completed

In confidence to: Division of Immunization
L.C.D.C., Tunney's Pasture 0603E1
Ottawa, Ontario K1A 0L2
(613) 957-1340 1-800-363-6456 FAX (613) 998-6413

IDENTIFICATION

PATIENT IDENTIFIER	PROVINCE/TERRITORY	DATE OF BIRTH				SEX	DATE OF VACCINE ADMINISTRATION			
		YEAR	MONTH	DAY		☐ Male ☐ Female		YEAR	MONTH	DAY

VACCINES

VACCINE(S) GIVEN	NUMBER IN SERIES	SITE	ROUTE	DOSAGE	MANUFACTURER	LOT NUMBER

ADVERSE EVENT(S)
Events marked with an asterisk (*) must be diagnosed by a physician. Report only events which cannot be attributed to co-existing conditions. Additional information for all events should be provided under SUPPLEMENTARY INFORMATION on reverse side. Record interval between vaccine administration and onset of each event in minutes, hours or days.

LOCAL REACTION AT INJECTION SITE

☐ INFECTED ABSCESS (tick one or both of the options below) MIN. HOURS DAYS
(i) positive gram stain or culture ☐
(ii) existence of purulent discharge with inflammatory signs ☐

☐ STERILE ABSCESS/NODULE MIN. HOURS DAYS
No evidence of acute microbiological infection

☐ SEVERE PAIN AND/OR SEVERE SWELLING MIN. HOURS DAYS
(tick one or both of the options below)
(i) lasting 4 days or more ☐
(ii) extending past nearest joint(s) ☐

☐ SCREAMING EPISODE/PERSISTENT CRYING MIN. HOURS DAYS
Inconsolable for 3 hours or more; OR quality of cry definitely
abnormal for child and not previously heard by parents

☐ FEVER MIN. HOURS DAYS
Highest recorded temperature (Report only 39.0°C (102.2° F) or above)
Temperature: _____ °C (or _____ °F)
Site: rectal ☐ oral ☐ axilla ☐ skin ☐ tympanic ☐
Temperature believed to be high but not recorded ☐
Should be supported by the presence of other systemic symptoms

☐ ADENOPATHY (tick one or both of the options below) MIN. HOURS DAYS
(i) enlarged lymph node(s) ☐
(ii) drainage of lymph node(s) ☐
Site(s) _____

☐ PAROTITIS MIN. HOURS DAYS
Swelling with pain and/or tenderness of parotid gland(s)

*☐ ANAPHYLAXIS OR SEVERE SHOCK MIN. HOURS DAYS
Explosive, occurring within minutes after immunization, and evolving
rapidly towards cardiovascular collapse AND requiring resuscitative therapy

☐ OTHER ALLERGIC REACTIONS (tick one or more of the options below) MIN. HOURS DAYS
(i) wheezing or shortness of breath due to bronchospasm ☐
(ii) swelling of mouth or throat ☐
(iii) skin manifestations (e.g. hives, eczema, pruritus) ☐
(iv) facial or generalized edema ☐

☐ RASHES (other than hives) MIN. HOURS DAYS
Lasting 4 days or more AND/OR requiring hospitalization
Generalized ☐ Localized (indicate site) ☐ _____
Specify characteristics of rash _____

☐ ARTHRALGIA/ARTHRITIS MIN. HOURS DAYS
Joint pain/inflammation lasting at least 24 hours
If condition is an acute exacerbation of a pre-existing
diagnosis, give details under Supplementary Information

☐ SEVERE VOMITING AND/OR DIARRHEA MIN. HOURS DAYS
Must be severe enough to interfere with daily routine

☐ HYPOTONIC-HYPORESPONSIVE EPISODE (in children < 2 yrs. only) MIN. HOURS DAYS
Characterised by all the features of: (i) generalized decrease/loss
of muscle tone; AND (ii) pallor or cyanosis; AND (iii) decreased
level of awareness or loss of consciousness
Should not be mistaken for fainting, a post-convulsion state, or anaphylaxis

☐ CONVULSION/SEIZURE MIN. HOURS DAYS
Febrile ☐   Afebrile ☐
Past history of: A) Febrile seizures Yes ☐ No ☐
                  B) Afebrile seizures Yes ☐ No ☐
Omit fainting, seizures occurring within 30 minutes of immunization,
and seizures occurring as part of encephalopathy or meningitis/encephalitis

*☐ ENCEPHALOPATHY MIN. HOURS DAYS
Acute onset of major neurological illness characterized by
any two or more of: (i) seizures; (ii) distinct change in level
of consciousness or mental status (behaviour and/or personality) lasting 24 hours or
more; (iii) focal neurological signs which persist for more than 24 hours

*☐ MENINGITIS AND/OR ENCEPHALITIS MIN. HOURS DAYS
Abnormal CSF findings AND an acute onset of: (i) fever with neck stiff-
ness or positive meningeal signs; OR (ii) signs and symptoms of encephalopathy (see
ENCEPHALOPATHY above)
Results of CSF examination should be provided under Supplementary Information

☐ ANAESTHESIA/PARAESTHESIA MIN. HOURS DAYS
Lasting over 24 hours
Generalized ☐ Localized (indicate site) ☐ _____

*☐ GUILLAIN-BARRÉ SYNDROME MIN. HOURS DAYS
Progressive subacute weakness of more than one limb
(typically symmetrical) with hyporeflexia/areflexia

*☐ PARALYSIS (Do not code if Guillain-Barré Syndrome is coded) MIN. HOURS DAYS
Limb paralysis ☐ Facial or cranial paralysis ☐
Describe _____

*☐ THROMBOCYTOPENIA MIN. HOURS DAYS
Give lab results under Supplementary Information

☐ OTHER SEVERE OR UNUSUAL EVENTS MIN. HOURS DAYS
Include any adverse event believed to be related to immunization,
that does not fit any of the categories listed above and for
which no other cause is clearly established
Report events of clinical interest which require medical attention, and particularly
events that are (i) fatal, (ii) life-threatening, (iii) require hospitalization, or
(iv) result in residual disability
DESCRIPTION
_____
_____
_____
_____

REPORTER'S NAME		TELEPHONE NUMBER	ADDRESS (Institution/No., Street, etc.)		
PROFESSIONAL STATUS: MD ☐ RN ☐ OTHER ☐			City	Province	Postal Code
SIGNATURE	DATE Year Month Day				

HC/SC 4229 (03-96) - 1

Canada

OUTCOME OF EVENT(S) AT TIME OF REPORT PLEASE FORWARD ANY FOLLOW UP INFORMATION	FULLY RECOVERED ☐	RESIDUAL EFFECTS (describe) ☐	FATAL ☐	LOST TO FOLLOW-UP ☐	PENDING ☐

SOUGHT MEDICAL ATTENTION (Emergency room, clinic, family physician etc.)　NO ☐　YES ☐　(If yes, include relevant details of treatment under **Supplementary Information**)

HOSPITALIZED BECAUSE OF EVENT(S)　NO ☐　YES ☐	LENGTH OF STAY (DAYS) ☐	DATE ADMITTED	Year	Month	Day

CONCOMITANT MEDICATIONS (exclude those used to treat the adverse event) DRUG(S) GIVEN	MEDICAL HISTORY　Please provide information on relevant medical history or concurrent illness (See detailed instructions on reverse)

SUPPLEMENTARY INFORMATION

INSTRUCTIONS FOR COMPLETING REPORT OF A VACCINE-ASSOCIATED ADVERSE EVENT

1. Please use dark ink when completing form to improve legibility of copies.
2. Report only events which have a temporal association with a vaccine and which cannot be attributed to co-existing conditions. **A causal relationship does not need to be proven, and submitting a report does not imply causality.**
3. Events marked with an asterisk (*) must be diagnosed by a physician. Supply relevant details in the SUPPLEMENTARY INFORMATION box.
4. Record interval between vaccine administration and onset of each event in minutes, hours or days.
5. Provide relevant information, when appropriate, in the SUPPLEMENTARY INFORMATION box. Includes details of events diagnosed by physician (see 3 above), results of diagnostic or laboratory tests, hospital treatment, and discharge diagnoses where a vaccinee is hospitalised because of a vaccine-associated adverse event. If appropriate, and preferred, photocopies of original records may be submitted.
6. Provide details of medical history that are relevant to the adverse event(s) reported. Examples include a history of allergies in vaccinee, previous adverse event(s), and concurrent illnesses which may be associated with the current adverse event(s).

TO BE COMPLETED BY MEDICAL HEALTH OFFICER RECOMMENDATIONS FOR FURTHER IMMUNIZATION

	SIGNATURE	DATE	Year	Month	Day
NAME: _____　PHONE: _____					

– Appendix III –
Vaccine Products
Available in Canada

The following list of immunizing agents and the companies licensed to manufacture and/or market them in Canada reflects the situation as of December 31, 2001, and is not meant to be exhaustive. Products are listed here if they are mentioned in this *Guide* or are related to preventive or therapeutic interventions described in it. Some products that are for specialized use or available only under a special access program may not be listed. In addition, new vaccine development has increased in the past few years and the number of products being licensed, sometimes replacing other products, makes it difficult to keep a table such as this one completely up to date. Further, not all licensed products of all manufacturers will necessarily be available in all parts of Canada at all times.

Readers should consult other sources, such as the *Compendium of Pharmaceuticals and Specialties* (the CPS), their local public health authorities or manufacturers for the latest information about product availability and accessibility. Also, the names used in this table are those in common use and may not be identical with the names used in pharmaceutical compendia.

For new products that are needed to treat patients in exceptional circumstances but that are not yet licensed or approved in Canada, practitioners should contact the Special Access Program of the Therapeutic Products Directorate, Health Canada, which has a mandate to authorize the sale of such products. Practitioners should contact the program at 613-941-2108 (phone) or 613-941-3194 (fax) (after hours 613-941-3061) to initiate a request.

Active Immunizing Agents

Antigen	Descriptive/ brand names	Company	Description or comments
BCG vaccine	BCG vaccine (freeze dried)	Aventis Pasteur	Intracutaneous (live)
		Shire Biologics	Intradermal (live)
Cholera	Mutacol Berna Vaccine	Swiss Serum & Vaccine Institute	Oral (live)
Cholera and typhoid combined	Colertif Berna	Swiss Serum & Vaccine Institute	Oral (live)
Diphtheria and tetanus toxoids (Td and D2T5)	Td - adsorbed (Adult)	Aventis Pasteur	Adsorbed D2 T5Lf/0.5mL (for individuals > 7 years and recall doses)
Diphtheria and tetanus toxoids Polio DT-Polio and Td-polio vaccine	Td-Polio adsorbed	Aventis Pasteur	Adsorbed D2 T5Lf/0.5 mL (for individuals 7 years and older)
	DT-Polio adsorbed	Aventis Pasteur	Adsorbed D25 T5Lf/0.5 mL (for children < 7 years)
Diphtheria and tetanus toxoids, and pertussis vaccine (acellular)	Tripacel	Aventis Pasteur	For primary series and 4th and 5th doses
	Adacel	Aventis Pasteur	For adolescents and adults
Diphtheria and tetanus toxoids, adsorbed per-tussis vaccine (acellular) and inactivated polio vaccine (DTaP-IPV)	Quadracel	Aventis Pasteur	For primary series and 4th and 5th dose
Haemophilus influenzae type b conjugate vaccine (diphtheria CRM 197 protein conjugate)	HibTITER	Wyeth-Ayerst Canada Inc.	Between 2 and 59 months
Haemophilus influenzae type b conjugate vaccine (meningococcal protein conjugate)	Liquid PedvaxHIB	Merck Frosst	Between 2 and 59 months
Haemophilus influenzae type b conjugate vaccine (tetanus toxoids conjugate)	Act-HIB	Aventis Pasteur	Between 2 and 59 months
Diphtheria and tetanus toxoids Pertussis vaccine (acellular) Inactivated polio vaccine and *Haemophilus influenza* type b conjugate vaccine (tetanus protein conjugate)	Pentacel	Aventis Pasteur	Act-Hib reconstituted with Quadracel for primary series and 4th dose

Active Immunizing Agents

Antigen	Descriptive/ brand names	Company	Description or comments
Hepatitis A vaccine (inactivated)	Havrix 1440	GlaxoSmithKline	For adults
	Havrix 720 Junior		1 year up to and including 18 years of age
	Avaxim Paediatric	Aventis Pasteur	Pediatric and adults
	Epaxal Berna	Swiss Serum & Vaccine Institute	Children ≥1 years and adults
Hepatitis A vaccine (purified inactivated)	Vaqta	Merck Frosst	
Hepatitis B vaccine (recombinant)	Recombivax HB	Merck Frosst	
	Engerix-B	GlaxoSmithKline	
Hepatitis A and hepatitis B combined	Twinrix	GlaxoSmithKline	For adults
	Twinrix Junior	GlaxoSmithKline	For children
Influenza vaccine	Fluzone	Aventis Pasteur	Split virus
	Vaxigrip	Aventis Pasteur	Split virus
	Fluviral	Shire Biologics	Split virus
Japanese encephalitis virus vaccine	JE-Vax	Biken – distributed by Aventis Pasteur	Inactivated
Lyme disease	LYMErix	GlaxoSmithKline	Recombinant
Measles virus vaccine		Aventis Pasteur	Live attenuated
Measles and rubella virus vaccine	MoRu-Viraten Berna	Swiss Serum & Vaccine Institute	Live, attenuated
Measles, mumps and rubella vaccine	MMR II	Merck Frosst	Live, attenuated
	Priorix	GlaxoSmithKline	Live, attenuated
Meningococcal polysaccharide vaccine	Group A and C	Aventis Pasteur	Groups A and C
	Menomune		Groups A, C, Y and W-135
	Mencevax AC	GlaxoSmithKline	Groups A and C

Active Immunizing Agents

Antigen	Descriptive/ brand names	Company	Description or comments
Meningococcal conjugate vaccine	Menjugate	Chiron – distributed by Merck Frosst	Group C
	NeisVac-C	Baxter – distributed by Shire Biologicals	Group C
Mumps virus vaccine	Mumpsvax	Merck Frosst	Live, attenuated
Pneumococcal polysaccharide vaccine	Pneumovax 23	Merck Frosst	Polyvalent: 23 capsular types
	Pnu-Imune 23	Wyeth-Ayerst Canada Inc.	Polyvalent: 23 capsular types
	Pneumo 23	Aventis Pasteur	Polyvalent: 23 capsular types
Pneumococcal conjugate vaccine	Prevnar	Wyeth-Ayerst	7 capsular types
Poliomyelitis vaccine (IPV)	Imovax Polio	Aventis Pasteur	
	Inactivated Poliomyelitis Diploid Cell Origin	Aventis Pasteur	Inactivated (Salk) trivalent: MRC5
Rabies vaccine	Imovax Rabies	Aventis Pasteur	Inactivated human diploid cell
Tetanus toxoids		Aventis Pasteur	Adsorbed T5Lf/0.5 mL
Tuberculin	Tubersol (Mantoux)	Aventis Pasteur	Tuberculin purified protein derivative
Typhoid vaccine	Typhim Vi Vaccine	Aventis Pasteur	*Salmonella typhi* Vi capsular polysaccharide
	Vivotif Berna Vaccine	Swiss Serum & Vaccine Institute	Live, oral, capsular, for individuals ≥6 years of age
	Thypherix	GlaxoSmithKline	
	Vivotif Berna L Vaccine	Swiss Serum & Vaccine Institute	Liquid, for individuals ≥3 years
Varicella	Varivax II Varilrix	Merck Frosst GlaxoSmithKline	Live, attenuated, for individuals ≥12 months of age
Yellow fever vaccine	YF-Vax	Aventis Pasteur	Live, attenuated

Passive Immunizing Agents

Antigen	Descriptive/ brand names	Company	Description or comments
Botulism anti-toxin (equine)		Aventis Pasteur	Type E
			Type A, B and E
Cytomegalovirus immune globulin	Cytogam	MedImmune Inc.	
Diphtheria antitoxin (equine)		Aventis Pasteur	
Hepatitis B immune globulin	Bayhep B	Bayer	Solvent detergent treated
Rabies immune globulin	Bayrab	Bayer	Solvent detergent treated
	Imogam Rabies	Aventis Pasteur	Solvent detergent treated
Tetanus immune globulin	Baytet	Bayer	Solvent detergent treated
Varicella-zoster immune globulin	VariZig	Cangene	Solvent detergent treated
		Massachusetts P.H. Biologics Laboratories	Solvent detergent treated
Respiratory syncytial virus immune globulin	Respigam	MedImmune Inc.	
Immune globulin (human)	Gammabulin N	Baxter	
	Baygam	Bayer	Solvent detergent treated
Immune globulin, intravenous (human)	Gamimune	Bayer	Solvent detergent treated 5% and 10%
	Gammagard S/D	Baxter	Solvent detergent treated 5%
	Iveegam	Österreichische Institut für Haemoderivate	5%

– Appendix IV –
Licensed Manufacturers or Distributors
(contacts for vaccines distributed in Canada)

Aventis Pasteur Limited
Connaught Campus
1755 Steeles Avenue West
Toronto, Ontario M2R 3T4
Tel: 1 888 621-1146

Baxter Corporation
4 Robert Speck Parkway, Suite 700
Mississauga, Ontario L4Z 3Y4
Tel: 1 800 387-8399

Bayer Inc.
77 Belfield Road
Toronto, Ontario M9W 1G6
Tel: 1 800 268-1432

Cangene Inc.
104 Chancellor Matheson Road
Winnipeg, Manitoba R3T 5Y3
Tel: 204 275-4200
or 1 877 226-4363

CHIRON (Canada) Inc.
2220 Argentia Road
Mississauga, Ontario L5N 2K7
Tel: 905 821-4975

GlaxoSmithKline Consumer
HealthCare
2030 Bristol Circle
Oakville, Ontario L6H 5V2
Tel: 905 829-2030

Massachussetts Department
 of Public Health
Biologics Laboratories
305 South Street
Jamaican Plain, MD 02130
Tel: 617 983-6400

MedImmune Inc.
c/o Genesis Bio-Pharmaceuticals
5334 Yonge Street, Suite 1007
Toronto, Ontario M2N 6M2
Tel: 1 800 828-6941

Merk Frosst Canada & Co.
16711 Trans Canada Highway
Kirkland, Quebec H9H 3L1
Tel: 1 800 567-2594

Österreichische Institut
 Für Haemoderivate
c/o Baxter Corporation
6635 Kitiman Road, Suite 30
Mississauga, Ontario L5N 6J2
Tel: 905 858-3539

The Reaserch Institute for Microbial
Disease of Oska University (BIKEN)
3-1 Yamadaoka
Suita City, Oska
565 Japan
Tel: 011 81 06 6879 8264

Shire Biologics
Division of Shire Bio Chem Inc.
2323 Parc Technologique Boulevard
Sainte-Foy, Quebec G1P 4R8
Tel: 418 650-0010

Swiss Serum and Vaccine Institute
c/o Berna Corp.
1555 Bonhill, Units 2 & 3
Mississauga, Ontario L5T 1Y5
Tel: 1 800 533-5899

Wyeth-Ayerst Canada Inc.
1025 Marcel Laurier Boulevard
St. Laurent, Quebec H4R 1J6
Tel: 1 800 361-1336

– INDEX –

A

Acetaminophen, 20, 174, 253

Active Immunizing Agents, 71

Adverse Events, 7
(see also individual vaccines)

Anaphylactic Hypersensitivity, 12

Anaphylaxis, Initial Management, 14

Anti-vaccine Reports, 51

Autism and MMR, 7

B

BCG Vaccine, 71
adverse reactions, 74
booster doses and re-immunization, 74
contraindications, 75
efficacy and immunogenicity, 72
other considerations, 75
preparations licensed for immunization, 72
preparations used for immunotherapy, 73
recommended usage, 73
simultaneous administration with other
vaccines, 74
storage requirements, 74
usual response to immunization, 74

C

Cautions and Contraindications
(see also individual vaccines), 4

Cholera Vaccine, 77
adverse reactions, 79
booster doses and re-immunization, 79
contraindications and precautions, 80
efficacy and immunogenicity, 78
epidemiology, 77
other considerations, 80
preparations licensed for immunization, 78
recommended usage, 78
route of administration, 79
serologic testing, 79
simultaneous administration with other
vaccines, 79
storage requirements, 79

summary of recommendations, 80

Communication about immunization, 43

Cost benefit, 2

D

Definitions for Reportable
Adverse Events, 262

Diphtheria Toxoid, 82
adverse reactions, 85
booster doses, 84
combined vaccines, 85
contraindications and precautions, 85
epidemiology, 82
preparations licensed for immunization, 83
recommended usage, 83

G

General Considerations, 1
administration of human immune globulin
products, 33
adverse events, 7
anaphylactic hypersensitivity, 12
anaphylaxis management, 14
cautions and contraindications, 4
cost benefit, 2
immunization and breast-feeding, 19
immunization of children and adults with
inadequate immunization records, 41
immunization of children with neurologic
disorders, 20
immunization of people with hemophilia, 31
immunization in immunocompromised hosts, 20
chronic illness or advanced age, 22
congenital immunodeficiency, 23
HIV, myelodysplasias, 25
immunoablative therapy, 24
long-term drug treatment, 24
splenic disorders, 22
travellers, 26
immunization of infants born prematurely, 31
immunization during pregnancy, 18
immunization records, 40
immunization technique, 38
storage and handling of immunizing agents, 33